THE SKILLED COMMUNICATOR IN SOCIAL WORK

THE SKILLED COMMUNICATOR IN SOCIAL WORK

THE ART AND SCIENCE OF COMMUNICATION IN PRACTICE

KAREN HEALY

First published 2018 by
PALGRAVE

Palgrave in the UK is an imprint of Macmillan Publishers Limited, registered in England, company number 785998, of 4 Crinan Street, London, N1 9XW.

Palgrave® and Macmillan® are registered trademarks in the United States, the United Kingdom, Europe and other countries.

ISBN 978–1–137–56348–4 paperback

This book is printed on paper suitable for recycling and made from fully managed and sustained forest sources. Logging, pulping and manufacturing processes are expected to conform to the environmental regulations of the country of origin.

A catalogue record for this book is available from the British Library.

A catalog record for this book is available from the Library of Congress.

Printed and bound by CPI Group (UK) Ltd, Croydon, CR0 4YY

CONTENTS

LIST OF FIGURES

PREFACE

"Mouths don't empty themselves unless ears are
sympathetic and knowing."

(Zora Neale Hurston,
Mules and Men, 2008, p. 185)

Social workers communicate with people in complex and challenging situations. We meet people who are at different points in the life course, from diverse cultures, and who may experience issues with spoken communication. Many of the people we meet have been exposed to trauma and injustice and this gives rise to heightened emotions including despair, sadness and anger. We need to build relationships based on confidence and trust in these challenging circumstances.

Recognising the diverse and complex communication situations social workers face, we seek to address two questions:

(a) How can we broaden the social work communication base to build our capacity to respond to the diverse communication challenges we, as social workers, encounter in our practice?

(b) What can research on and about communication, particularly emerging research about emotions, offer the communication base of social work?

Turning to the first question, the book evolved in part from our concern about the assumptions underpinning the communication foundation of social work. Often it is assumed that social workers and the people who use our services share common communication capacities and preferences. This view reflects a Euro-centric and adult-centric worldview and often privileges spoken communication. People whose capacities and preferences are "other" to these assumptions, such as children or people from non-European cultural backgrounds or people with sensory differences, are inadequately acknowledged in the foundation communication literature.

Of course it is true that social workers often specialise in practice with specific populations. However, regardless of our practice field, social workers need also to *communicate* with people with diverse capacities and needs. So social workers need both depth of knowledge and skill in the field in which they practice, and breadth of knowledge and skill to engage with the diversity of people we meet in practice. By broadening the foundation of the communication base of social work we seek to recognise the rich variation in capacities and needs of the people with whom we communicate in social work.

The second question we seek to address concerns extending the contribution of social and behavioural science research, particularly emerging research on emotions, to the communication base of social work. This involves strengthening the scientific basis of communication in social work. We acknowledge that communication in social work has a strong element of artistry by which we refer to the inherent creativity involved in forming and maintaining a working relationship with another person. Building rapport means effectively conveying to another person that we "get" them, we understand and empathise with their thoughts and feelings, and that we are on the same "wave length." This involves much more than formal knowledge and skills, though these help; it involves using our "whole" selves including our emotional selves.

While we continue to recognise the artistic dimensions of communication, we consider that science has much to offer the communication base of social work as well. By science we refer to the large and diverse body of social and behavioural sciences research on and about communication. Of particular interest is the research on emotions that has emerged over several decades in the social and behavioural sciences. Social workers have long recognised elements of emotions in practice, particularly emotions such as empathy that build the working alliance. Emerging research has the potential to dramatically expand our understanding of emotions in practice. We now have evidence that emotions are important to all aspects of decision-making, of the profound influence of emotions and emotional regulation on many dimensions of communication, and the importance of emotional intelligence to productivity in a range of human service fields (see Fox, 2008; Gross, 2008, 2015; Keinemans, 2014; Hochschild, 2012). This evidence is important to revaluing the role of human relationships and of emotions in social work, both of which have been under sustained assault by managerialism over many decades (Howe, 2008; Munro, 2011; Saario and Stepney, 2009). The research encourages us to recognise heightened emotions, including the so called negative emotions such as anger, as part of the usual conditions we will encounter in social work practice. Developing our capacity to recognise and regulate heightened emotions in ourselves and others needs then to be recognised in the broad communication base of social work.

There are many people I want to thank for their insights and support as I wrote this book. Thank you to the following colleagues and friends who have inspired me with their practice and insights particularly on communication in challenging and complex situations: Karyn Walsh, Peter Walsh, Lisa Chung, Brenda Clare, Christine Craik, Julie Conway, Joel Cullin, John Drayton, Penny Gordon, Jo Lee, Rolv Lyngstad, Barbara Moerd, Maria Merle, Jane Miller, Tom O'Brien and Mary O'Brien, Siv Oldetal, Anita Phillips, Pam Sayeg and Cindy Smith. My thanks also the people at Palgrave, especially Peter Hooper and Louise Summerling for their interest in this project from the outset and their helpful communications along the way. Thanks and appreciation to my niece Khloe Healy who as a community support worker has shared with me her many insights about promoting dignity and respect. Thank you (again) to my husband Dennis Longstaff for his love, support and his always helpful and highly analytic insights into what makes us all tick.

1

The Skilled Communicator in Social Work

Everyday social workers communicate with people who are at different points in the life course, who are from diverse cultures and backgrounds, and who are facing a range of life challenges. These encounters can be further complicated in situations of heightened emotions or where the people experience communication challenges such as those associated with mental health challenges, sensory differences, cognitive losses or impairments, or challenges in spoken expression. Our capacity to communicate effectively in these diverse and challenges circumstances is vital to building constructive working relationships.

In this book we focus on communication with people who use social work services and the people who support them. In Part 1 of the book we outline the foundations of skilled communication. We focus on the knowledge and skills that are central to forming and maintaining the working alliance between social workers and service users in a broad range of practice contexts and situations. We draw attention to heightened emotional states in ourselves and others as a frequently encountered aspect of social work communication and we discuss research evidence about the nature and experience of these emotional states. We discuss strategies for promoting emotion regulation in ourselves and others so as to strengthen the working alliance in circumstances where heightened emotions are generated.

In Part 2 we extend the foundations of skilled communication to include communication with people who have diverse capacities and needs. Here we consider communication in the context of: cultural and linguistic diversity; communication with children, young people and older adults; mental health challenges; and differences an individual's capacity to receive, process and express spoken communication. We incorporate evidence from a range of social and behavioural sciences to inform the communication base of social work as seek to respond to people with diverse communication challenges and needs. While communication skills in direct practice are our focus, the theory and skills discussed in this book are relevant also to interpersonal communication with colleagues and in teams.

Skilled communication in social work: What is it?

Skilled social work communicators are purposeful, reflective and responsive to the communication needs of others. By purposeful communication we refer to communication that facilitates the identification, development and achievement of our shared purpose. Our shared purpose is negotiated with the service user and involves an amalgam of our institutional and professional obligations and capacities with the services user's aspirations and expectations of the practice process and outcomes (Healy, 2014; see Chapter 2, this volume).

Reflective communication involves analysing how our personal characteristics and capacities as well as our professional experience can inform communication. Self-knowledge of one's own characteristics, capacities, and emotional states enables the skilled communicator to anticipate and address possible challenges in communication encounters. Reflection also involves the capacity to analyse critical incidents to develop insight into the assumptions and practices that contributed to the incident and to use this insight to form the basis for developing new knowledge and skill in our practice (Fook and Gardner, 2007; see also Chapter 2, this volume).

By responsive communication we refer to the skilled communicator's capacity to recognise and adapt to the communication's capacity needs of those with whom they interact. Social workers need both depth and breadth of communication capacities to respond to this diversity. Social workers within specific practice domains often develop "depth" of knowledge and skill by which we refer to the development of specialised communication capacities relevant to that context. But this is not sufficient to be an effective communicator. Alongside depth of communication capacities specific to our domain of practice, social workers also need a broad base of knowledge and skills. This is due to the inherent diversity people's communication needs and capacities even within the "same" practice setting. For example, a person who experiences mental health challenges may experience age related sensory changes that affect the communication encounter. A further issue is that social workers often work in partnership with people's families, support people and community members, who may have different communication needs and capacities to those of the service user.

The art and science of skilled communication

An aim of this book is to introduce the reader to the art and science of skilled communication in a wide variety of practice situations and in diverse and challenging circumstances. As Nevo and Slonim-Nevo (2011,

p. 1178) remark: "Practice is as much an art as it is a science, and as such it is the application of empirical findings to clients' unique characteristics and context." We use the term "art" of communication to refer to the creative aspects of communication through which we interpret and respond to the communication capacities and needs of each individual with whom we interact.

We use the term "science of communication" to recognise the large body of social and behavioural sciences research on and about communication. A key question motivating this book is: what can research on and about communication, particularly emerging research about emotions, offer the communication base of social work? This research spans several domains including: social work research on or about communication in practice including systematic studies of aspects of communication (see Green, 2017; Keinemans, 2014; Trotter, 2013, 2015) the study of the practices of communication, such as research of intercultural communication practices (Jandt, 2016; Liu, Volčič and Gallois., 2014) as well as research on the psychological, social and political processes that influence communication. This includes empirical research in social neuroscience (Gross, 2008; Werner and Gross, 2010), cognitive and social psychology (Fox, 2008; Hargie, 2011); and sociology and political sciences (Jasper, 2011; Hochschild, 2012).

We recognise that the diversity of disciplines engaged in research on or about communication presents both challenges and opportunities for social workers in building an evidence informed approach to communication. The research can enhance our understanding of the biological, psychological and social dimensions of effective communication in social work. This knowledge can be applied to understanding and responding to the diverse and challenging communication situations social workers regularly encounter. Yet, this literature is expansive and there are many areas of debate. Furthermore, these diverse research studies rarely focus on social work communication practices. We acknowledge then incorporation of communication related research into the communication base of social work is an ongoing project.

The dynamic model of communication

Skilled communication is dynamic. While the working alliance remains a central feature of effective communication, the knowledge and skill required to communicate effectively can vary from context to context and in response to the diverse capacities and needs of the people with whom we communicate. In Figure 1.1 we present our dynamic model of skilled communication which we use throughout this book.

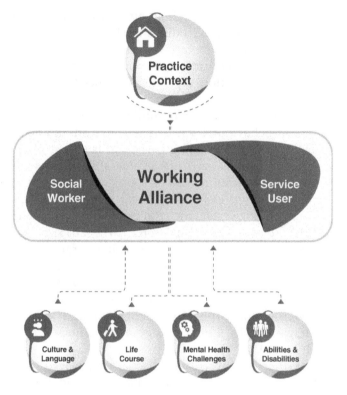

Figure 1.1   The Dynamic Model of Skilled Communication

The working alliance between the social worker and service user lies at the centre of our dynamic model of communication. The practice context provides the institutional parameters that shape the working alliance. The working alliance is underpinned by recognition of differences among people that influences their communication needs and capacities. In this book, we will consider four domains of human diversity that are often encountered in social work practice and which profoundly shape communication processes between social workers and service users. We turn now to outline of each of the elements of the dynamic model of communication.

The working alliance

The working alliance refers to the "joint involvement and emotional relationship" between workers and the people using our services (Jensen et al., 2010, p. 462). The importance of the working alliance, also referred as the "therapeutic relationship," is widely acknowledged in social work and cognate fields (Killian et al., 2017; Knight, 2015; Richards and Viganó, 2013). The working alliance is the vehicle through which our practice purpose, goals and processes are negotiated and achieved (Von Braun et al., 2013). We enhance our capacity to build a working alliance through reflection on, and adaption of, our "use of self" prior to, during and after practice encounters.

Building the working alliance requires attention to both the rational and emotional dimensions of communication. McCabe and Priebe's (2008, p. 404) observation about communication in the field of psychiatry is equally relevant to social work, namely that "Communication is not only technical. It also involves emotions, particularly when communicating about profoundly disturbing experiences."

Modern social work theory and practice has valorised the rational dimensions of the working alliance. There is considerable focus in modern social work practice on the rational processes through which the worker and service user negotiate their purpose, set goals, engage in problem-solving and evaluate their practice (see Trotter, 2013, 2015). The focus on rational thought is consistent with the humanist philosophy which "attaches great importance to the capacity of human beings to use rational thinking to manage their lives and their environment" (Payne, 2011, p. 5). While rational thought is powerful and important, the emphasis on rationality has perhaps occluded the importance of emotions as well (Howe, 2008; Keinemans, 2014). Emotions in social work communication have been further marginalised by rise of managerialism with its focus on the achievement of outputs and outcomes and neglect of the relational dimensions of practice (Howe, 2008; Morrison, 2007; Munro, 2011; Reimer, 2013).

We propose there are several reasons why social workers need a strong grounding in understanding and responding to the emotional dimensions of communication. First, emotions have a powerful influence on communication. Emotions shape our thoughts, feelings and behaviour; sometimes in ways we or others find difficult to regulate (see Fox, 2008). For example, when we are in heightened emotional states we may find ourselves unable to concentrate, to process information and that our bodily responses such as tone of voice are affected. To communicate effectively with others we need to become skilled at identifying the emotional states that may be conveyed in through para-vocal and non-verbal cues and also in managing these cues in ourselves.

Second, social workers work with people who are experiencing life challenges and these challenges often evoke strong emotional states. These emotional responses have high information content about how a person perceives a situation and what matters to them (Roberton, Daffern and Bucks, 2012). Taking notice of and exploring emotional responses can deepen our understanding of the service user's needs and perspectives.

Another reason that social workers need a sound understanding of the emotional dimensions of communication is because it matters to service users (see Healy and Darlington, 2009; Sheldon and Macdonald, 2009). As skilled communicators we need to be able to identify our emotional responses and those of others. In working with people experiencing life challenges we are very likely to encounter people in heightened emotional states. We need to understand the impact these elevated emotional states have upon people's capacity to engage in aspects of communication such as information processing. For example, psychological research shows that people in states of heightened emotions can experience difficulty in hearing or processing and recalling information (Fox, 2008, Chapter 7). In Part 1, we incorporate recent research on emotions into the foundation knowledge and skills for communication in social work practice (see also Howe, 2008; Morrison, 2007; Munro, 2011). We discuss strategies we, as social workers, can use to respond to heightened emotional states in ourselves and in others.

The practice context

The second element of our model is the practice context. We use the term "practice context" to refer to the laws, policies, obligations and professional responsibilities that shapes our communication encounters (Healy, 2014). The practice context influences communication as it provides the rationale for the meeting of social work and service user and it shapes at least some of the boundaries, norms and expectations influencing the communication. Understanding the impact of practice context is important to communication generally and to professional communication in particular. Hargie (2011, p. 24) observes:

> What takes place when people come together and engage in communication is partly a feature of particular attributes and characteristics that make each other a unique individual, and partly due to the parameters of the shared situation in which they find themselves.

The recognition of the influence of institutional context on professional communication is not unique to social work. However, the institutional context can cause particular tensions in social work practice. The humanist ethos of social work which prizes personal autonomy is often in tension with institutional obligations of social workers (Healy, 2014). The nature of these institutional obligations may place particular constraints on social workers including the requirement to act against the wishes of the service user in some circumstances. For example, social workers in mental health services may be involved in the implementing involuntary treatment orders for people who are unwell, in child protection services we may be involved in the forced removal of children from their families, and in probation and parole services we may be required to make recommendations for the continued detention of a person who poses a threat to public safety.

While these constraints on the autonomy of both the worker and the service user are most visible when working within mandated clients (see Trotter, 2015), they are, nonetheless present in almost all social work practice. In both for-profit and non-profit services, social work services are usually shaped by third party funding arrangements as the person using the service (the "service user") is not the same agency paying for the service (usually a government or non-government funding body and, occasionally, an insurer). In our communication then, social workers must walk a fine line between recognising institutional mandates while also promoting a constructive working relationship with those who use our services (Healy, 2012). Social workers need to transparently communicate their institutional obligations to the people with whom we work. In Chapter 2 we discuss how social workers can prepare to communicate their professional obligations to the service user.

Communication and diversity

Our dynamic model of communication recognises that the working alliance is underpinned by a recognition of, and responsiveness to, people with diverse communication capacities and needs. We propose that diversity of communication capacities and needs is a usual condition of social work practice. This approach stands in contrast to taken for granted assumptions about the communication capacity and needs of service users.

Social workers in a broad range of practice domains have noted that social work communication foundations often assume an adult-centric and Euro-centric approach (see Kampfe, 2015; Petr, 2003; Yip, 2004). Disability advocates, particularly members of the Deaf community, have criticised the emphasis on spoken communication or hearing privilege among health and human services professionals (Murray, 2015). We note this emphasis on spoken communication also marginalises the communication needs of those who face challenges in processing spoken communication or expressing themselves in spoken words (Pardoe, 2012). As we have observed, the humanist assumptions underpinning modern social work accord privilege to "rational" communication (Payne, 2011). Taken together these assumptions have often contributed to an implicit expectation that the service user is a "white," rational, middle-aged adult whose preferred mode of communication is spoken communication. This view has led to the neglect in much of the foundation communication literature in social work to the communication capacities and needs of those who are "other" to this norm (for exception see Koprowska, 2014). Where these differences are acknowledged, they often considered as special practice domains or special needs groups, such as social work in mental health services or aged care services. This belies the reality that regardless of the setting in which practice social workers frequently communicate with people who have diverse communicate capacities and needs. Of course, emerging social workers cannot be expected to develop a depth of capacity in all aspects of social work practice across all domains of practice. However, it is important we have a broad foundation of communication knowledge and skill across the range of communication challenges and needs we can expect to encounter in practice.

In Part 2 of this book we consider four areas of human diversity that are both commonly encountered by social workers and that also affect communication processes. In Chapter 6, we outline the knowledge and skill required for culturally competent communication in situations of cultural and linguistic differences. We propose that communication with people of diverse cultural and linguistic capacities and needs is, and will increasingly become, a usual condition of social work practice. Worldwide the flow of migration has been away from areas of high conflict and poverty towards the wealthy countries particularly those of the United Kingdom, Western and Northern Europe, Canada, USA, Australia and New Zealand (Czaika and de Haas, 2014). In the context of these global demographic shifts, social workers must regard culturally competent communication skills as an essential component of our professional base.

Social workers need also to demonstrate awareness of, and sensitivity to, the ongoing impact of colonisation on practice between social workers and Indigenous people. In countries with histories of European colonisation, such as Australia and New Zealand, Canada, the United States, South America and the Nordic nations, Indigenous people have experienced intergenerational oppression and trauma directly linked to health and social welfare policies and practices (Bennett, Green, Gilbert and Bessarab, 2013; Harrison and Melville, 2009). Social workers in these countries are likely meet to with Indigenous people as colleagues and also as service users (Barker, Alfred and Kerr, 2014). As we discuss in Chapter 6, recognition of the history of colonisation and its ongoing impact is vital to culturally competent communication with Indigenous people.

A second dimension of diversity we consider is the influence of life course on communication processes. We share the concerns of many commentators that the foundation literature on communication in social work has the neglected diverse communication needs of those other to the "norm" of the middle-aged adult service user (for discussion see Kampfe, 2015; Petr, 2003; Storlie, 2015). We seek to raise awareness of, and the reader's capacity to respond to, the diverse communication needs of people at different points of the lifespan, particularly children, young people and older adults.

The third area of diversity we consider is knowledge and skills for communication with people experiencing mental health challenges. While some social workers specialise in mental health services, social workers across a variety of fields regularly communicate with people who experience mental health challenges. These challenges are ubiquitous with for example depressive and anxiety disorders affecting more than 600 million people worldwide (WHO, 2016). Furthermore, mental health challenges, particularly serious and chronic mental health conditions, are associated with a range of social hardships (Gallagher, Jones, McFalls and Pisa, 2006). For these reasons, we recognise that knowledge and skills in communication with people experiencing mental health challenges must be included in the broad communication knowledge and skill base of social work.

The fourth area of diversity we consider pertains to differences in the capacity to receive, process and express oneself through spoken communication. Most literature on interpersonal communication in social work and the human services assumes parties' capacity to engage in, and preference for, spoken communication. This assumption has marginalised the communication needs of those with different sensory capacities, such as people who are Deaf or who experience vision impairment. Similarly the needs of those who experience cognitive differences that impact on their capacity to process verbal information are similarly neglected as are those who capacity to express themselves in spoken words. In Chapter 10, we consider the foundations of communication with people who experience challenges with spoken communication or who have capacity in other modes of communication.

The structure of the book

The book is divided in two parts. Part 1 presents The Foundations of Skilled Communication. This section has four Chapters focused on core knowledge and skills for building and maintaining the working alliance. In Chapter 2 we concentrate on preparing to communicate. We consider the tasks associated with building a sound background knowledge for the communication encounter, understanding our professional obligations and capacities, and preparing for the use of self in forming the working alliance. We discuss the importance of reflection on one's characteristics and emotional states and developing one's capacity for emotion regulation as important dimensions of preparing to communicate. In Chapter, 3 we outline core communication skills. These are skills in: listening; non-verbal communication; use of touch; observation; and verbal or spoken skills. The thoughtful and deliberate use of these skills is essential to building the working alliance and provides a basis for responding to people with diverse communication capacities and needs discussed in Part 2. In Chapters 4 and 5 we turn to consideration of heightened emotions in social work practice. In Chapter 4 we define heightened emotions, the causes and effects of these emotional states and their importance to communication in social work. We then discuss how social workers can respond to heightened emotional states with a focus on preventing emotional escalation, responding to escalated emotions and de-escalating heightened emotional states. In Chapter 5, we discuss heightened emotional states of anger and aggression. We consider that these commonly encountered emotional states can present significant challenges for social workers and the people and yet skilful response to these emotional states can strengthen the working alliance (Monds-Watson, 2011).

Part 2 focuses on Communication and Diversity. This Part is comprised of five Chapters and we concentrate on building a broad base of knowledge and skills for communicating with individuals with diverse communication capacities and needs. In Chapter 6 we focus on intercultural communication. Our approach to intercultural communication has three elements: understanding of cultural and historical context; intercultural awareness; and intercultural communication skills. We discuss the practical application of this approach to communication in social work practice. In Chapters 7 and 8 we turn to communication at early and late stages of the life course. In Chapter 7 we consider the knowledge and skills for developmentally sensitive communication with children and young people. In Chapter 8 we consider communication with older adults.

In Chapter 9 we turn our attention to communication with people experiencing mental health challenges. We discuss how a person's communication capacities can be affected by mental health challenges and how social workers can communicate effectively with people experiencing these challenges.

In Chapter 10, we consider communication with people who experience challenges and differences in their capacity to receive, process or express themselves in spoken communication. In Chapters 7, 8, 9 and 10, we include discussion of communication with families in because of the important role families often play in providing support to people at early and later points in the life course and in relation to people facing challenges associated with mental health or disabilities associated with challenges in spoken communication.

In Chapter 11, we review the themes of the book and the implications for research and practice development on skilled communication.

We also consider the implications of advances in information and communication technology (ICT) for skilled communication in practice.

The book is designed to build readers' capacity for skilled communication. In each Chapter we include practice exercises, review questions, an annotated bibliography and reference to websites where available.

Conclusion

Social workers and the people with whom we communicate bring a range of communication capacities, challenges and needs to our work together. In this Chapter we have introduced the dynamic model of communication we have developed to recognise and respond to the diversity of communication challenges and needs we encounter in practice. Our approach recognises the artistic elements involved in the creative use of self in building and maintaining the working alliance. We also seek to strengthen the evidence base of communication by incorporating social and behavioural science evidence on and about communication relevant to the diverse and challenging situations we face in social work practice.

Review questions

1. What does the term "working alliance" mean and why is it important in social work practice?

2. What experience do you have in communicating with people:

   ➢ with different cultural identities to your own?

   ➢ with different linguistic abilities to your own?

   ➢ with people at different points in the life course to your own?

   ➢ who are facing mental health challenges?

   ➢ who face challenges in receiving or processing spoken communication or in expressing themselves in spoken communication?

3. Drawing on your life experience, what have you learnt about communicating with people who have different communication needs and capacities to your own?

4. What have you learnt from the social and behavioural sciences that would inform your approach to communication in social work?

PART 1

The Foundations of Skilled Communication

In Part 1 we consider the foundations of skilled communication. In this section we outline: preparation for communication; core communication skills; understanding and responding to heightened emotions. The four Chapters in Part 1 provide a foundation for skilful communication in the variety of contexts of social work practice and the knowledge and skills discussed here provide the basis for communication with diversity we present in Part 2 (Figure P1.1).

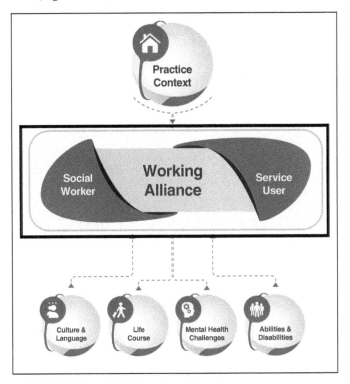

Figure P1.1   The Dynamic Model of Skilled Communication

2

Preparing to Communicate

Preparing to communicate refers to the actions we take to become ready to engage with others in a professionally purposeful way. While we may be most aware of the need to prepare for our first encounter with a service user, preparing to communicate is important at every phase of the social work process. In this Chapter, we begin with a discussion of the nature and role of preparation for communication in practice. We then discuss three elements of preparing to communicate, these are: practical tasks of preparation at each phase of the social work process; analysis of professional purpose; and the skilful use of self.

The nature and role of preparation for communication

Effective communication requires preparation. By preparing to communicate we aim to enhance our capacity to:

➤ convey to the service user a clear sense of our purpose and capacity to assist them.

➤ use our time and the service user's time effectively and efficiently.

➤ prepare to adapt and use ourselves to build a working alliance with the service user, including preparing ourselves emotionally to communicate with the service user.

➤ communicate to the service user that we value them, that is we have committed seriously to understanding their situation and to acting to achieve outcomes appropriate to our purpose which includes response to their needs.

In this Chapter we consider three elements of preparation for communication in social work. These are:

➤ practical tasks involved in preparing to communicate. We focus here on tasks associated with gaining sufficient information to anticipate and respond to the service user's challenges and needs.

> analysing our organisational and professional obligations. Transparently communicating our organisational and professional obligations to the service user is an important foundation for building a congruent understanding of our purpose with them.

> preparing for the use of self. Our purpose here is to understand how our social identity characteristics and our emotional state and responses are likely to influence the formation and maintenance of the working alliance. Through reflection on our "selves" we enhance our capacity to support the working alliance.

Let's consider the following example. Imagine it is Monday morning and you have arrived at work in a busy community services centre. The receptionist informs you there is a young family, Omar and Fatimar Azim and their two children waiting to meet you. The receptionist has provided you with a sketchy outline of the family's needs. It appears that family does not want to return to their home which is an apartment in a community housing complex. They need accommodation urgently. The family has previously contacted your agency for assistance in paying utility bills. The receptionist tells you that Mr Azim speaks English well and was able to communicate the family's needs to her. Mr Azim appeared to be angry. Mrs Azim is reported to be tearful and spoke only to her husband. The receptionist is unsure of the language in which Mrs Azim spoke to her husband and it is unclear whether Mrs Azim can communicate in English. Their two children, aged 3 and 5 years, are sitting closely by their parents and are described by the receptionist as distressed and clingy.

As you prepare to communicate with this family there are several questions you may ask of yourself. These include: what is my professional purpose? How do I communicate with this family in ways that enable us to work together to address the life challenges they face? What capacities do I bring to this situation? What barriers or challenges might I face in communicating with this family?

This scenario is typical of some of the challenges social workers face as we prepare to communicate with others. We often need to communicate with people in situations where the information is incomplete and where people may be experiencing significant crisis and heightened emotions arising from the challenges they face. Other challenges may include possible differences in world views and language barriers.

As social workers we need to be skilled in communicating with people in the context of uncertainty and individual and social challenges. We need to communicate in ways that create emotional engagement, a common understanding of the situation and a shared sense of purpose. We turn first to describe the phases of the social work process and to outline our purpose and practical tasks involved in each phase.

Practical tasks in preparing to communicate

Communications between social workers and service users often involve three phases; preparation to communicate is important to each of these phases as indicated in Figure 2.1.

The three phases of communication are: connecting, working together and endings. These three phases underpin each communication encounter and also are reflected in communication with service users over time. In a crisis service we may meet with the service user once, or over a very short amount of time, and in this meeting we will need to connect, to undertaken work together, and conclude the working relationship. Yet, the three phases remain relevant to ongoing relationships though the focus of our communication and hence of our preparation may shift over time. For example, on our second or third meeting with a service user the focus may turn to greater emphasis on our work together.

We turn now to preparing to connect in our first meeting with the service user. The first meeting, particularly the first part of our meeting, with the service user can have an enduring effect on the working

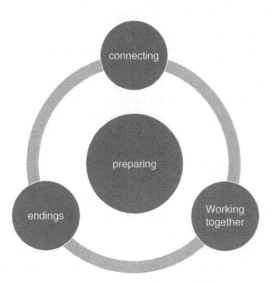

Figure 2.1   Preparing to Communicate at Each Phase of the Social Work Process

relationship and so the preparation may be more demanding for this first meeting. The primary task of the first meeting is to establish the working alliance which, as we have defined in Chapter 1, refers to "the joint involvement and emotional relationship" between the worker and service user (Jensen et al., 2010, p. 462). In this part of the Chapter we discuss the practical tasks associated with preparation to communicate and later in the Chapter will turn to analysis of professional purpose and developing the use of self.

As part of preparing to form a working alliance, it is important to gain a preliminary understanding of the service user's situation. This preliminary understanding can include the history of their involvement with our agency and any other relevant personal background, an understanding of the presenting reason for your meeting with the service user and any information about likely practical or emotional needs in the situation. Gaining a preliminary understanding is important for many reasons including: to anticipate the needs of the service user; to recognise any professional obligations we bear; to prepare ourselves to communicate with the service user.

Preparation is, in part, an information gathering exercise. This can include reviewing case notes and other written records, referral information which can be formal (such as a referral letter) or informal information, such as the observations of staff who have had previous contact with the person. The importance of gaining a good understanding of background information cannot be overstated. Indeed, in his review of the tragic death of Victoria Climbie, Lord Laming (2003) observed that the failure to review the child's case records substantially contributed to the social workers' failure to understand the gravity of the child's situation. Yet, while background information is very important, we need to view it critically, recognising gaps or contradictions in the information. We need also to maintain an open view of the service user and their situation. The background information is a guide but we need to recognise that these are other people's views of the person's situation. In our first meeting with the service user we seek to gain their perspectives on their situation and their hopes and expectations for our work together.

The location of our meeting is also important to consider as part of our preparation (Koprowska, 2014). Social workers meet people in a wide variety of physical environments including: health and social service agencies; hospitals; courts; and people's homes. There are a wide variety of issues to consider in our environment. These can include practical consideration about physical access where people have disabilities and the appropriateness of the space for the nature of the meeting and the number of people who may be present. In Chapters 4 and 5, we discuss the importance of creating a physical and emotionally safe environment. In later Chapters we also discuss the importance of ensuring our environment is responsive to people with diverse communication needs and capacities. In the case of the Azim family, possible practice environment considerations may include provision of a private space to discuss their situation and whether we can provide any written material in their preferred language.

While preparation to connect with the service user is important in the first phase of the social work process, it remains highly relevant at later phases as well, though the nature of the preparation may change in these later phases. In later meetings our goal shifts from building to maintaining the working alliance. Like all relationships, maintaining the working alliance requires attention. As we commence our work together we prepare to meet with the service user by reviewing previous agreements, goals and concerns and any information about our progress on these matters (see Trotter, 2013, 2015). Our preparation also involves reflection on self to be adaptive to the needs of the service user. We will have become aware of the unique communication capacities and needs of the service user and we can prepare by adapting ourselves to these needs.

The ending phase is an opportunity to consolidate any gains made by the service user during your work together and to empower them by acknowledging strengths and their options to continue to address issues that are ongoing or that may arise in future. Preparation for this phase should involve reviewing information, including the presenting problem and any progress made towards understanding and addressing that problem, as well as acknowledging service user's strengths and capacities that have emerged in the course of your work together. Reviewing insights gained and progress made can be important to making these changes visible to the service user.

Practice exercise

Returning to the Azim family case study, let us consider what background information we have and how this might inform our preparation to communicate with the family. We have some informal referral information about possible language difference that alerts us to assess the need for an interpreter. We are aware also of the heightened emotional state of the family members. We understand that the family has used the agency services before and so we can also access the case notes. As we look at the case notes, what information might we seek? What other information might we seek and where would we seek it?

Analysing our organisational and professional obligations

Developing and maintaining a working alliance requires that we build a congruent view of the purpose of our work with the service user. Professional purpose refers to our intentions in practice. It describes what we do in practice, why we do it and how we do it. Our intentions in practice are shaped by institutional and professional capacities and obligations. It is important then that we reflect on these obligations and capacities and to ensure that these are transparent in our work with the service user (Trotter, 2013, 2015).

As outlined previously (Healy, 2014), construction of our professional purpose includes recognition of:

➢ our institutional responsibilities. These include the laws and policies that shape our practice environment and any obligations one may have to a team or third party such as a Court in relation to your work with the service user.

➢ our professional practice base. This includes theories, knowledge, values and skills drawn from social work and cognate fields.

➢ our developing framework for practice. By this we refer to the sense of professional identity and approach that emerges from our practice experience over time.

Our sense of professional purpose is contextual and dynamic. Our institutional context includes our organisational setting of practice as well as the broader legal, policy and social environment that shape the organisation. Our institutional context places obligations upon us which include formal protocols and informal expectations about how we will relate to the service user. For example, the implicit expectations of how a social worker will communicate vary between more formal settings, such as Courts and statutory authorities, and other settings, such as youth services. By understanding our institutional obligations we build our capacity to transparently communicate these to the service user and to build a congruent understanding of our purpose with them.

Our sense of purpose is dynamic because it is negotiated. While preparing for practice we can develop an initial sense of professional purpose based on the known elements of our purpose, such as our institutional obligations, our purpose will alter in response to the service users' needs. An important element of our first meeting with the service user to gain insight into their expectations and needs from the social work process and to consider these in the development of a shared professional purpose.

The elements of our professional purpose may change over time (Healy, 2014). For example, the service user's needs may evolve and as the demands of the situation alter. For instance, a family working with a social worker on a palliative care team will have different needs as the primary patient's health status alters. We ourselves as workers may change and adapt our practice over time as we gain new evidence and insights into practice and as our practice framework evolves (see Fook, Ryan and Hawkins, 2000). The dynamic nature of professional purpose means that reflection on purpose is an important part of preparation to communicate at every phase of the social work process.

Our activities as agents of change may also contribute to alterations in our professional purpose. In accordance with our systemic outlook and our values base we are obliged to advocate for social justice in the organisations and societies where we practice. Our point is that in understanding our institutional context on our professional purpose we should not see it as static or beyond our responsibility to influence.

Referring to our case example of the Azim family, our professional purpose would be informed by:

➤ our institutional responsibilities. This would include attention to any statutory obligations and organisational protocol related to the family's situation and needs.

➤ our professional practice base. We refer here to theories, knowledge and values that inform our practice. For example, we would need to be mindful how our values influence how and what we communicate with and to the family. These values include: respect for and promotion of individual's right to self-determination; promotion of welfare or well-being; equality; and social justice (Banks, 2012). Theoretical perspectives such as anti-oppressive theory would encourage us to work alongside the family to gain and communicate a critical understanding of the social and structural factors that have contributed to the current difficulties they face. Knowledge about intercultural communication would inform our sense of purpose and approach to the family including consideration of whether or how to engage an interpreter (see Chapter 6).

➤ the Azim's family's expectations and needs as they see them. Social workers recognise through our values and theoretical frameworks the importance of collaborating with service users to define the nature of the challenges they are facing, and how to respond to them. So in preparing to communicate we would aim at minimum to anticipate what the service user might expect or need from us. In this situation, the fact that the Azim family have already expressed to the reception staff their needs in terms of a housing need provides an initial basis for understanding their expectation of you. We are aware that the parents are expressing heightened emotions that require our attention. We are alerted also to the possibility that we may need to engage an interpreter to facilitate communication.

➢ our developing framework for practice will inform our response. How we respond to this situation will be informed by our previous experiences and how we have integrated these into our evolving practice framework and this will vary among workers (Fook et al., 2000). For example, a worker may adopt a "housing first" approach giving priority to the presenting housing problems as their primary concern, while another worker may seek to prioritise the family's emotional state as their highest priority before considering the housing issues.

Practice exercise

Review the elements of our professional purpose that would inform our initial meeting with the Azim family. To what extent do you agree with our outline of the factors that would be considered within each of the elements of: institutional responsibilities; professional practice base; family expectations and needs; and our developing practice framework?

What other factors would you include within each of these elements to inform your professional purpose?

Articulating our professional purpose

Our sense of professional purpose informs how and what we communicate with the people we meet in direct practice. We may be called upon by colleagues and members of interdisciplinary teams, by service users and sometimes by external stakeholders such as Courts or review panels to describe our professional purpose. It is important then that we can not only describe our professional purpose but also to demonstrate how it influences our approach to practice.

Drawing on what we know of the Azim family from the brief case introduction and consideration of our purpose, we could describe our purpose is to work in partnership with the Azim family to provide emotional support and to address housing concerns. This description of our purpose reflects a value position (our desire to work in partnership) and an understanding of both the service users' stated needs and the organisational mandate for involvement in their lives. Our desire for partnership should be reflected in how we communicate with the family such as in how we involve them in defining their needs and their proposed solutions to the challenges they face.

As discussed earlier, our sense of professional purpose is dynamic. As part of the preparation phase we must develop an initial sense of professional purpose, and we need to be prepared to continue to negotiate our professional purpose as the working alliance evolves and more information comes to light. For example, we may learn that the Azim family have been experienced racial discrimination, or have been a victim of crime at the community housing complex. We may learn that a family member is ill and this has contributed to difficulties in paying rent. Our sense of professional purpose may alter in response to this information to be restated as: to work in partnership with the Azim family to advocate for their right to remain in their home and to provide support services to them.

Preparing for the "use of self"

The term "use of self" is widely used in social work and in related literature to refer to self awareness and deliberate use of self in developing and maintaining the interpersonal relationship with the service user (Arnd-Caddigan and Pozzuto, 2008; Wang, 2012). This involves understanding how we can use and adapt ourselves including our social identities, personal capacities, and our emotional responses to build and support the working alliance.

In Figure 2.2 we present two elements of the use of self in social work. We use the term "formal role" to refer to our formal professional title or role description. The "personal self" refers to the social identity characteristics and emotional states of the worker. Critical reflection on both elements is important to the use of self in practice.

We turn first to our formal role. We recall that our formal role contributes to, but does not entirely define, our professional purpose. The formal role refers to the social worker's designated work role, such as "child protection worker," "hospital social worker" or "community worker." The service user is likely to be aware of the social worker's formal role description in their initial encounter with us because this description will be implied or explicit in the practice context. The description and formality of the social worker's role varies significantly by context and the formal role may be a point of confusion or even threat for the service user. For example, in contexts where social workers have been referred by a third party such as a multi-disciplinary team, the service user may be confused by the reason for the social worker's presence. Challenges to our initial communication with the service users are likely to arise in circumstances where negative views of our formal role prevail. In particular, in services where our role is associated with the use of coercive power, people may express a range of negative perceptions related to fear or even a sense of failure arising from the involvement of social work services in their lives (Trotter, 2015). These perceptions, especially when tied to strong emotional reactions, such as fear, are likely to influence the service user's communication with us. Even in roles with less formal authority, such as that of family support worker, counsellor or community health worker, the service user is likely to have assumptions about how the first meeting will proceed based on our formal role title.

In preparing to communicate with the service user, it is helpful for us to consider the previous experiences the person may have had with social workers and any perceptions and expectations they may have of our role. These experiences and perceptions should be explored in the initial stages of building the working alliance particularly where they might otherwise act as a barrier to an alliance. Over the course of our work with the service user it can be helpful to return to discuss our evolving role with the service user particularly to ensure that all parties to the communication are mindful of obligations and boundaries in the role (Trotter, 2015).

Understanding and adapting the personal "self" in practice

We turn now to focus on the second element of the professional "self," namely, the personal self (Figure 2.2). We use the term "personal self" to refer to our social identity, emotional capacities and our attitudes and values. Each of these elements profoundly shapes the formation and main tenance of the working alliance and so requires critical reflection in our preparation for practice.

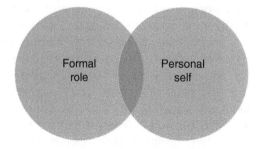

Figure 2.2   Elements of the Use of Self in Social Work Practice

Our social identities

We turn first to our social identities and their influence on the formation of the working alliance. Perceptions of our social identity characteristics play an important role in the formation of the working alliance including whether the service user has confidence in our ability to be helpful to them. In preparing for practice, then, it is important to ask "What does the service user see when they see you?"

Many of our social identity characteristics are those over which we have limited influence, which may be visible to others, and may be important to our sense of identity. The social characteristics found to influence communication include:

> age and age differences between the parties to a communication (see Froemming and Penington, 2011);

> cultural background including differences in world views and communication norms (Jandt, 2016);

> gender (Cottingham, 2015; Hochschild, 2012);

> physical presence, such as height and appearance;

> abilities and disabilities;

> sexuality;

> class and social status.

Our social identity characteristics shape how we communicate and also affect how others perceive and communicate with us. As communication is a shared enterprise between two or more parties the influence of our social identity characteristics cannot be fully understood prior to meeting with the other. In addition, a social identity characteristic that might be regarded as a challenge in one context may be an advantage in another. For example, a social worker in their twenties might be perceived by an older service user to be "too young" to help them, while a young service user may perceive they are more able to connect with a younger worker. Further social identities are socially constructed and thus how these characteristics are understood and experienced vary across social and cultural contexts.

A related issue is that our social identity characteristics have varying degrees of visibility. For example, some characteristics are visible, such as age or gender, while others are not necessarily so such as social class or sexuality. In addition, even within a social identity group there are varying degrees of visibility with, for instance, variations in the forms and experiences of physical disability.

As part of our preparation to communicate we can anticipate the possible influence of our social identity characteristics and to consider how we may respond to possible challenges. At issue is whether it is possible or desirable for us as workers to adapt in ways that anticipate and address possible communication challenges. In some situations we may be able to communicate in ways that directly or indirectly address the communication challenges associated with our social identity. For example, a young social worker may overcome an older service user's concerns about their perceived youth and inexperience by demonstrating herself to be well prepared, knowledgeable and respectful in her approach. In some circumstances, a female Indigenous social worker may overcome barriers to communication with a male Indigenous service user by demonstrating a high level of cultural awareness and sensitivity to gender roles and expectations in her communication with the service user (see Casey, 2003).

However not all communication challenges associated with our social identity characteristics can be addressed through personal adaption. It may become necessary to refer the service user to a social worker whose personal characteristics are appropriate to the situation. For instance, in some contexts it will be challenging or inappropriate for a male social worker to speak with a female service user or for a person of a particular cultural background to speak to a worker from a different cultural background on specific issues.

Our key message here is that our social identity characteristics influence how others perceive us and can shape the possibilities for building a working alliance. As social workers we need awareness of our social identity characteristics and their likely influence on communication particularly in the diverse circumstances and with the variety of people we meet in our practice. On the basis of this awareness we can then decide the extent to which it is desirable, necessary or possible for us to adapt our communication approach to address possible communication challenges associated with these characteristics.

Practice exercise

This exercise is intended to assist you to reflect on how your personal characteristics may influence the formation of working alliance with service users, particularly where the other person's characteristics differ from your own.

▶

◀

How do you identify yourself in relation to the following characteristics?

➤ age

➤ cultural background including differences in world views and communication norms

➤ gender

➤ health

➤ abilities and disabilities

➤ sexuality

➤ class and social status

Are there any other social identity characteristics that are important to how you see yourself and how others see you?

In what circumstances are the characteristics you have identified likely to be a strength in forming a working alliance with the service user?

What circumstances if any might these differences provide challenges?

How will you manage these challenges?

Our emotional capacities

We turn now to our emotional capacities which are important in all communication and especially for forming and maintaining a working alliance. We refer to emotional capacities as our ability to understand our emotional states and those of others and to regulate our emotions in ways that support the working alliance. Sheppard and Charles (2015, p. 1839) observe that "Social work is, in many respects, emotional work, and a capacity to work interpersonally is a necessary feature for social work to take place at all." In developing the working alliance, social workers need to be able to recognise and regulate our own emotions as well as to identify and respond to others emotions (Howe, 2008).

As we have established, emotions are not only feelings. Emotions are a multi-system response to stimuli (events, experiences and perceptions) and reflect, as well as shape, our understanding, our bodily responses, feelings and actions. Furthermore, our emotional responses may be conscious or unconscious (Fox, 2008). Unconscious emotions are those of which we are not aware but which may exert influence our thoughts and actions. For example, a "flight" response may precede our awareness that we are experiencing fear.

There are many reasons why social workers need to become attuned to our own emotional states and the emotional states of others. First, our capacity to communicate emotions is very important to the working alliance. Numerous researchers in social work and cognate fields have identified that the expression of empathy, warmth and genuineness are central to the development of the working alliance (Sheppard and Charles, 2015; see also Howe, 2008; Spratt and Callan, 2004). Sheldon and Macdonald (2009) summarise the research on how service users would prefer social workers to relate to them and each of these preferred dimensions has a strong emotional dimension component. They report that service users' prefer social workers who demonstrate:

> ➤ **Non-possessive warmth.** This means that the service user perceives that the worker likes them and supports them to make their own choices. To put it differently, the warmth of the worker does not depend on the service user's compliance with him or her but instead arises from an unconditional positive regard for the service user;

> ➤ **Genuineness.** This means that the service user perceives that the worker cares about them and their situation;

> ➤ **Accurate empathy**. This means that service user perceives that worker listens to them and is able to demonstrate that they understand the service user's thoughts and emotions in relation to their experience.

Other research also points to service users' preference for workers are helpful and responsive to their needs (Healy and Darlington, 2009). Service users' preferences for workers to demonstrate non-possessive warmth, genuineness, accurate empathy and helpfulness all point to the emotional dimensions of communication in social work. The people who use our services want us to be emotionally attuned and responsive to them.

Second, awareness of our emotional states is important to recognising and responding to the emotional states of others. As Howe (2008, p. 185) observes:

> Before the worker can be in touch with the feelings of the client, she must first be able to acknowledge and understand her own emotional states and the power they have to affect her, particularly as she relates to others in need, distress, anger and despair (Shulman, 1999, p. 156). The reference point for an understanding of others is oneself.

Within the traditions of humanistic psychology and social work it is recognised that the workers capacity to understand their own emotional responses is important to connecting to the emotional state of the service user (Morrison, 2007). Even if we are unaware of our own emotional state it is likely that service users will be attuned to it. Morrison (2007, p. 253–254) asserts that service users with experiences of trauma may be acutely attentive to our emotional expressions due to having developed "emotional antennae which is highly attuned to the emotional demeanour of those whom they have to have to depend."

Third, our emotional responses are important also to other aspects of the social work process beyond the working alliance (Keinemans, 2014). Morrison (2007, p. 259) proposes that understanding of "emotions is a critical aspect at every stage of the social work task: engagement, assessment, observation, decision making, planning and intervention." Munro (2008, 2011) proposes that our rational and emotional responses provide important information that we should critically scrutinise and draw upon in our decision-making. Munro (2011, p. 91) states:

> Research in neuropsychology suggests that our intuitive and emotional responses occur automatically and outside conscious awareness; we cannot choose to be only logical, thinking machines... Appreciating the importance of both logical and intuitive understanding and the contribution of emotions offers guidance on the different training needs in using them to best effect.

Our emotional responses provide us with important information about the situations in which we are involved (Munro, 2011; see also Keinemans, 2014; Morrison, 2007). Our emotions, much as our thoughts, hold important information that can positively influence our practice.

While many researchers agree that emotions play a vital role in assessment and intervention, a failure to reflect on our emotions can also lead to distortions in what we attend to and how we process information (Munro, 1996, 2008, 2011; see also Howe, 2008; Morrison, 2007). This view is also supported by the work of Nobel Prize–winning decision theorist, Daniel Kahneman (2011) who proposes that intuitive thinking, which is often strongly informed by emotions, can contribute to good decision-making but may also be subject to predictable biases and errors of logic (see also Munro, 2008). These biases include intuition being vulnerable to reliance on prior and emotionally charged experiences, risk aversion and protecting group relationships. For these reasons, it is important to critically scrutinise intuitive and emotional responses to situations we encounter in practice. An uncritical approach to our emotional responses may contribute to decision-making errors.

Overall, our emotional responses influence the formation and maintenance of the working alliance. Emotions also provide us within insights
that we need to recognise and review in our assessment and decision-
making processes (Keinemans, 2014; Munro, 2011). Our own emotional
responses can also influence our capacity to fully present in situations,
for example in situations where we ourselves experience strong emotional responses. Emotions are difficult to ignore and can shape
communication encounters in ways that are both positive, such as in
forming a connection with the service user, and negative, such as making
it difficult to engage in analytic thinking process that are important for
decision-making.

Practice exercise

Reflecting on our emotional responses

Let's refer back to the case study of the Azim family introduced at the beginning of
the Chapter.

What do you recall about the emotional states of the family members?

What are your emotional responses to the family members?

How might your own and the family members' emotional states influence the communication process?

With your peers discuss your answers to these questions. Together discuss how you
might acknowledge your own and others emotions in ways that promote a working
alliance.

Regulating our emotions

Emotions are an important part of communication. Social workers need
to be skilled at identifying and responding to the emotional dimensions
of communication and to being able to critically scrutinise the information content of our emotional responses. As skilled communicators we
need also to be to regulate our own emotions. As Howe (2008, p. 13)
observes: "The ability to regulate your own emotions affects the skill
with which you are able to manage your dealings and relationships with
others."

The concept of "emotion regulation" refers to the "processes that
serve to decrease, maintain or increase one or more aspects of emotion"

(Werner and Gross, 2010, p. 17). McRae et al. (2008, p. 145–146) further explain:

> Emotion regulation can be deliberate or habitual, conscious or unconscious, and can involve changes in the magnitude, duration, or quality of one or several components of an emotional response. Emotion regulation strategies can target one's own emotions or those of another individual, at a variety of time points in the emotion generation process.

Emotion regulation involves recognising our emotions and managing the behavioural and physiological expressions of these emotions, and may also involve changing the way we experience these emotions.

The concept of emotion regulation has received considerable attention in the social and behavioural sciences literature (see Biron and van Veldhoven, M., 2012; Hochschild, 2012; Mende-Siedlecki, Kober and Ochsner, 2011). In her ground-breaking sociological study originally published in 1983, Hochschild (2012) pointed to the important but often devalued role of emotion regulation in service work across a variety of industries. She used the term "the managed heart" to refer to service workers' management of their own and others emotions in providing a variety of human services. Over the past two decades, an expansive research literature has emerged on the psychological aspects of emotion regulation (see Gross, 2015; Lewis, Haviland-Jones and Barrett, 2008; Kring and Sloan 2010). This literature has highlighted the importance of emotion regulation for effective communication and outlined strategies for achieving emotion regulation for both givers and receivers of services (see Gross, 2008, 2015). Psychological researchers recognise that emotion regulation is multi-dimensional and includes behavioural, experiential and physiological aspects (Dvir et al., 2014, p. 149; Werner and Gross, 2010).

Emotion regulation is a particularly important concept for communication in social work. At the heart of communication in social work lies a paradox. The paradox is that the relationship between ourselves and the people with whom we work must be both authentic and yet we must regulate our emotions sufficiently that we remain purposeful and helpful to the other. This paradox is perhaps especially acute in situations of heightened emotions such as when a person is distressed, angry or aggressive. In such circumstances, social workers need to maintain a high level of emotional self-regulation and to invoke the deliberate and thoughtful use of communication strategies in order to promote the safety and well-being of themselves and others.

Emotion regulation involves "the imposition of higher rational control over lower, more basic emotional systems to accomplish adaptive goals" (Thompson and Goodman 2010, p. 38). The reference here to emotions as "more basic" is not intended as a value judgement but rather to recognise that the parts of our brains that store and process emotions are more automatic and less subject to conscious control than the higher ordered parts of the brain enabling rational thinking. Emotion regulation does not mean the absence of emotions. It refers instead to the attempt to consciously recognise our emotional states and to use both emotional and rational processes to inform our responses to situations, particularly situations where heightened emotions are provoked.

Furthermore by regulating our own emotions, we can also assist others to do the same. Some of the people with whom we work with may experience particular challenges in regulating their emotions and this will impact on their capacity to communicate with us and others. Challenges in emotion regulation can be due to difficult childhood situations, such as being subject to abuse or neglect or to other issues such as some forms of mental illness or developmental disabilities (Dvir et al., 2014). By modelling emotion regulation, we can assist others to learn to regulate their own emotions in a range of circumstances.

Strategies for emotion regulation

We turn now to strategies for regulating our emotions. Research psychologist James Gross and his colleagues (see Gross, 2008, 2015; Gross and Thompson, 2007; Werner and Gross, 2010) identify these strategies as:

1. situation selection

2. situation modification

3. attentional deployment

4. cognitive change

5. response modulation.

In this section, we explain and evaluate the strategies in relation to preparing ourselves to communicate in social work practice.

Notably, the first two strategies involve seeking to alter our exposure to emotionally evocative situations, the next two strategies involve altering how we experience emotionally evocative situations while the final strategy involves changing how we respond once emotions have been generated.

The first two strategies we consider here involve seeking to alter our exposure to an emotionally evocative stimulus. The first of these is "situation selection." This refers to making a choice about whether or not to enter into an emotionally evocative situation. The nature of our work limits our capacity to make choices about whether or not we enter into emotionally challenging situations. One reason is that our role may require us to enter circumstances that are, for most people, uncomfortable or distressing. For example, our roles may oblige us to meet with a family following the suicide of a family member or undertake a child protection interview with a parent who is angry or to be exposed to details of the horrific suffering of victims of abuse. A further reason that situation selection is a limited strategy for regulating our emotions is that our work can be unpredictable. We may for example choose not to work in a field because it elicits strong emotions for us, such as we may choose not work in the field of mental illness if we have a personal history of this or we may choose not to work with survivors of sexual abuse for the same reason. However, even when we choose not to work in a specific field, we may not be able to avoid particular situations that are emotionally evocative. For example, a child protection worker will still work with families where mental health issues are a concern; a social worker working in community support services will still encounter people suffering the impact of childhood abuse.

The second of these strategies, "situation modification" involves modifying aspects of the situation to "change its emotional impact" (Werner and Gross, 2010, p. 23). For example, to reduce our fear of a visiting a person's home, we may ask a colleague to accompany us on the visit. However, our capacity to modify situations we find emotionally evocative are limited because we work in a variety of contexts and often in environments over which we have limited control. Nonetheless it is still worth identifying elements of a situation that may be emotionally evocative and reviewing the options available to assist us in regulating our emotions.

The third strategy is "attentional deployment" which refers to distracting our attention from the emotionally evocative aspects of a situation. This can involve actively ignoring those elements of a situation we find distressing, such as zoning out to verbal abuse. To an extent, our practice frameworks can enable us to deploy our attention in ways that reduce the emotional impact of a situation or behaviour. For example, faced with a person who expressing anger towards us, we may seek to understand the information contained within that anger and how we might draw on this information to make sense of what matters to the service user (Bosly, 2007).

A fourth strategy is referred to as "cognitive change" and involves "changing how we appraise the situation to alter its emotional significance, by changing how we think about either the external or internal situation or our capacity to manage the demands it imposes" (Werner and Gross, 2010, p. 26). This strategy involves thinking about a situation in ways that enable us to find a way to understand and respond to the emotional challenges. For example, we may feel overwhelmed by the large and significant problems facing the person with whom we are communicating. In order to build a working alliance and shared sense of purpose we need to regulate our emotional response sufficiently not to be swept into a sense of helplessness or hopelessness. One way we can do this is encouraging ourselves and the person with whom we are communicating to break down the problem into parts and to work together on the most urgent matters first. In this way, we can build our and the other's confidence and hope in finding solutions to the challenges being faced.

The fifth strategy is "response modulation" which refers to influencing the experiences, behaviours or physiological responses that have been evoked in the situation (Werner and Gross, 2010, p. 29). Response modulation can involve strategies to regulate emotions within the situation. For example, faced with a situation in which we experience strong emotions of anger or fear, we may seek to regulate our physiological responses through deep breathing and deliberately quietening our vocal tone.

As we prepare to communicate with the other, we may also develop a range of response modulation techniques to assist us to regulate responses that may get in the way of forming a working alliance. Self-knowledge about our own signals of emotional elevation, such as physiological signals, can assist in implementing the techniques. Typical early behavioural and physiological signs of emotional arousal include:

➤ quickening of breathing or heart rate.

➤ increased sweating.

➤ change in vocal tone and volume, particularly a heightening of tone and volume.

➤ quickening of speech rate.

➤ change of facial expression.

➤ involuntary muscular movements, such as clenching of fists, moving away from the other.

Some behavioural and physiological strategies for moderating these responses can include:

➤ deliberate slowing of breathing.

➤ lowering of vocal tone and slowing of speech.

➤ purposeful change of facial expression towards a calmer expression.

➤ focusing on relaxing our posture.

Practice exercise: Regulating our emotions

Imagine you have been given a referral to attend a situation that you are likely to find emotionally challenging. The emotion you might experience could be: anger, fear, sadness.

1. Describe the situation that would be likely to evoke at least one of these emotions for you.

2. Now consider how you would use any of the five strategies of emotion regulation discussed here to regulate your emotions.

3. Consider what impact your approach to emotion regulation would have on your capacity to build and maintain a working alliance with the service user.

Our attitudes and judgements

We turn now to consider how our judgements and perceptions can impact on the working alliance. We refer to judgements or perceptions as beliefs about a situation or person that draw on our experiences, values or views. These judgements or perceptions can impact upon us in ways that affect how we engage with the person and may prevent us from being open and focused on our professional purpose. Judgements can also be referred to as prejudices in so far as we draw on previous experience or stereotypes to make an evaluation of a person or their circumstance in ways that deny the unique characteristics of the current situation. Typically we use the term prejudice to refer to negative judgements but prejudices can also lead to overly optimistic views of person and their situation as well. In her review of child protection decision-making, Munro (1996, p. 806; see also Munro, 2008, 2011) concluded that the social workers' beliefs about the situation impacted on how, and whether, they could process new information, she observed:

> The common human failing of tending to notice evidence that supports one's beliefs while overlooking of dismissing evidence that challenges them. When social workers believed a child was a risk they displayed a good standard of investigation and monitoring. When they became optimistic about a family's

progress, they were slower to notice and recognize the evidence of problems that challenged their optimism.

In essence the judgements can be formed prior to or during our communication with service users impacts on how we engage with them and what sense we make of their circumstances.

Judgements and perceptions inevitably arise in all human service work and indeed in all human interaction. Judgements enable us to form mental short cuts that make it possible for us to manage often complex and large amounts of information (Kahneman, 2011). At the same time, judgements can interfere with our ability to engage in an open and focused manner with the person with whom we seek to communicate.

The point is not to avoid judgement, for such a goal is unrealistic, but rather being aware of and subjecting our judgement to critical scrutiny (Keinemans, 2014). Prior to meeting the service user we may have limited time to review our judgements, but we can at the very least be aware of our judgements and perceptions and to be mindful of limiting their impact on how we engage with the service user in initially building the alliance.

The practice of critical reflection can assist us to become mindful of our judgements and increase our capacity to minimise the negative impact of judgements on practice. Reflective practice involves "the unsettling and examination of hidden assumptions in order to rework ideas and professional actions" (Fook, 2013, p. 6). Fook (2013; see also Fook and Gardner, 2007) draws on critical incident techniques to outline a two-step process involving first critical examination of our assumptions in relation to specific events in practice. The second step then involves re-working those assumptions in ways that enable us to promote a working alliance with service users and which promote individual and social change. A critical approach to reflective practice requires us to critically examine how our assumptions and judgements are linked to existing social arrangements (Fook, 2013). For example through critical analysis of a practice situation we may be able to see how a person's individual situation reflects broader social conditions. Critical reflection then reduces the likelihood of negative value judgements compromising our capacity to communicate respectfully.

Critical reflection requires us also to understand other people's responses to us as social workers in the historical and structural context of our practice. For example, an older person may react with caution and apparent suspicion towards a social worker out of fear of the workers' capacity to act in ways that reduce the older person's authority over their

Practice exercise: Practising critical reflection

Returning to the Azim family case study, imagine that Mr Azim has informed you he no longer wishes to live in the community housing project because his wife has formed strong friendships among the women living there. Mr Azim believes that these friendships are interfering with Mrs Azim's focus on the family and has created disrespect for his role as the head of household. Yesterday Mrs Azim and the children arrived home 30 minutes later than expected because they had lost track of time while visiting the home of a family living in the neighbourhood. Mrs Azim is tearful throughout the interview. At one point she quietly points out that the children have made friends among other children living there. Mrs Azim is willing to agree to Mr Azim's wish to leave the community house.

1. What are you assumptions about what is happening in the relationship between Mr and Mrs Azim?

2. What challenges are there to forming a working alliance with Mr and Mrs Azim?

3. How would you manage this situation to ensure that the value of respect for person was evident in how you communicated with Mr and Mrs Azim?

own lives. By encouraging us to identify and analyse our own assumptions and to consider the ways in which an individual's behaviour and situation may reflect broader social arrangements, critical reflective practice can promote respectful communication with others.

Conclusion

We lay the groundwork for the working alliance prior to meeting the service user. In this Chapter, we have outlined three elements of preparing to communicate, these are: practical tasks associated with gaining sufficient information to anticipate and respond to the service user's challenges and needs; analysis of our professional purpose; and developing our capacity for the purposeful use our "selves." We have incorporated emerging research on emotion regulation to provide strategies we may use to build our emotional readiness for practice. We have also considered the role of critical reflection in enabling us to recognise and minimise the impact of assumptions and judgements that may interfere with the formation of the working alliance.

Review questions

1. Why is it important that we prepare to communicate?

2. What are some practical tasks a social worker can undertake to prepare to communicate?

3. What are the elements of professional purpose that we need to communicate to service users?

4. What is emotion regulation and why it is important to preparing to communicate in social work practice?

5. Why is it important to reflect on our judgements and attitudes as we prepare to communicate?

Recommended further reading

Fook, J. & Gardiner, F. (2007). *Practising critical reflection*. London: McGraw-Hill Education.
This book offers a practical guide to the theory and practice of critical reflection. It provides practical illustrations of the use of critical incident techniques to review practice assumptions and to prepare to build knowledge in practice.
Healy, K. (2014). *Social work theories in context: Creating frameworks for practice*. Basingstoke: Palgrave.
In this book is a detailed analysis of the construction of professional purpose in social work practice. The book assists the reader to analyse the influence of institutional context, professional capacities and practice frameworks on the construction of our professional purpose.
Howe, D. (2008). *The emotionally intelligent social worker*. Basingstoke: Palgrave.
Professor David Howe provides an informative guide to emotional intelligence and its relevance to the social worker's capacity to develop and maintain a working alliance with the service user. This book offers a thought-provoking and evidence informed account of the importance of emotions and emotional intelligence to many domains of social work practice.
Hochschild, A. (2012). *The managed heart: Commercialization of human feeling*. Berkeley, CA: University of California Press.
Professor Arlie Hochschild first published this pioneering sociological study of emotions in contemporary work in 1983. In this research monograph she demonstrates the centrality of emotions and emotion regulation to contemporary modes of work, particularly in service industries. Professor Hochschild highlights the social and economic benefits arising from the emotional capacity of service workers and argues for the recognition and reward of emotional labour in the workplace.

Lewis, M., Haviland-Jones & Barrett, L. (2008). *Handbook of emotions* (3rd edition). New York, NY: The Guildford Press.
This is a collection of papers by leading researchers on the psychology of emotions. The Chapter by James Gross, an eminent authority on emotion regulation, is important reading for those seeking deeper understanding of the science of emotion regulation. The book provides a range of evidence based insights into the role and nature of emotions and their impact on many aspects of our lives.

3

Core Communication Skills

We now turn to the use of communication skills in social work practice. Professional communication in social work draws on the skills we use in everyday interactions. The key difference between everyday and professional communication is that the latter involves the deliberate and thoughtful use of communication skills to achieve our professional purpose including in developing and maintaining the working alliance. Allen and Langford (2008, p. 53) assert that "Communication skills are the range of learnt techniques that help social work professionals to communicate clearly, warmly with a wide range of people, even those who may have impaired communication, or whose first language might not be English." A core set of skills underpin effective communication in the diverse contexts of practice and with people of varied cultural and social backgrounds, at different points of the life course and with a range of abilities and needs. In this Chapter, we discuss the core skills of effective interpersonal communication in social work practice. These are skills in: listening; non-verbal communication; use of touch; observation; and verbal or spoken skills. These skills serve as a foundation for everyday practice and as a basis for the more advanced communication skills we will discuss in later Chapters.

Listening skills

Perhaps the most important communication skill a social worker can have is the capacity to listen well. Listening is an active process of engaging with, and facilitating articulation of, the perspectives of the people with whom are communication. Listening is an active process of engaging with the people with whom are communicating to encourage them to express themselves.

How we listen as social workers has many similarities with how we listen in everyday life. For example, in both professional and non-professional contexts we demonstrate listening by being attentive to the speaker. But there are also important differences. One of the most important differences being that listening in social work is a purposeful activity. Even while listening, the social worker will often subtly direct the speaker to particular topics that are important for developing an assessment or intervention plan regarding the issue at hand. While we may consider ourselves to be good listeners in most situations, as a social work professional we are likely to need to further develop our listening skills to respond to the many challenges of listening well in our professional role. Some of these challenges pertain to the pressures of our working environment, such as time limitations, while others relate to the challenges the person may present such as expressing anger and aggression (Chapter 5).

Empathetic listening is important to building and maintaining the working alliance and to developing an understanding of the service user's perspective. "Empathetic listening" refers to the message receiver accurately understanding what the "sender is feeling and thinking" and conveys this understanding in their non-verbal behaviour and verbal tone and expression (Boyle, Hull, Mather, Smith & Farley, 2006, p. 107). Empathetic listening skills are important to almost every social work encounter (Lishman, 2009). Exceptions to this include emergencies where the social work must gain information quickly, such as in a situation where a person is at risk of immediate harm. Even in these situations the social worker needs to demonstrate concern and recognition of the thoughts and feelings of the other person.

To demonstrate that we are listening, we need to create a physical environment in which we can give our undivided attention to the service user. Many practice environments present practical obstacles to achieving this. For example, the lack of physical space for private conversation can be an obstacle. Similarly, interruptions by colleagues, telephones or pagers as we interact with the service user can also disrupt our capacity to give our undivided attention to the service user. There is a risk is that we fail to notice these obstacles because we have become used to them. Nonetheless, they can convey to those with whom we are communicating that we do not have the time to listen to them.

Another component of empathetic listening is that of understanding the speaker's perspective. Our own expectations of the conversation and our prejudices can form barriers to understanding the perspective of another. For example, the expectation that we should focus on risk assessment can prevent us from hearing the service users' perspective on the matter at hand. In contexts where we are listening to a group of people, such as in group work or community development practice, we need to ensure that we are able to hear the range of perspectives present, not only the loudest or most influential voices. A lack of focus on service users or the diverse views of community members' perspective can contribute to a lack of rapport and is likely to deny us important information we need to make sense of the situation in which we are engaged.

Facilitation is also an important element of listening in all methods of direct practice. Facilitation refers to the listener directing the speaker, often in subtle ways, to express their thoughts and feelings in a way that will help them and the worker to understand and act on their situation. An important way we can facilitate discussion is by the use of "continuers" or "minimal encouragers," these are short verbal utterances or non-verbal cues for the other to continue the conversation (Harms, 2015). Examples of verbal minimal encouragers are: "Hmm," "Yes," "I see." Encouragers can also extent to brief statements of empathy, such as, "That must be difficult," or specific invitations for more information, "Tell me more about that." Non-verbal encouragers include nodding to show you understand, or agree with, the speaker's view, or leaning forward to show interest in the speaker's words. Verbal and non-verbal signs of encouragement can also enable you steer the conversation towards the disclosure of information needed to form an assessment and intervention plan with the individual, family, group or community or team with whom you are working.

In nutshell, we can demonstrate that we are listening by:

> minimising distractions and interruptions to the conversation.

> approaching the conversation with an open mind. This may involve being aware of, and putting aside, our pre-existing assumptions.

> encouraging the speaker to express themselves. We can assist this by purposeful use of encouragers and focused questions aimed at bringing attention to parts of the narrative that appear important either for the service user or to the professional purpose on which we are focused.

Listening exercise

Over the next week take note of how you listen in conversation. For this reflective exercise, choose three conversations in which you have been engaged over the week. Try to ensure there is some variation in the examples you choose. Ideally choose an example where you believe you listened well, another where you were dissatisfied with your listening and a third example somewhere in the middle of these two levels of satisfaction. This variation is likely to help you to reflect on your strengths and areas for development as a listener. Complete the following table as you reflect on your examples. In each row, briefly describe the example, such as,

▶

◄

"conversation over lunch with my friend." Then provide a rating from 1 to 5 (with 1 being completely untrue to 5 being completely true) for each of the following elements and outline:

1. I focused entirely on the speaker (consider what helped you focus and what prevented you from focusing, such as distractions)

2. I maintained an open mind (consider what helped you maintain an open mind and any challenges you faced to keeping an open mind)

3. I encouraged the speaker to express themselves (consider how you created or limited opportunities for the speaker to express themselves)

In the final column note your reflections on any other aspect of how you listened, or what prevented you from listening well in the conversation.

	I focused entirely on the speaker	I maintained an open mind	I encouraged the speaker to express themselves	Other reflections
Example 1	(rating 1–5)	(rating 1–5)	(rating 1–5)	
Example 2	(rating 1–5	(rating 1–5)	(rating 1–5)	
Example 3	(rating 1–5)	(rating 1–5)	(rating 1–5)	

Practice reflection: Reflection and discussion questions

After you have completed the listening exercise, consider the following questions.

What have learnt about your strengths as a listener?

What have you learnt about your areas for further development?

Identify two strategies for improving your listening skills.

Listening with two or more people

Many social work practice situations involve listening to more than one person. For example, when communicating with families and with groups it is important that we demonstrate we are listening to each person. By demonstrating we are listening to each person we build their confidence as someone who wants, and is able, to assist the family or group. In addition, by listening to all members perspectives we can develop a comprehensive picture of the situation that recognises similarities and differences in the viewpoints of members of the family or group.

There are a number of strategies that social workers can use to ensure that they are able to listen equitably to different viewpoints. These strategies include:

➤ establishing ground rules or principles at the outset of a meeting that encourage recognition of all perspectives.

➤ ensuring that equivalent time is allocated to hearing different perspectives.

➤ subtly facilitating equivalent speaking space to each person. For example, in a family meeting, the social worker may direct open questions to specific individuals, rather than asking open questions to the whole family group.

➤ being explicit about ensuring equal speaking space, for example, stating that a particular group member has already spoken and asking for another person to speak.

➤ increasing awareness within the family or group of patterns of inequality in speaking and inviting the group to take responsibility for ensuring greater equality in speaking. For instance, we can provide members of the group with visual cues that show who is speaking most often in a group.

➤ ensuring the safety of each person to speak. In some situations, such as abuse or violence within the family, it may be necessary to hold separate meetings for different family members.

Non-verbal communication

We turn next to non-verbal communication. This refers to communication through our physical presence and behaviour. Non-verbal behaviour includes: facial expression, posture, pitch and tone of voice, and cues such as nodding, distance to the other person. We will also consider presentation of self and use of touch as part of our discussion of non-verbal communication. It is important that we give at least as much attention to our non-verbal communication as our spoken communication for two reasons (Lishman, 2009). The first is that non-verbal communication is a highly influential form of communication. Studies on communication have indicated that up to 85 per cent of the communication is conveyed through non-verbal interaction (Harms, 2015, p. 36). The second reason is that attention to non-verbal communication is vital to developing a working alliance based between the social worker and the service user.

Achieving congruence in non-verbal communication helps to demonstrate to the other person that we understand and empathise with them. Social workers need to be able to reflect upon their non-verbal behaviour and to adjust this behaviour to communication needs of service users and their specific practice environment. One of the challenges in communicating non-verbally is that much of this behaviour is unconscious to us. For example, we may be unaware of a habit that can, in a practice environment, become distracting to the service user. Also, non-verbal communication "habits" that we may have developed in one context, may be inappropriate another context. For example, in some practice environments, it may be appropriate to have open, smiling and engaging facial expression and in other contexts, such as some legal contexts or in situations dealing where clients are dealing with sudden trauma, such facial expressions may be inappropriate.

A number of models of non-verbal communication have been developed to assist social workers, and other helping professionals, to reflect upon and to demonstrate non-verbal behaviour that is appropriate to facilitating a constructive and purposeful interaction. Most of these guides have been developed for counselling and casework interactions but, nonetheless, have utility for other situations where the social workers seek to demonstrate engagement, interest and empathy with others. One of the most well-known models of non-verbal communication for health and social care professionals is S.O.L.E.R. This model was developed by Gerard Egan (2010) for counsellors and caseworkers, however can also be used as a framework for reviewing our non-verbal behaviour in other contexts. The meaning of the acronym S.O.L.E.R. is as follows:

S: Sitting squarely, that is facing the person we are communicating.

O: Open body posture. This involves avoiding crossing one's arms across one's body or placing an object across one's body, such as a folder. However, crossed legs are acceptable as long as it is does not compromise the perception of an open body posture.

L: Leaning towards the other sufficiently to demonstrate interest and engagement, but not so far as to imply a level of intensity that could be uncomfortable for the person with whom we are communicating.

E: Eye contact. Maintaining an appropriate level of eye contact with the service user to demonstrate that we are listening and interested in their story, but no so much as to intimidate.

R: Relaxed. Appearing relaxed in one's facial expression and body posture is important to putting those with whom we are communicating at ease.

Egan's model is helpful on a number of levels. The simple acronym, S.O.L.E.R. covers many dimensions of non-verbal behaviour and it is easy to recall enabling us to quickly assess and adjust our non-verbal behaviour even in the midst of a practice situation. While some may regard the model as prescriptive, it is sufficiently broad to be relevant to a range of contexts of professional communication.

Nonetheless, the model does not address some cultural, gender and contextual differences that can impact on effective non-verbal communication. The model places great emphasis on the postural aspects of non-verbal communication but less on other equally important aspects of non-verbal communication such as facial expression, interpersonal distance, and appearance. In Chapter 6, we consider how we can demonstrate cultural sensitivity in our non-verbal communication.

Another issue to consider is the behavioural adjustments needed if the person with whom we are communicating is not seated in a chair, which can be case in some health care settings. Storlie (2015, p. 77) notes if the person "is lying in bed or sitting in a wheelchair, the provider should position him or herself at the eye level of the individual rather than talking over a side rail or standing above them." The worker should be sensitive to the continuing need to maintain a posture that facilitates engagement with the other as a partner in communication.

Appearance, identity and communication

Our physical appearance, particularly our clothing, personal grooming and general demeanour, communicates a great deal about ourselves, particularly our identity, to others. This information can be important to the service users' assessment of whether they regard us as a credible source of assistance to them. Like all aspects of ourselves, our appearance is the also a dimension of the use of self in social work and, no less than our verbal and non-verbal communication, should be subject of critical reflection. Some aspects of our appearance reflect aspects of our identity and, as such, we may not want to change these aspects of our appearance or these aspects may be unalterable. How we manage these aspects of our appearance and identity in our interactions with service users is likely to be quite different to those aspects of our appearance, such as our clothing and general demeanour.

Let's turn first to those aspects of our appearance that are amenable to change and which may have significant influence of service user's perceptions of us and our capacity to be of assistance to them. These aspects include our clothing, our personal grooming and our general physical appearance and demeanour. Very little attention is paid in the social work literature to these aspects of our appearance. This is surprising given the large body of literature in other fields, such as business, on the importance of appearance to effective impression management and engagement with the service users. In some practice contexts, such as health services, there are formal dress codes which apply to a broad range of staff including social workers. Beyond these specific practice contexts, the issue of appearance is rarely discussed. It is as though many of us assume, incorrectly, that our presentation has little impact on our relationships with service users or in service users' assessment of our capacity.

Like all aspects of self in social work, our appearance should be subject to critical reflection. In addition to sending a message of respect for others, social workers should convey in their words and actions a clear statement of their professional purpose which should always include the ability and willingness to be of assistance to service users and community members (Sheldon and Macdonald, 2009). In reflecting a capacity for personal self-care, our appearance can also promote service user's confidence in our capacity to be assistance to them.

A neutral clean appearance helps to reduce the chance that your appearance will be distraction for the service user. Our attire and demeanour should reflect the accepted standards of the variety of services and individuals with whom we are likely to engage in our daily work, not only the standards of the service we are employed within. For example, working in a service for young people we will be likely to interact not only with the young people, but perhaps also their families, the police service, schools and the legal profession. We need to ensure that we respect the dress codes of Courts of Law and other environments, such as public talks, where you seek to advocate or publicly represent service users. Failure to reflect these codes will limit your credibility and may negatively affect your capacity to convey your message.

Let's turn now to those aspects of our appearance which may be difficult or impossible to alter. Unalterable or difficult to alter aspects of ourselves that are likely to influence our appearance can include: our age; our gender; our height and weight; our skin tone and facial shape; and signifiers of ability or disability. These elements of our appearance reflect aspects of our personal and cultural identity (or identities) to service users and can be the subject of positive or negative assessment by them. For example, the service user may comment that they would prefer to have a social worker of a different age, gender, or ethnicity to your own. In some cases, we may be required by law to accommodate these requests, such as services where clients have a right to be served by a person of their gender or ethnic group. In some, but not all cases, we may work in a service where the workforce is sufficiently large and diverse to accommodate the service user's request for another worker based on perceived greater compatibility between themselves and a worker with a similar set of identities to them.

Anti-oppressive practice theory emphasises that practitioners should be able to critically reflect on their identities and how this shapes their interactions with service users (Healy, 2014; Dominelli, 2002). Accordingly, it is important that we are able to critically reflect on our appearance and our identities and, as appropriate, to explore the service users' concerns with them. For example, a child protection service user may complain about the involvement of an "older worker whose kids are grown up" or a "young, childless worker." The social worker could respond to this by acknowledging and exploring the service user's concerns; these concerns may include the perception that the worker will not understand or may judge them. If the social worker can explore these concerns and commit both in their words and actions to the values that the service user would like to see in the relationship, such as understanding and a non-judgemental attitude, the worker is likely to overcome the service user's concerns. While it is easy to become defensive when aspects of our identity are questioned, it is more productive for our relationship with the service user if we can explore the basis of their concerns and put strategies in place to address these concerns. In so doing, we demonstrate a genuine willingness to be of assistance and this attitude is positively correlated with client satisfaction with social work services (Maiter et al., 2006; Sheldon and MacDonald, 2009).

Touch

Touch refers to bodily contact between two people. Touch is a complex area of communication with a variety of possible meanings depending on its context and on the nature of the touch. Touch can be used to convey a range of intentions including affection, reassurance and solidarity or, conversely, touch can convey dominance (Green, 2017; Lynch and Garrett, 2010). Where touch is discussed in social work, it is often in relation to the possible risks associated with touch between the worker and people using our services. Insights from trauma-informed practice have contributed to social workers awareness of the potential for touch to trigger traumatic memories (Havig, 2008). In addition, Green (2017, p. 774) notes social workers "may be inhibited from utilizing supportive touch because of concerns about crossing professional boundaries and fictitious abuse allegations." Growing awareness of the historical abuse of vulnerable people, particularly children, in institutional care where inappropriate touch was integral to the abuse suffered may contribute also to a reluctance to incorporate touch particularly in relation to children (Lynch and Garrett, 2010). The National Association of Social Workers (NASW, 2008, p. 1) Code of Ethics instructs that social workers "should not engage in physical contact when there is a possibility of psychological harm to the client as a result of the contact (such as cradling or caressing clients)." The NASW further asserts that social workers are responsible for setting clear, appropriate and culturally sensitive boundaries when physical contact occurs.

Cultural differences in the use of touch are frequently observed (see Chapter 6, this volume). Some cultures have higher levels of casual touch than others (Jandt, 2016). Cultural differences extend to the use of touch in professional communication. While engaged in residential social work practice in the Republic of South Africa, Lynch and Garrett (2010) observed workers to much more frequently engage in positive displays of affection and support using touch than occurs in the Republic of Ireland.

Despite the risks associated with touch, appropriate use of touch can support the working alliance through demonstrating a wish to connect with the other and empathy with them. In their small exploratory study, Lynch and Garrett (2010, p. 392) report that residential social workers working with children regard touch as appropriate when "initiated by the child; carried out for practical reasons (e.g. transporting a child); ensured safety (e.g. holding hands crossing a road); play focused; offered comfort and reassurance; facilitated communication; accompanied greetings and saying 'goodbye'." As with other forms of nonverbal communication, the social worker needs to be attuned to the other person's response to the use of touch. Green (2017) proposes that touch should be limited at least initially to touching of hands, such as the back of the hand, or forearm to support. As the social worker becomes more known to the service it may be appropriate to extend this further. For example, Green (2017, p. 786) suggests that "touch can also be offered rather than imposed, such as offering a hug to a distressed service user."

The use of touch in social work communication is controversial. Touch can be both beneficial and harmful to the working alliance. When used skilfully and appropriately, touch can support social workers to communicate care and empathy for the other. To use touch skilfully the social worker needs to commence with the tentative use of touch on safe zones of the body, such as the hand of the other person, and to learn through implicit and explicit feedback about whether the use of touch supports effective communication with the person (Green, 2017). Where the social worker uses touch in their communication, they should do in ways that support the professional working alliance and which are responsive to the cultural context of the communication (NASW, 2008). In addition, the social worker should refrain from using touch in situations where a person is angry or aggressive as this may exacerbate their heightened emotional state (see Chapter 5, this volume)

Practice exercise

Undertake a role play involving person who is in emotional distress due to loss. Practice the role play without any use of touch by the social worker and then practice it again with the deliberate use of "safe" touch, such as touch on the hand or forearm of the person who is playing the distressed service user.

Review what impact if any the presence and absence of touch had on the worker's capacity to convey empathy and support for the service user.

Observation skills

Observation refers to taking note of, and analysing, what we see and experience either in our direct interaction with service users and community members or when we observe them in interactions with others, such as family or community members. The profession's recognition of the importance of observation has varied at different points in our history and among different groups in the profession (Le Riche, 1998). Observation of infants and children, particularly in interaction with their parents, has been a cornerstone of psychodynamic approaches to social work (Tanner, 1998). Within the psychodynamic approach, observation is distinct from active engagement with service users and may involve the social worker in observing the service user(s) from a distance, such as behind a two way mirror (Trowell and Miles, 1991, cited in Tanner, 1998, p. 11). Ferguson (2011, p. 206) has argued for renewed acknowledgment of the role of observation as part of what he defines as "intimate social work practice"; that is practice which recognises "the centrality of the emotions and the body and the mind of the worker and service user in doing and experiencing" social work. In this section, we refer to observation as part of the active engagement between us as social workers and those with whom we work.

Observation provides us with information about the emotional state and reactions of those with whom they work. This information can enhance our capacity to communicate with a diverse range of individuals and communities. For example, in working with a family where there is conflict between a young person and their parent, we may use our observations about the relative disengagement of the young person to allow him/her as much space as possible in determining whether and how they will join our meeting with his or her family.

By sharing some of our observations with the service users we can also build a common understanding of his/her circumstances. Sharing observations can be seen as a form of clarification in that we invite the service user to comment on our observations. For example, as part of developing a case plan with a young person leaving out-of-home care, we might share with him or her that while he/she appears to be relieved to have left the care system, he/she also seem sad about the loss of connection with a foster parent. This reflection could help us to explore the service user experiences in care and what points of connection, if any, he/she would like to maintain with their foster family or the care system.

In a cross-cultural context, much information is to be gained by observing norms about interaction. For example, we may observe that there appears to be age hierarchy determining who speaks first in any interaction or we may notice that facial expression and vocal tone is subdued. By observing and reflecting these patterns, you enhance your ability to communicate effectively with people from cultures other than your own.

Observations about service users and community members' response to us, as workers, can also provide a basis for critical reflection on our practice (Le Riche, 1998). By reflecting on circumstances in which we experience an unexpected or unpleasant response from a service user, or community member, we might reflect on what contribution we have made to that reaction. It may be that the service user's response has valuable information for us about our role and how we might improve our communication in this role. For example, reflecting upon a situation in which we appeared to trigger an angry response from a service user, we may find that we failed to communicate difficult information in a sufficiently sensitive way or that our timing of the communication contributed to the service user's response. Of course, it also needs to be acknowledged that the very nature of some social work roles is more likely to give rise to negative responses from service users, such as any role that involves curtailing service user's individual rights, such as roles in statutory social work services. Even so, reflecting on how we might most clearly and sensitively communicate with service users is likely to enhance our capacity to build an effective working relationship in these roles (Trotter, 2004, 2013; see also Miller, 2009).

Observation about our own responses to circumstances we encounter in our practice are important to critical reflection. Our own intuitive reactions to situations, particularly strong reactions, should not be ignored. By subjecting our reactions to critical scrutiny, we may uncover personal biases but, equally, we may also recognise that there is an issue that needs further exploration. For example, a strong negative "gut" reaction to a parent we meet in the context of a child protection assessment may, upon reflection, be found to be due to the fact that the parent has similar physical features to an abusive parent with whom you have previously worked. This insight can enable us to avoid allowing previous practice encounters to negatively impact on the current practice situation. Alternatively, upon reflection, we might conclude that our reaction was a response to parent's negative description of the child and the sad demeanour of the child, and we may decide that further assessment of the situation is required.

Building a shared understanding: Reflective listening and speaking skills

In many contexts of social work practice, we need to develop an accurate and detailed picture of the other person's perspectives. Developing this understanding is an active process requiring good listening skills, facilitation skills and the capacity to check the accuracy of our emerging understanding with those with whom we are interacting. Whereas in everyday conversation, we might engage in a two-way expression process, in social work practice our communication process should be focused on enabling the other person to express themselves. For example, if a service user tells us they are grieving the breakdown of their relationship with a partner, it is more important for us to explore with them their experience of grief than sharing our experience of grieving over a similar loss. Of course, it may be appropriate to share that we have had a similar experience, but only in so far as it enables the service user or community member to express themselves. In a professional practice context, the focus of the interaction should remain on the service user or community member and not be on expression or exploration of the social worker's experience.

We now turn to communication skills that we use to: stay on track and to develop a shared understanding with the service user of their situation and the focus of our work together. Paraphrasing involves a brief statement reflecting back to the service user or community members, our understanding of the thoughts or feelings underpinning, or evident, in what is he/she said and which may also be evident in the demeanour of the service user. For example, in response to a young person happily discussing the apartment they have just moved into, we might say: "It sounds like you are happy in your new home."

Accurate paraphrasing demonstrates we are listening. Paraphrasing helps to ensure the accuracy our understanding, as through paraphrasing we can provide the service user with an opportunity to correct our view. Paraphrasing is used more frequently in casework and counselling than in everyday conversation. This is because one function of paraphrasing is to keep the discussion focused on the issue at hand and on enabling the service user to express their views; this contrasts with the mutual exchange of viewpoints that characterises everyday conversation.

Parroting involves repeating back the exact words of the service user and is used to emphasise key points in the statements to you. For example, in the following statement, "After hearing the news, I went into shock," we might parrot back "Went into shock." Parroting can be part of demonstrating understanding and empathy of the service user's or community members' situation.

The third of these tracking and focusing skills is the skill of "clarification." Clarification involves seeking a more complete understanding of the person's situation. Clarification is important for ensuring that you understand who and what is important to the service user or community member. In seeking clarification, it is important to avoid sounding inquisitorial. For example, it is important to avoid terms like "please explain" when asking for further information. Instead, it can be helpful to put forward your understanding as a clarifying question such as: "So Joanne is your daughter, is that right?" This question allows the service user to clarify their relationship to "Joanne." We can also avoid sounding inquisitorial by asking in sensitive way for more information, such as "Can you tell me a little more about your relationship with Joanne?" Clarifying statements and questions can also relate to service users' experience of an event. For example, at a community meeting you might ask: "Can I please clarify then, the community was not informed about the government consultation of the plan to build a block of apartments on the land?" It is important that clarifying statements include the option for respondents to correct your interpretation. An explicit questions, such as "Have I interpreted that correctly?" can help to let respondents know you are seeking their viewpoints.

While clarifying questions, paraphrasing and parroting are important for keeping us on track and for ensuring the alignment of our interpretation with the view of the service user, clarification needs also to be used sparingly. An overuse of clarifying questions can create an impression that we are not listening attentively or that we do not have the capacity to understand the service users' or community members' story. A person can become frustrated if they are asked, too frequently, to explain or clarify points that they believe should be obvious to the service provider. For example, a community worker would be expected to have some understanding of recent events, particularly high-profile events in the community and of key members of the community, such as formal and informal leaders.

The skill of summarising refers to the use of statements that bring together the key issues raised and points covered and will often involve a statement of future action. Because of the range of topics covered, summaries will tend to be significantly longer than paraphrases. Summaries can also facilitate some power sharing in the casework interaction by providing service user with both clarity about the caseworker's understanding of the major themes and proposed directions for future action and with the opportunity to clarify misinterpretation. Summaries need to be used sparingly as their overuse can lead to too greater focus on the sense the worker is making of the interaction rather than facilitating the service user's expression views.

The use of questions

The effective use of questions is important in all forms of social work to gain a clear understanding of the service users' situation. Yet, the inappropriate use of questions can have a negative effect on your relationship with the service user. Perhaps most obviously, the overuse of closed questions, can lead the service user to feel they are being interrogated. As we develop our communication skills for practice it is important that we consider the different forms of questions and their effects of our professional relationships.

Open questions refer to questions that are intended to elicit an answer that encourages the client to answer in an extended or narrative form. According to Boyle et al. (2006, p. 123) "Open-ended questions allow the client to answer as he or she chooses, giving whatever detail the client deems appropriate based on the client's interpretation of the situation." Open-ended questions can be helpful in indicating the service user that you are actively seeking their view of the situation and as such as important for building rapport and gaining a shared understanding of the situation.

Open-ended questions may begin with words such as "what," "how," "when" and "who" or with questioning statements hinting at information you might be looking for. For example, we may state "John, can you tell me a little more about what has happened at home to make you so unhappy there." This hinting style of questioning, which is intended to invite the service user to tell of their perspective, can be especially important when working with services users from non-Western cultures. For instance, indigenous service users can find direct questions including open questions intrusive and intimidating (Eades, 2013; for further discussion see Chapter 6 of this book).

We should avoid questions beginning with "why" because such questions can appear inquisitorial and imply that the worker does not believe, understand, or empathise with the service user's view. For example, the question "Why didn't you leave the situation" can imply that the service user should have left the situation. Similarly "Why did you take the pills?" can imply that the person should not have taken the pills or that the worker is finding it hard to understand their actions. The intention to explore the motivations for taking "the pills" could be put more openly as: "What were you feeling when you took the pills?"

Open-ended questions can be limited or create problems in some situations. Open-ended questions may not be helpful in situations where specific information is needed, such as in possible medical emergencies or in referring clients to services. For example, in a situation where you suspect a client has overdosed on medication, you may need to know the amount of medication taken. Similarly, open-ended questions may not be helpful in gaining information needed to determine client eligibility for a service. Open-ended questions can also be unhelpful when the client is an emotional state that can impede their capacity to express themselves fully. For example, a person in a state of emotional shock may be too overwhelmed to answer open questions. Also, it is also important to limit open-ended questions in situations where you have limited time to hear the answers. When we are under significant time pressures, it is better to communicate this to the service user than to cut off the service user as they respond to questions from us.

Closed questions are questions that call for a short answer of a single word, such as yes or no, to a short sentence. Closed questions can be helpful for gathering specific information. This information may be needed to gain an overview of the service user's situation, to determine their eligibility for a service, or to investigate a particular concern. In some instances, these questions might form part of the initial engagement with the service user, such as "I just need to ask some questions before we can discuss your matter in more detail."

Closed questions should be used sparingly in social work practice. A key problem is that closed questions reinforce the power of the worker to direct the interaction. For this reason, the extensive use of closed questions can be a direct contradiction of our value of promoting the service user's capacity for self-determination. The extended use of closed questions creates an inquisitorial tone to the interview that is likely to alienate the service user. Boyle et al. (2006, p. 124) also suggest that the overuse of closed questions can reinforce the view of the service provider as expert and so erroneously lead the service user to believe that "Once they have supplied all the answers, the social worker will provide a solution."

In recent years, with the growth of strengths-, narrative- and solution-focused approaches to practice, there is increased development of questions as part of the assessment and intervention process. Despite their different philosophical origins, narrative, strengths and solution focused approaches all recognise the power of language in shaping service outcomes. Across these different approaches, language is recognised as much more than a vehicle for expression and instead can shape our awareness of the possibilities open to us. One shared characteristic of these different approaches is the optimistic view of human capacity, and hence there is some emphasis on questions that reveal and explore those capacities. We turn here to some examples of these types of questions.

Coping questions are questions that explore how the client has coped with their situation. For example, instead of only exploring a range of problems a service user has experienced, the worker may also ask "Given everything that's going on for you right now, how have you managed to get the children to school every day?" Coping questions can help to focus our and the service user's attention on the service user's capacities and in so doing counter the focus on failure or pathology that can easily dominate social work interactions, such as risk assessments. Coping questions also can demonstrate that you are seeking to understand and empathise with the service user's circumstance.

Exception questions are questions that ask service users to report on situations where they experienced a breakthrough, or at least a break from, the issue of concern. For example, when working with a young person who has missed two of the past five days at school, the worker might ask "What was different about the two days that you were able to get to school?" Like coping questions, exception questions challenge a focus on the problems facing the individual and instead draw attention to exceptions to the problem. We can use these exceptions as a way of assisting people to develop solutions that may work for them.

Scaling questions are questions that ask the service user to rate their experience on a continuum. For example, the worker might ask "On a scale of one to ten, with one feeling completely anxious and with ten feeling completely calm, can you tell me how you feel about your anxiety today." The scaling questions allow enable a person to "externalise" a problem. This means that the worker and the person with whom they are working view the issue as something external to the client and this can assist us to reconceptualise a problem as more amenable to change then if it were an integral part of the person. For example, a person might reconceptualise themselves a person who battles, and sometimes beats, anxiety, rather than as an "anxious person."

Miracle questions invite the service user to consider their situation without the problem or issue of concern. The term "miracle" is used to refer to the fact that the worker is inviting the client not to engage in a step by step analysis of their concern but rather to imagine a completely different situation. For example, the worker may ask, "If this nightmare was over tomorrow, how would your life be different?" or "If a miracle happened tonight, what would your life be like tomorrow?" Like coping and exception questions, the miracle question is intended to counter a focus on pathology or failure. It is also intended to invite us, as workers and those with whom we work to spend at least as much of our energies on creating a different and more positive future and we do on understanding the problems of the present.

Demonstrating sympathy and empathy

In many social work contexts the demonstration of sympathy and empathy are important for expressing concern for the service user and understanding of their situation. These concepts are helpful to building rapport with the service user.

Sympathy refers to acknowledging and being moved by the experience of the other. For example, in hearing about a young mother's struggle to complete school, a social worker may sympathetically comment on the difficulty of the young person's struggle with words such as "That must be really difficult." Similarly, in hearing that a service user has recently been widowed, the social worker might state "I'm sorry for your loss." An expression of sympathy shows that you hear the difficulty being experienced, and expressed, by the other person. Sympathy has been described as "passive understanding" (Trevithick, 2005, p. 154) because it requires only that the sympathiser observe and reflect back the other's expression of their experience. Even so, sympathetic responses can be helpful for demonstrating our willingness to acknowledge the experience of the other. On the other hand, too much sympathy can be experienced as unhelpful because it can lead the service user to conclude that the social worker did not "really understand" or could not "identify" with their situation.

Empathy refers to a willingness to imagine and, in that imagining, experience some of the pain or difficulty of the service user. By empathising we put ourselves in the position of the other person and reflect back to them what you imagine their experience to be like. Empathy is often regarded as more active than sympathy because it requires us to more fully enter into the experience of the service user. The demonstration of empathy involves a number of elements, including:

➤ identifying the experience of the service user.

➤ imagining what that experience is like for the service user (in other words, trying to enter into the lived experience of the service user).

➢ putting that understanding, borne of imaginatively entering into the service user's world, into words.

➢ providing them with the opportunity to further explore that understanding.

The following example demonstrates the difference between a sympathetic and empathic response.

Practice example

Service user: Since the diagnosis, I feel I can't go on, I have no motivation, everything seems bleak.

Practitioner: I'm sorry this is such a difficult time for you **(sympathetic response).**

Practitioner: The diagnosis has left you feeling sad and frightened. It seems that it is difficult to find a reason to go on with your future seeming so uncertain. Is that how you are feeling? **(empathetic response).**

I have concluded the empathic statement with a question because it is important for the service user to have the opportunity to correct your understanding of their situation. This can be achieved by including an vocal inflection at the end of the sentence, to indicate that a correction is welcome, or by the inclusion of a direct question, such as "Have I understood you correctly?"

Practice exercise: Developing sympathetic and empathetic responses

Consider the following service user statements and develop a sympathetic or empathetic response to the statements. Statement from young woman whose partner has become increasingly verbally hostile towards her, "Rob has been really angry lately and, after last night's violent outburst, I'm frightened to go home."

Sympathetic statement:

Empathetic statement:

Strengths and limits of empathy

The demonstration of empathy is widely regarded as a cornerstone of effective social work practice because of its potential to: demonstrate care for the service user; build rapport; and promote service user insight into how their experience may be viewed by others. Trevithick (2005, p. 155) states:

> the importance of being understood by another human being is enormously important, not least because it can lead to self-understanding. Self-understanding can last a lifetime: longer than our professional involvement, which may be fleeting. Nevertheless our role in this process of self-discovery may be deeply significant.

Many social workers view that demonstration of empathy is integral to achieving change especially in interpersonal and group work practice. When we demonstrate empathy we can create a safe space in which in the service user and community member can explore the challenges facing them.

Demonstrating empathy is also important in community practice and policy contexts. However, much less has been written on empathy in macro practice contexts. Empathy is important in macro practice contexts for demonstrating to community members or to other participants in the policy process that you understand their point of view. Indeed, if the community worker or policy worker is unable to demonstrate empathy for a range of positions on an issue they risk being perceived as "captured" by a particular interest group or community. Empathy is important for negotiating across differences, such as differences within a community or different perspectives on a policy outcomes, and thus for achieving a workable solution to community or policy problems.

The capacity of the worker to demonstrate empathy has been shown to be an important factor in service user satisfaction with service provision (Maiter et al., 2006; Trotter, 2002). Workers' use of empathy has been linked to positive outcomes in child protection, for example, children being in care for shorter periods, families making more progress (see Trotter, 2013). Lack of empathy, as indicated by workers making judgemental comments about families or individuals has been linked to negative outcomes, such as greater levels of continued offending among juvenile offenders than would be anticipated by their case history (Trotter, 2015).

While the importance of the capacity to demonstrate empathy is well established, research points to some problems in the use of empathy also. The first is that workers' inappropriate use of empathy has been linked in some circumstances to negative service outcomes. For example, referring to research on juvenile offenders, Trotter (2013) concluded that workers who demonstrate high levels of empathy may inadvertently imply that they not only understand but endorse the service user's behaviour including anti-social behaviour. In his study of child protection services, Trotter (2002) stated that it was necessary for workers to combine an empathetic and positive approach to service users with clear expectations and willingness to gently confront families with abuse and neglect concerns.

Trotter (2015, pp. 164–168) states that empathy should be linked to a clarity of purpose and a "pro-social" perspective on the part of the service provider. Pro-social perspective means reinforcing behaviours and attitudes that are consistent with the goals you are trying to achieve with the service user (e.g. reduced violence, increased school attendance) and challenging anti-social or criminal comments or actions (Trotter, 2015). Trotter (2015, Chapter 4) identifies four steps in promoting pro-social attitudes in our communication with service user, these are:

1. the worker identifies pro-social attitudes or behaviour by the service user or community member (e.g. attending parenting group)

2. the worker rewards and encourages pro-social attitudes and behaviours, through for example, noticing and praising those attitudes and behaviours

3. the worker models prosocial actions and comments in the way they relate to the service user (e.g. being respectful, punctual).

4. the worker challenges anti-social behaviours or comments (e.g. "everybody does it" "it doesn't harm anyone").

A further limit to empathy is its potential to lead us to over-identify with the service user and in so doing leave us unable to confront aspects of the service user's outlook or behaviour that may harm others. Writing on the problems of over-identification in child protection work, Killen (1996, p. 793) defines over-identification as:

> a form of projective identification where we project onto the parents our own feelings and qualities or feelings or feelings and qualities we believe that we have towards children, instead of empathizing with and facing the parents' and children's realities.

Avoiding over-identification can be a particular challenge because the demonstration of empathy inherently relies on our capacity to imagine what it would be like to walk in the service user's shoes. Assuming how we would feel and react if we were in the situation of the service user can prevent us from understanding service user motivations or attitudes that may be far different to our own, or at least to the motivations we are willing to attribute to ourselves. In other words, we are likely to attribute to ourselves and to service users more positive motivations than might necessarily be the case. At its most problematic, over-identification can prevent us from seeing how the service user may hold attitudes or engage in behaviours that inadvertently or deliberately harm others. For example, the belief that all parents care for their children, if given the right circumstances, may prevent us from identifying the very small proportion of parents who present a true danger to their children. Similarly, assuming that the juvenile offender violent behaviour was an expression of their desperate circumstances can lead us to underestimate the experience of the victim and to perhaps underestimate the violent intent of the offender. Engaging in critical reflection with peers and with a professional supervisor can be helpful in recognising when we have begun to over-identify with service users and it can help us in facing the service user in their "reality" rather than in the reality we might imagine. Of course, it is important that your supervisor has the capacity themselves to stand outside the practice situation. This can be a particular problem where the supervisor also has developed a position or perspective in relation to particular cases as can happen when the supervisor is also involved with the same practice situation. In some instances, therefore, it may be necessary to seek external supervision.

Conclusion

In this Chapter we have considered the core skills that underpin effective communication in social work practice. These skills are also used in every day conversation however in social work practice we deploy these skills purposefully to build and sustain the working alliance and to achieve other professional purposes, such as developing a shared understanding of the life challenges facing the service user. These skills also provide a foundation for communication with people who have diverse capacities and needs discussed in Part 2 of this book.

Review points and questions

1. Outline three reasons why it is important for social workers to listen well in practice.

2. Discuss how non-verbal communication affects a social worker's capacity to effectively engage with people from diverse cultural groups.

3. What are some arguments for and against the use of touch in social work communication?

4. Discuss why observation is an important part of communication in social work.

5. Discuss the meaning of empathy and its uses and limits in social work practice.

Practice exercises

1. Undertake a role play of the following situation to experiment with the use of different types of questions in social work communication.

Imagine you work in the rehabilitation ward of a hospital where your role involves helping people who experience a range of health challenges in returning to their homes. Part of your role involves assessing the level of support the patients have in their home and their community as this support can make a substantial difference in the capacity of people to manage the challenges of daily living. In this role play, imagine you are meeting Betty Miller, a 75-year-old widow who lives at home. She is about to return home after five days in hospital following a hip fracture sustained after a fall in her home. Following the fall, she spent a night on the floor of her home unable to move or to reach a phone to call for help. Although the rehabilitation team has organised a personal alarm for Betty to wear at all times so that she can call for help if she needs it, and they have organised for a range of home improvements, Betty is anxious about returning home. Other members of the team have noted that Betty seems anxious not only about another fall but also about returning to living alone as she appears to be socially isolated.

In this role play, your purpose is to explore with Mrs Miller her concerns about returning home. Try first to explore these concerns using closed questions. Note what impact the use of closed questions has on the interaction. Try conducting the role play again, this time using more open questions and using at least two of the following question types: coping questions; exception seeking questions; scaling questions; and miracle questions. What impact do these questions have on the interaction with Mrs Miller?

2. Communicate skilfully to build the working alliance

Imagine you work at a non-government organisation that provides practical assistance (such as food, assistance with bills and accommodation) as well as referral to specialist services to many disadvantaged people living in the area. Today you are

▶

◀

about to meet Nadia, a 28-year-old woman from Sudan. She and her husband fled Sudan five years ago. Together they have two young children and she is five months pregnant with her third child. Nadia and her family live in public housing and experience financial hardship. Nadia and her husband regularly visit your service and they have good English-language skills. Nadia's husband, Omar is unwell today, so you are meeting her alone. The receptionist says that Nadia has asked to see a social worker about financial help and a "personal" matter.

➢ Identify and discuss what might be the challenges in forming a working alliance with Nadia.

➢ Discuss how you would use the communication skills discussed in this Chapter to build a working alliance with Nadia.

➢ Role-play the scenario using the communication skills we have discussed in this Chapter.

Recommended further reading

Harms, L. (2015). *Working with People: Communication Skills for Reflective Practice* (2nd edition). South Melbourne, VIC: Oxford
This book introduces core skills and foundational theoretical perspectives for the social work interview.
Lishman, J. (2009). *Communication in Social Work* (2nd edition). Basingstoke: Palgrave.
This book provides a practical guide for communication skills in direct practice with individuals and families.
Trotter, C. (2013). *Working with Involuntary Clients* (3rd edition). Crows Nest, NSW: Allen and Unwin.
This book offers a very helpful guide to the evidence base for effective communication with people who are involuntary users of social work services. The book outlines a person-centred and pro-social approach in which the social worker uses the working alliance to recognise and support pro-social attitudes and behaviours. The book is particularly helpful for circumstances in which the social work role involves encouraging behavioural or attitudinal change.

4

Communication and Heightened Emotions

People facing life challenges are likely to experience heightened emotional states. These heightened emotions including elevated states of fear, sadness, despair and anger can profoundly influence communication. Social workers need to be able to recognise and respond to these emotions which are commonly encountered by people experiencing life challenges in ways that support and sustain the working alliance. In this Chapter we outline the importance of emotions in communication. We then define heightened emotions and the causes of these emotional states. We then discuss how social workers can recognise these emotions while also supporting service users to regulate their emotions sufficiently to enable thoughtful and emotionally informed responses to the challenges they face.

Communication and emotions

In Chapters 1 and 2 we discussed the importance of recognising the emotional dimensions of communication. We have noted that attending to the emotional dimensions of communication is vital to building and maintaining the working alliance and to gaining a shared understanding of the service user's situation. This is particularly so in situations where people experience emotional distress (McCabe and Priebe, 2008). We have observed also that regulating our own emotions is important to being present with the other and to building their capacity to regulating their emotions.

Emotions have a powerful influence on communication. Winkielman, Berridge and Sher (2011, p. 207) observe "emotional reactions come with a sense of urgency." In addition, "emotions are *embodied* and manifest in clearly recognizable and stereotyped, behaviour patterns and facial expression, comportment and autonomic arousal" (Dolan, 2002, cited in Fox, 2008, p. 25, italics in original). The urgent and embodied nature of emotions makes them difficult to ignore and is likely to be unhelpful to do so. This means that our and others emotional reactions may require recognition and response before any other purposes of our communication can be achieved.

Emotional responses can be conscious or unconscious (Winkielman et al., 2011). Conscious emotions are emotional states that we are aware of and could express in words if needed. We can tell, for example, if we are feeling happiness, anger or grief. While researchers recognise that many animal species experience emotions, according to Ward (2012, p. 71) "What may 'make us human' is our ability to consciously reflect on our emotions and share them socially via our language and culture..." Our capacity to identify and reflect on our emotions into words is very important for a variety of reasons. This capacity for reflection on emotions makes the information underpinning emotions available to us and to others. For example, in practice we may encourage a person who is experiencing frustration with our service to help us understand the cause of the frustration so that we can improve our services to them. Similarly, we may experience a sense of discomfort when talking with a person whose account of a situation is inconsistent with the facts before us (see Munro, 2011). Paying attention to this emotional discomfort can lead us to the explore situation further and may ultimately enable us to gain a more comprehensive view.

Unconscious emotions refer to emotions that we are unaware of but which influence our behaviour. One type of unconscious emotion is that associated with immediate responses to situations of threat (Winkielman et al., 2011). For example, our fast physical response to avoid contact with a poisonous animal is an unconscious emotional response to threat and has obvious survival value. Unconscious emotions are often powerful and because they are unconscious can be difficult to analyse or control. These emotions can have a strong influence on communication in ways the person experiencing them may find difficult to explain. Yet, unconscious emotions also contain information that can be useful to explore with the service user in gaining a shared understanding of their situation.

What are heightened emotions?

Social workers often meet people at a point of crisis or life challenge. These situations are likely to generate heightened emotions. We use the term "heightened emotions" to refer to emotional arousal that is of sufficient intensity to substantially impact on one's feelings, physiological responses, cognitive processes and actions. The range of heightened emotional states is broad and can include states that a likely to be experienced positively, such as such as euphoria. Our focus here is on states that often experienced as negative and which are likely to arise from life challenges. Negative emotions are emotions are usually associated with a threat to us and "makes us feel agitated or uncomfortable" (Howe, 2008, p. 26). Examples of "negative" heightened states include:

- sadness
- despair
- grief
- fear
- anxiety
- anger
- shame
- disgust.

Many researchers postulate that these negative emotions have survival value as they cause us to avoid threats to our physical survival and social inclusion (see Fox, 2008; Howe, 2008; Ward, 2012).

Our experiences and expressions of emotions are culturally bound. Consequently emotions that are experienced as distressing to the self or others vary by culture. Fischer et al. (2004, pp. 193–194 cited in Howe, 2008, p. 68) notes that many collectivist cultures emphasise the maintenance of harmony and this elicits "the norm of suppressing emotions that create tensions or distance between people, such as anger, contempt, annoyance or pride... In individualistic cultures the opposite pattern can be found. Westerners are reluctant to show emotions, such as shame that display their faults and weaknesses..." Cultural norms around gender and emotional expression may lead to gendered differences in the experience and expression of heightened emotions. For example, in many western cultures men are discouraged from expressing despair and sadness which may instead be expressed as anger. By contrast because women are often discouraged from expressing anger, these states may be expressed as despair or sadness.

Heightened emotional states are likely to influence our actions. The "fight or flight" response is a well-known example of how humans, and other species, immediately and often unconsciously respond to a perceived threat. The fight response is expressed in emotional states of anger and can be associated with verbal and physical aggression including violence. The flight response refers to attempts to evade the threat and can include emotional or physical withdrawal.

Factors contributing to heightened emotional states

Emotions are important to how we experience the world and express our-selves. All of us experience heightened emotions are some points in our lives. Social workers meet people at points of crisis and life challenge that are likely to generate heightened emotions. Emotionally distressing expe-riences can be acute, such receiving devastating news about our health or the health of a loved one, or may occur over time, such as the breakdown of an intimate relationship. Many people who use social work services are also highly likely to also experience additional number of factors that increase their chances of experiencing heightened emotion states. We will consider some of these factors here.

Past emotional trauma, also referred to as complex trauma, may con-tribute to a person's level of emotional arousal. Sandra Bloom (2013, p. 27), an expert in trauma informed mental health care notes:

> People who have been severely or repeatedly traumatised may lose their capac-ity to modulate their level of arousal... They are prepared to fight or flee, even where there is no danger. They may also become flooded with memories, images and sensations that are overwhelming.

Some researchers propose that the impact of traumatic events on children is even more profound and long-lasting than people who have expe-rienced trauma as adults (Bloom, 2013). Later in this Chapter, we will discuss the neurological bases of emotional responses to past trauma.

Social and environmental factors can contribute to heightened emo-tional states. Injustices and inadequacies within a person's environment may generate heightened emotions particularly of anger and despair. Bosly (2007, p. 16) notes that social workers frequently encounter people who are "disempowered, disillusioned and disenfranchised and therefore more likely to be angry." Understanding the experiences and perceptions triggering the emotional state can be important to effective advocacy. For example, a person whose relative is not receiving the health care they need may become frustrated and angry at the service provider. By recog-nising the concerns underpinning these heightened emotional states we can effectively advocate for improvements to service responses and ser-vice systems.

Heightened emotional states can also reflect a person's learnt responses to achieving wants and needs. People who as infants and chil-dren have experienced or been exposed to heightened negative emotions from caregivers may model these emotions themselves (Howe, 2008). For example, children who have been exposed to emotional abuse directly or witnessed it between their parents are likely to model these states in their interactions with other children. People may have learnt that expressions of sadness, anger or aggression are useful in certain circumstances to achieve an objective. For example, various researchers in the field of domestic violence propose that perpetrators use violence to gain power and control (see Bosly, 2012; Kernsmith, 2005).

Altered neurological states can also contribute to heightened emotional responses. Some neurological diseases, such as dementia, and injuries, such as traumatic brain injuries, can contribute to changes in individual's emotional states and their capacity to regulate their emotions (Howe, 2008; Kampfe, 2015). Developmental conditions such as autism and cognitive impairments may impact on a person's capacity to regulate their emotions. Mental health conditions can be associated with heightened emotional states such as euphoria, sadness and anger. Drug and alcohol use has also been associated with heightened emotional states including states of anger and expressions of aggression (Milner and Myers, 2007).

The brain and heightened emotions

Neuroscience offers helpful insights into the neurobiological bases of heightened emotions. From neuroscience we learn structures within the brain can contribute to powerful emotional responses in circumstances where individuals perceive threat or intrusion or that evoke traumatic memories. The amygdala, a structure within the brain, is believed to be central to the perception of threat and to processing of the emotional content of memories (Ward, 2012, p. 81; see also Bauman et al., 2011). The amygdala can function independently of conscious thought with one consequence being that people can experience strong emotional reactions to events or circumstances that are separate to their conscious or rational understanding of that situation (Bauman et al., 2011). For example, a person who has previously experienced severe abuse may understand that they are now safe from that abuser but can nonetheless have memories of those events triggered by apparently unrelated events, actions, sights or smells. These memories can be so powerful that the person experiences the same level of emotional intensity as when the abuse occurred. Havig (2008) noted that adult survivors of childhood sexual abuse find that some forms of medical and health interventions particularly those involving physical touch can trigger traumatic memories and the powerful emotions of fear and distress associated with those memories.

People who have experienced complex trauma, particularly repeated trauma from early childhood, may find it difficult to understand or articulate heightened emotional states arising from traumatic memories.

This is particularly where these memories have been laid down prior to language acquisition. Howe (2008, p. 81) observes that:

> Under stress, children and adults who have suffered unresolved abuse, neglect and trauma find that the primitive parts of the emotional brain take over from the reflective cognitive cortex. Under stress – any kind of stress including difficult and tense relationships – these individuals are catapulted into survival mode. They become alert, tense and fearful.

Neurobiological research also indicates that early developmental stress or trauma may contribute to enduring changes in how people respond to stressful events later in life. It is proposed that early developmental stresses negatively impacts on the Hypothalamic-Pituitary-Adrenal (HPA) Axis and can contribute to the "enduring hyperarousal states" (Corbin, 2007, p. 543). This means that people who have experienced significant prior trauma, particularly early in life, may experience frequent states of alertness as their body and mind prepares to mobilise against threats to their survival (Corbin, 2007). In this state of alertness the person may be vulnerable to emotional triggers that are associated with escalation to a state of heightened emotions.

Of course, social workers have long known of the enduring nature of emotional trauma and neuroscientists have added to our understanding that the experience of this trauma has a biological as well as a psychological and social basis. The insights from neuroscience on how experiences, particularly traumatic experiences, are retained and retrieved help us to understand the challenges individuals may face in predicting or controlling distressing emotional states.

Heightened emotional states and communication

Heightened emotional states can shape communication in a myriad of ways. As we have discussed, emotional states often come with urgency and as such gain priority in our thoughts and actions. When a person experiences a heightened emotional state, their entire experience of an interaction is likely to be affected by that state. Howe (2008, p. 31) notes that:

> when we are in an aroused emotional state, what we see, what we think and how we behave are deeply influenced by that emotion. Emotions ensure that we pay attention to the things that matter until the matter is dealt with.

Furthermore, a person experiencing a heightened emotional state may find it difficult to hear, focus or respond to another person (Bloom, 2013; Bowie, 2013; Dvir et al., 2014). In other words, emotional triggers may lead us, or the person with whom we are communicating, to be so overwhelmed by our emotional response as to limit to engage with a person or to accurately interpret their message (Froemming and Penington, 2011).

Heightened emotional states influence how we receive, process information and store or retrieve information (Bauman et al., 2011; Winkielman et al., 2011; Ward, 2012). One impact is that we may more readily recollect events or experiences that generated heightened emotions. In particular, people who have experienced very traumatic events may experience frequent and intrusive recollections of the event (Howe, 2008). Conversely, people may also find an event or experience so distressing they recall little of it. An example of the impact of heightened emotions on information processing and memory formation can be found in the in the documentary "How to die: Simon's choice" (Deacon and Open University Press, 2016). Aired by the British Broadcasting Corporation in 2016, the documentary showed the final months of the life Simon Binner, a man with aggressive motor neurone disease who had chosen to end his life through euthanasia. In the last minutes of his life, Simon who was now devoid of speech due to his disease, played a speech (recorded by an actor) to his wife, Debbie, who was at his bedside. In his speech, Simon communicated his love for his wife and appreciation of their life together. Two weeks after his death, the BBC crew visited Debbie who recollected that Simon had played a speech but, she observed, she could not remember what was said. This lack of recollection most likely reflects the acute emotional state that Debbie experienced at the time of her husband's death. It may also reflect the ongoing effect of grief and loss on Debbie's capacity to recall information from that time.

Heightened emotional states can help us to survive by enabling us to quickly perceive and respond to threats. Yet, heightened emotions also lead to actions that are unpredictable, unconstructive or dangerous. Wolvin and Coakley (1996, cited in Froemming and Penington, 2011, p. 115) note that heightened emotions may "arouse immediate, unthinking, positive or negative reactions within the listener." The fight or flight response that is often an immediate response to threat can lead an individual to be socially withdrawn (the flight response) or verbally or physically aggressive (fight response). Unless managed skilfully both responses can be damaging to the development or maintenance of the working alliance.

Heightened emotional states and social work practice

Understanding and responding to service user's heightened emotional states and assisting them to regulate their emotions is an important part of social work practice. Howe (2008, p. 8) notes that: "Helping service users and clients feel in control of their lives, to be able to regulate their emotions, and to achieve emotional well-being is much of what social work is about." By skilfully responding to heightened emotional states in ourselves and others we can build confidence and trust in us.

We turn now to outline how we can assist people to regulate their emotions when faced with a situation has that generated, or is likely to generate, a heightened emotional state. Our goal is not the suppression of emotions but to support the person to gain greater control over how and when they experience and express their emotions. Mende-Siedlecki et al. (2011, p. 277) remind us that "humans possess an astonishing faculty for regulating these [powerful] emotions and adapting to situations from which they arise." This adaptive capacity can enable the person with whom are communicating to regulate their emotions sufficiently to respond thoughtfully and purposefully to their situation.

Our approach to supporting emotion regulation in the face of actual, or likely, heightened emotional states focuses on four points in the emotion generation cycle (McRae et al., 2008, pp. 145–146). These phases are outlined here (Figure 4.1).

The cycle of emotional escalation occurs over a varied time period – minutes to days or weeks. By understanding the cycle of emotional escalation our aim is to prevent escalation or to manage the escalation in a way that enables the person to gain control of their emotional state (Stubbs and Dickens, 2008).

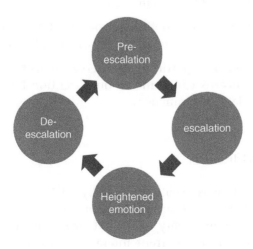

Figure 4.1 The Cycle of Emotional Escalation and De-escalation

Phase 1: Pre-escalation

Pre-escalation is the phase prior to the commencement of emotion escalation. Pre-escalation is most relevant to circumstances where heightened emotions are generated in response to environmental stress or an ongoing concern rather to an acute event. In some acutely stressful events there may little or no pre-escalation phase. For example, in the event the sudden death of a loved one, a person may move directly into a heightened emotional state with little or no pre-escalation phase.

By environmental stress we refer to a point of tension between a person and their environment including the social relationships in their environment. For example, in a group work situation a person may perceive that their opinions are being stifled. Over time this may lead to frustration that the person initially expresses subtly such as through critical comments or withdrawal from the group process. If this frustration is not recognised and responded to, a cycle of escalation may commence.

We can reduce the likelihood of escalation by addressing potential sources of emotional stress in those aspects of the working environment we and the service user have control. Strategies for reducing potential stressors in our environment can include:

➤ creating an environment that is calming to our senses. For example we should consider how the colours, lighting and sound environment of the environments where we meet the service user might contribute to heightened alertness and seek to reduce these stimuli.

➤ being transparent about principles for the allocation of resources and ensuring these principles are fair.

➤ involving service users in defining ground rules for service protocols and any processes, such as group processes, in which they are involved.

➤ providing a range of opportunities for service users to provide feedback so that any concerns can come to our attention before the cycle of emotional escalation commences.

Phase 2: Escalation

Escalation of emotions is usually sparked by a trigger event. While emotional triggers reflect the meaning a person associates with a particular stimuli, emotional triggers vary in the extent to which they are predictable and generated by the current interaction. Trigger events are often events that in some way threaten the person's sense of social or physical well-being, integrity, or safety.

The concept of emotional trigger is important to understanding the process of emotional escalation. The term emotional "trigger" refers to stimuli that arouse strong emotional states in individuals (see Carello and Butler, 2015; Havig, 2008). Emotional "triggers, also known as 'hot buttons,' may cause such a significant emotional reaction that the listener can no longer fully engage in the interaction" (Froemming and Penington, 2011, p. 115). Triggers can be any stimulus, such as words, smells or events, that provokes an emotional response. Triggers can be conscious, for example, we may have an awareness of issues that particular situations or actions are likely to arouse a strong emotional response in us. Triggers can also be unconscious, such as emotional triggers associated with traumatic memories.

Some emotional triggers are obvious in that we can reasonably predict that a person may react strongly. For example, in social work practice we can reasonably predict that a person being faced with a life-threatening event such as a car accident or physical assault may experience strong emotional responses to that event long after its occurrence. We also know that people can experience heightened emotions when confronted with the threat posed by statutory power. Hence, social workers in roles of authority, such as those working in child protection, statutory mental health services, and probation and parole services, are likely to encounter people who express heightened emotions such as despair or anger towards them.

While some emotional triggers can be predicted many are also highly individual and some can be unpredictable. A number of factors including one's life history, current social circumstance and personality will also affect whether one experiences a particular action or event as triggering. For example, survivors of childhood sexual abuse report that some forms of physical touch can trigger traumatic memories of abuse (Havig, 2008). The apparently well-meaning act such as to touch the arm of a client in distress in distress may be experienced as highly intrusive or inappropriate.

Emotional triggers can have a significant impact on communication. In a positive sense emotional triggers can give us information about pressing concerns for people. Exploration with the other person with whom we are communicating about a strong emotional trigger can reveal useful information on how to direct our work with them. For example, an older person may respond strongly to a recommendation from their medical practitioner that their driving license be removed. Acknowledging and exploring the person's response may enable us to communicate beyond the presenting issue of loss of driver's license to further concerns about maintaining social connection and autonomy. By contrast, if we ignore the powerful emotions triggered for the person we may lose important information about we can be most helpful to them.

Types of triggers

There are three main types of emotional triggers. The first are interactional triggers. This refers to situations where the behaviours between the parties contribute to the escalation of emotions. Escalation can happen over varying periods of time from very long simmering tensions over months or even years, to matters escalating in a few moments (Richter, 2006). Interactional factors such as perceptions that workers are denying or ignoring one's legitimate needs, perceptions of being unheard or of being unfairly treated by the worker or authoritarian/dismissive/judgemental approaches that contribute by workers the person feeling unheard or blamed. Similarly organisational structures that reinforce authoritarian relationships or that frustrate the expression of, or adequate response to, needs can also lead to escalation of emotions.

A second type of trigger are emotionally provocative events. An event that is likely to threaten a person's sense of safety or well-being for themselves or those to whom they are attached is likely to provoke a heightened emotional response. Indeed, the absence of such an emotional response in situations likely to evoke heightened emotions might be cause for concern. For example, we can predict that a person faced with devastating news about the health of or injury to a loved one will experience heightened emotions. Similarly a person who has experienced an assault or threat of assault. We can also predict that many people may respond with anger to a statutory child protection worker or mental health worker given the potential threat to their liberty that statutory power invokes.

The third type of trigger are those associated with past trauma and which may have very little to do with the current interaction with the worker or the situation. These triggers can be difficult to predict because they are unique to person's experience and memory. Furthermore some triggers are unconscious, meaning that the person may not be able to articulate why emotions are being generated for them. For example, an item of jewellery with a religious symbol worn by a worker may evoke a person's memory of institutional abuse.

People who have experienced trauma may experience powerful emotions in response to situations or communication acts that may not, on the face it, have strong emotional content. In addition, we need also to be aware that people who have experienced trauma may be distrustful or hostile towards health and welfare professionals (Knight, 2015). We need in these circumstances to be particularly mindful of communicating both verbally and non-verbally in ways that demonstrate respect. This includes being clear about our role, demonstrating appropriate professional boundaries and showing understanding of the powerful emotions that our presence and role may trigger.

Recognising and responding to heightening emotions

By being attuned to signs of emotional distress at this stage we can intervene to prevent further escalation of emotions. Signs of emotional distress can include:

➢ physiological signs: change of facial expression particularly intensification of eye contact or avoidance altogether of eye contact, increase pace or audibility of breathing, signs of aggression such as clenched fists.

➢ expression of "negative" feelings such as frustration or despondency.

➢ actions and behaviours: changes in behaviour particularly behaviours that would suggest emotions associated with a fight or flight state. This could include an provocative acts such as breaking agreed group rules (a fight response) or removing oneself from a situation (a flight response).

We can take a number of actions at this stage in an effort to prevent the further escalation of emotions, these actions include:

➢ distraction or distancing from the trigger event or experiences. This involves removing the person from the situation or helping them to understand the trigger in a way that dampens the emotional response.

➢ providing genuine reassurance of emotional and physical safety. For example, a person who has experienced a physically traumatic event, such as an assault, should be accommodated in a location where their physical safety can be assured.

➢ engaging in activities that help to reduce the heightened physical arousal. For example, a person who is in an aroused emotional state may benefit from going on a short walk with the social worker rather than having a seated conversation.

➢ sharing with them your observations that they appear to becoming distressed and ask what support they need.

➢ empowering the person to recognise their strengths and capacities to manage the emotions they are experiencing. Utilising the person's previous experiences of managing similar emotions can help build an evidence base with them of their capacity to manage current challenges.

Phase 3: Experiencing heightened emotional states

The next point in the cycle is the phase where the emotions are height-ened. Heightened negative emotional states can be expressed in a variety of ways. While our words provide insight into emotional states, much information is provided non-verbally. Our facial expression and vocal tone provide a great deal of information about our emotional state, and it would seem that we are hardwired to quickly recognise the emotional state of others. Howe (2008, p. 50) notes that "One of the remarkable things very young babies appear able to do is recognize and discriminate between different emotional expressions on other people's faces and in their voices." Heightened emotional states are often expressed in way that are instantly recognisable such as: crying or wailing; verbal defensiveness; heightening or increased pitch of vocal tone; sweating. In addition, the person experiencing heightened emo-tions may also report physiological changes such as: heart palpitations; increased breathing rate; and hypersensitivity to stimuli such as sound, light or colours.

The person experiencing an acute state of alertness is likely to find that their thoughts and actions are negatively affected. The person's capacity to receive information is likely to be altered. The state of alert-ness affect their capacity to hear, recollect or process new information. The person may also find it difficult to reason or reflect on their situation and they may appear confused (France, 2007).

In a "fight" state the person may focus on minute detail of the other person's statement alert to points of dispute. The person's control over their physical co-ordination may be affected. For example, a person in state of shock or sadness may find it difficult to perform everyday tasks such as making a cup of tea or coffee or preparing a meal. One of the risks of heightened emotional states is that these states can contribute to people acting out in a way that is dangerous to themselves or others, for example, when a person is state of anger or frustration physically hits out at another.

Phase 4: De-escalation

Finally, there is de-escalation where the heightened emotional state passes. The person's emotional responses return to a resting or normal state and the emotional state loses its intensity and priority. Depending how the de-escalation occurred the person may experience physiological after effects, such as weakness or some continuing alterness, or psycho-logical effects such as feeling shaky, sad or embarrassed.

Because emotional states are transient states we should expect changes in emotions to pass in time. The time period in which this cycle occurs may be brief, as short as a few minutes to much longer, hours or days (Fox, 2008). When the heightened emotional state has passed the person is likely to still feel the emotion but it no longer pervades thoughts and actions. One aim of de-escalation is to speed up the process through which the person reaches the point of de-escalation.

We turn now to explain what we as social workers can do to recognise these emotional states in others and communicate in ways that support the other to regulate their emotions either through preventing escalation or through assisting de-escalation of emotions.

Responding to heightened emotions

Heightened emotional states are transient states (Fox, 2008). These states are often experienced as acutely distressing to people experiencing them and have negative impact on communication. Our goals are to respond to heightened emotional states in ways that build and maintain the working alliance and assist people to regulate their emotions so as to build their capacity to respond thoughtfully to their situation, and to reduce the risk of harm to self and others. We recognise heightened emotional states as providing important information about what matters to a person and, further, when well managed can lead to the strengthening of the working alliance. Yet, heightened emotional states also pose risks to the working alliance and also the potential for physical or psychological harms to the parties involved in responding to, or experiencing, the heightened emotional state.

A variety of approaches exist to responding to heightened emotional states. Our approach draws on trauma informed practice (Carello and Butler, 2015; Havig, 2008), verbal de-escalation techniques (Price and Baker, 2012), low arousal model of behaviour management (Sturmey and McDonnell, 2011) and crisis intervention theory (France, 2007). These approaches share common themes about the importance of recognising and responding to heightened emotional states in ways that build the working alliance. These approaches also recognise that heightened emotional states are multisystemic in that these states affect our thoughts, emotions and behaviours.

When communicating with a person in a situation where emotional escalation is likely to or has already occurred, our focus should be on supporting emotion regulation. We refer here to processes that decrease the impact or experience of negative emotional states on the development and maintenance of the working alliance. This involves balancing the need to acknowledge emotions, supporting the safe expression of emotions and

reducing emotional arousal while also maintaining our professional purpose and boundaries. By safe expression of emotions we refer to ensuring
expression of emotions does not lead to actions that may harm the self
or others. By reducing emotional arousal we refer to supporting the
de-escalation of the emotional state sufficiently to enable the person with
whom we are communicating to gain (or re-gain) sufficient control of their
emotions to respond thoughtfully to their situation and to reduce any risks
of harm to themselves or others. This balance is outlined in Figure 4.2.

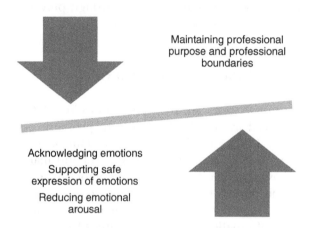

Figure 4.2   A Framework for Supporting Emotion Regulation

Supporting emotion regulation: key themes

Supporting emotion regulation requires us to communicate in ways that
minimise emotional escalation, recognise and respond to heightened
emotions, and promote emotional de-escalation. In this section we discuss four elements of this approach.

Communicating confidence, calmness and non-reactivity

Regulating our own emotions is important to our response in each
phase of the cycle of emotional escalation and de-escalation (see Carello
and Butler, 2015; France, 2007; Price and Baker, 2012; Sturmey and
McDonnell, 2011). A person experiencing a heightened emotional state
is experiencing emotions that are overwhelming and may be distressing
to them. The worker's own demonstration of confidence, composure and
professional purpose can assist in promoting a sense of emotional safety.

The worker's capacity to be clear about their role and communicate this consistently in their words and behaviours can help the person gain a sense of shared purpose and of boundaries to the relationship. Several authors note the importance of workers appearing calm even we are experiencing heightened emotions (Fauteux, 2010, Price and Baker, 2012). By demonstrating calmness we model behaviours that may help the other person do the same despite the presence of strong emotions. Active listening and awareness of facial cues to show concern are important. We use the term non-reactivity to refer to the capacity to recognise strong emotions without letting them control our, or the other person's, response to the situation.

We can achieve non-reactivity by developing awareness of our own and others' emotional states. As some emotional states are unconscious, we need to be skilled at monitoring our physiological and cognitive processes and to be aware of any changes to these processes in ourselves. In addition, we need to develop the capacity to modulate our thoughts and actions in response to these states. Gross and his colleagues use the term "response modulation" to refer strategies aimed as deliberate containment of our responses to achieve emotion regulation in ourselves and also others (see Gross and Thompson, 2007; Werner and Gross, 2010).

Response modulation has both thinking and behavioural elements. The thinking elements involve monitoring and adjusting how we think about a situation. When faced with a strong emotional state in others we can enhance our capacity to maintain our own emotional equilibrium though self-talk that builds our confidence in responding to the situation. For example, we can remind ourselves of the training we have undertaken to prepare ourselves for responding to these challenging situations. Behavioural elements include acting in ways that do not reflect a fight or flight response, but rather a capacity to remain present in the face of strong emotions.

Achieving physical and emotional safety

Heightened emotional states are usually triggered by a perception of threat to a person's physical or emotional safety and well-being. Furthermore, the fight or flight response that is often associated with heightened emotional states can lead to behaviours and actions that are harmful to the self or others. It is important that the worker ensures the physical and emotional safety of the environment so as to reduce escalation of emotions, to reduce risk of harms to self or others, and also to de-escalate heightened emotions (Fallot and Harris, 2009). Physical safety involves minimising actual or perceived physical threats in the environment. For example, the risk of harm may be increased when a person feels physically cornered (Price and Baker, 2012). Promoting physical safety can also involve reducing the stimulants in the physical environment that could incite emotions. For example, moving a person in acute distress to a quiet space can help to them regain emotional composure.

Creating emotional safety involves creating an environment in which the person perceives they are safe from further emotional trauma. Fallot and Harris (2009) suggest that the social worker should be alert and responsive to signs of discomfort or potential escalation of emotions among the people with whom they are communicating. Creating emotional safety involves validating and normalising the person's experience and engaging in ways that recognise triggers.

Promoting collaborative communication

Engaging in ways that enable the person experiencing the heightened state to feel heard, and that their contribution is valued, is important to building and maintaining the working alliance. Within the crisis intervention and verbal de-escalation literature several techniques for promoting collaboration with people in heightened emotional states are emphasised. These techniques include:

➤ encouraging the "open expression of emotions and thoughts" about whatever concerns the person (France, 2007, p. 37). This sometimes referred to as ventilation.

➤ helping the person to focus their thoughts. France (2007, p. 37) notes that "individuals overwhelmed by a crisis sometimes displays muddled thinking. When that happens the worker may need to encourage the person to focus on one or two topics" (France, 2007, p. 37).

➤ demonstrating reflective listening. Using communication skills such as clarifying, paraphrasing and summarising can assist in communicating your understanding of the person's situation and in building a shared focus to your communication.

➤ providing space to calm one's emotions. The term "time out" is sometimes use to refer to deferring the active communication so that person has time to regain emotional composure. A change of physical scene, such as encouraging a walk outside or in a different location to the current environment can also help to calming the emotions.

➤ explaining and maximising choice. We demonstrate our commitment to partnership by helping the person experiencing the heightened emotional state to understand the choices available to them and to assist them in making those choices.

Prioritising empowerment

Situations in which heightened emotions are provoked create challenges and learning opportunities. Heightened emotions often emerge in situations of crisis and we can use these as opportunities to assist the person with whom we are communicating to develop skills in emotion regulation and problem solving.

We recognise that a person experiencing a heightened emotional state may experience constraints on their capacity to receive and process information, and to reason (Sturmey and McDonnell, 2011). Nonetheless, it may be necessary to engage in a process of decision-making such as in a crisis where an outcome needs to be achieved. For example, a parent who has been informed that their child is to be removed pending further investigation may still be involved in decision making about where the child would reside. Furthermore, a focused problem solving process can also assist in de-escalating the situation by providing a clear focus to the communication and a boundary about the issue to be addressed.

Structured problem-solving conversations can help the person regain a sense of control over a situation which has generated heightened emotions. France (2007, pp. 40–41) suggests three questions to guide the structured problem-solving conversation with a person experiencing a crisis. These are:

a. What have you tried so far to deal with the situation?

b. What have you thought about trying?

c. Right now, what other possibilities come to mind?

France further proposes that on the basis of a systematic exploration of answers to these questions, the worker then collaborates to develop a plan of action to respond to the crisis that has generated the heightened emotions. France (2007, p. 45) notes that:

> When clients have faith in the plan that is developed, they experience fewer negative emotions because they devote much of their mental and physical energy towards accomplishing tasks they believe will be productive.

An action plan that is realistic and grounded in the person's own experience of what works for them is relevant to both problem solving and also to supporting emotion regulation. The action plan can help to create order and develop the person's confidence in their capacity to respond to current and future challenges. In addition, the collaborative process of building the plan grounded in the person's experience helps to create commitment to the working alliance between ourselves and the people with whom we are communicating.

Reflection, recovery and resilience

Heightened emotions present challenges for the person experiencing the emotions and those responding to them. The period after the heightened emotional state passes is an important phase in the development and maintenance of the working alliance. During the period of heightened emotions the person is likely to have limited capacity to receive and process information. After the heightened emotional state has passed, the worker should check in on what the person has understood of that time and what information they take from it. Any decisions made during that period should be reviewed and any further decision-making needs should be discussed.

The person may also have a reaction to their emotional response during the period of elevated emotions. It is common for people having negative emotional responses to have distressing recollections of the heightened emotions and their actions during these states. These recollections can generate negative emotional states, including embarrassment, anger or guilt. Left unaddressed these negative emotional states can also damage the working alliance. It is important then for the worker to explore the person's recollections of the heightened emotional state and to proactively address any ongoing concerns arising for them. For example, feelings of embarrassment can be responded to by normalising heightened emotional states, this means to reassure the person that they are not alone in their experience of heightened emotions and to convey our commitment to building the working alliance.

Reflection on heightened emotions can also provide an opportunity for empowerment. Reflection on heightened emotional states can provide new insights into what matters to the person who has experienced the state and what triggers these states. Emotional states can be generated by unconscious triggers and providing opportunities to reflect on what generated the emotional state can help the person gain greater insight into themselves and to actively engage in emotion regulation strategies.

Finally we turn to recovery and resilience following heightened emotional states. The experience of heightened emotions can have an ongoing impact on the parties to the communication. Even though a well-managed response may assist and empower the person and may foster a sense of professional purpose and achievement among those who responded, these states can have a powerful negative impact (Savaya,

Gardner and Stange, 2011). As workers, we can benefit from supportive supervision to assist us in making sense of the heightened emotional states and their impact upon us. In their study of social workers responding to trauma survivors, Gil and Weinberg (2015) identified a positive association between weekly supportive supervision and reduced incidence of secondary trauma among practitioners. Witnessing another in an intense state of distress may trigger strong emotional responses that, if left unaddressed, can impact negatively on us. Exposure to people in heightened emotional states can be so overwhelming as to reduce our professional confidence, reduce our capacity to process information, or cause us to act in ways that are not consistent with our professional obligation, such as avoiding people or situations that are likely to generate strong emotional states (Savaya et al., 2011).

Supportive supervision that incorporates critical reflection and critical incident de-briefing can foster recovery and resilience. Critical incident de-briefing enables us to reflect on challenging events and experiences in an emotionally safe environment (Fook and Gardner, 2013; Sturmey and McDonnell, 2011). In critical incident de-briefing, the person who has been subject to a critical incident is encouraged to recount that event and to reconsider the event in ways that enable learning from the event and to reduce the ongoing impact into the future (Fook and Gardner, 2013). For example, where a worker has been subject to a client in high distress that, in turn, triggered a distressed state in the worker, he/she can use the critical de-briefing approach for reflecting on the emotions generated in the incident and to develop strategies for reducing the negative impact of the event upon them. This can include encouraging the worker to recognise and adapt their physiological response to memories of the event, such as deliberately containing the flight response, and re-framing their emotional response. For instance the worker can be encouraged to accept how they responded, and reframe their response in becoming distressed as an indication of deep empathy rather than as weakness. The person then may use the critical incident technique to consider how they would choose to respond to future critical incidents of a similar nature. This technique is intended to help us make sense of the experience in order to reduce its negative emotional impact into the future, and to foster professional learning from the experience.

Conclusion

Social workers often communicate with people experiencing heightened emotional states. Negative emotional states are often acutely distressing to those who experience them. By understanding heightened emotional states we can support people as they experience these states, assist in the de-escalation of these states and assist people in developing skills to recognise and response effectively to these states in future. While they are an inevitable part of social work practice, heightened emotional states can negatively affect the worker, the service user and the working alliance between them. We outlined processes for recognising and responding to heightened emotional states in ways that promote learning, recovery and resilience for workers and service users.

Review questions

1. What does the term "heightened emotions" mean?

2. When a person is in a heightened emotional state how is their capacity to communicate likely to be affected?

3. What is "emotion regulation"?

4. What are the four phases of the cycle of emotional escalation and de-escalation described in this Chapter?

5. What can social workers do to support a person who is experiencing heightened and distressing emotions?

Practice exercise

Imagine that you are a family support worker conducting a weekly family support group for young parents. Margaret is a 19-year-old mother of Tony, who is 6 months old. Margaret was removed from her family when she was around 2 years old and lived in a series of foster homes. Margaret has been quite isolated and it is only by the concerted efforts of the young mothers' support worker that Margaret has agreed to attend the support group.

The groups occur in a community centre where there are separate rooms for group work and child care. At the first support group meeting, Margaret appeared shy but participated in the group activities while Sheena her support worker was present. This week Margaret has again come to the group and you have welcomed her. There are 11 young women at the meeting. You have encouraged the other young women to be supportive to new members. The first activities in the group are warm up activities which began with a reflection on the week during which time some of the young mothers shared struggles they had had with managing their children's sleeping patterns. Margaret initially contributed to the conversation saying that Tony was sleeping

▶

◄

well. At some point, Sheena (Margaret's support worker) left the room to answer a phone call and has been away for around 20 minutes. The next group activity was about developing an activities booklet about local area events and places to go for young families. The group was brainstorming how they spend their weekend when you noticed that Margaret had physically withdrawn from the group and had gone to sit in the corner. You left Janelle, the peer worker (another young mother) in charge of the brainstorming so you could speak with Margaret. As you got closer, you notice that Margaret is softly crying and rocking back and forth. As you sit quietly next to her she says "I want to get my son and go home, I hate it here." You suggest that you could both go find Sheena, to which Margaret again responds more forcefully "I want to get son and go home."

➢ How would you describe Margaret's emotional state?

➢ What factor(s) appear to have triggered her emotional state?

➢ What would you, as a worker do next, to support Margaret?

➢ If you were meeting Margaret a few days after this incident what issues might you explore with her and how would you explore those issues?

➢ What emotional responses would working with Margaret raise for you and how would manage your emotional responses?

Recommended further reading

Fox, E. (2008). *Emotion science: Cognitive and neuroscientific approaches to understanding human emotions.* Basingstoke: Palgrave
The book provides an accessible yet detailed account of psychological and neuroscience research into emotions. It is helpful for providing insights into the processes of emotional arousal and the impact of heightened emotions on thought, feelings and actions.
Fook, J. & Gardner, F. (2013) *Critical reflection in context: Applications in health and social care.* Oxford: Routledge.
This edited collection includes a range of reflections on how to use critical reflection to examine critical incidents in practice, so as to promote professional learning and skills development.

5

Anger, Aggression and Violence

Anger is one of the emotional states a person may experience in response to life stressors and injustices. Yet this emotion and the frequently associated behavioural response, aggression, are not well recognised in the foundations of social work communication. This remains so even though many social workers report being subject to anger and aggression including threats of violence (Criss, 2010; Robson, Cossar and Quayle, 2014; Schraer, 2014). Social workers also report being inadequately prepared to communicate with people who are angry or aggressive and to respond where there is a threat of violence (Savaya, Gardner and Stange, 2011). This lack of preparation can lead to inadequate communication in situations where people are angry, behave aggressively or threaten violence and to loss of confidence by the social worker in their professional capacities. By developing our ability to respond to anger and to diffuse aggression and potentially violent situations, we extend our ability to be present to this commonly encountered emotional reaction to life challenges, and to demonstrate that we can assist the service user to build knowledge and skills in regulating their emotions.

We begin this Chapter by defining anger, aggression and violence and we outline why it is important for social workers to respond to anger and the related behavioural consequences of aggression and violence. We then present the phases of the escalation and de-escalation and outline strategies social workers can use for communicating in ways that recognise the emotion of anger but which can help to diffuse aggression.

Anger

Anger is an emotional state, while aggression and the potential for violence are possible expressions of this state. While these concepts are not the same, they are interrelated. Ronan et al. (2013, p. 3) notes: "Human anger, aggression, and violence are interrelated concepts, all associated with verbal or physical actions which inflict discomfort or pain."

Turning first to anger, we adopt Ronan et al. (2013, p. 3) definition of "anger as a commonly experienced emotional state that often results from the perception of a personally meaningful injustice." Anger arises from a disjuncture between person's experience of their situation and their perception of what is right, fair or appropriate. These perceptions may align with general community expectations. For example, a parent who is angry about the failure of health care staff to adequately meet their children's health care needs is a situation that many in the community would regard as justified anger. Other situations may not align with community expectations, for example, a person may become angry because they believe they are entitled to special treatment or privileged access to a resource. Anger may ensue when this expectation is unmet. The personal nature of the perceptions that give rise to anger means that we cannot always predict when a person is likely to respond with anger to an interaction or situation. Nonetheless, understanding how the angered person perceives their situation is an important element of de-escalation as we will discuss later in this Chapter.

Anger can also be caused by issues others than a perception of injustice. Anger can be a response to a perception of threat to one's physical or emotional well-being. For example, an older person may be angry towards the social worker involved in assessing their capacity for continued independent living. In this situation, the older person may perceive the worker's role to threaten their emotional well-being.

Anger is a powerful emotion that can provide us with information about what matters to the person with whom we are communicating (Bosly, 2007). Acknowledgement and exploration of the person's anger can contribute to the development of a shared understanding with them of their situation. It can also contribute to shifts in the goals of our work together. For example, a person who is angry that a social worker cannot provide them with permanent housing at this time may be helped to understand what resources are available immediately to temporarily address the situation, and what needs to happen to achieve permanent housing.

Aggression and violence

We turn now to aggression and violence. Ronan et al. (2013, p. 3) state that "Aggression can be broadly defined as hostile, injurious, or destructive behavior." Aggression may involve acts of psychological or physical aggression. Anger and aggression are not always linked. "While anger is unquestionably a motivating force in many acts of aggression, it's certainly not always present. Experiencing anger does however increase the likelihood that a person will behave aggressively" (Monds-Watson, 2011, p. 8). Violence can be understood as a subtype of aggression. "Violence" is the term used to describe extreme forms of aggression that are likely to cause serious psychological and physical injury or death (Dewall, Anderson and Bushman, 2012). Anderson (2000, p. 163) notes that "All violence is aggression, but many forms of aggression are not violent." (2000, p. 163). While anger is a frequent precursor to aggression including acts of violence, this is not always the case. We note also that some forms of aggression can be performed with little emotion and with the intention of intimidation or other forms of harm.

Aggression can be distinguished between "reactive" aggression and "instrumental" aggression. Monds-Watson (2011, p. 9) uses the term "reactive" aggression to refer to:

> impulsive or thoughtless aggressive acts that arise from feelings of anger. The primary motivation underpinning affective aggression is the instinctual urge to harm the victim (who is usually the person or thing perceived to be provoking anger in the perpetrator). (Brackets in original.)

Reactive aggression, which is also referred to as affective aggression, can be a conscious or an unconscious response to perceived injustice, threat or frustration. When experienced or expressed unconsciously the aggressor may not be aware they are behaving in ways others perceive as aggressive.

Another form of aggression is instrumental aggression. This is the deliberate use of aggression to achieve an end goal (Liu, 2004; Monds-Watson, 2011). Instrumental aggression "is characterized as controlled, purposeful aggression lacking in emotion that is used to achieve a desired goal, including the domination and control of others" (Liu, 2004, p. 697). Instrumental aggression is not necessarily preceded by anger nor indeed by any other emotional state. Instead it is aggression deliberately deployed by the aggressor to achieve an end goal, such as the domination of another person. For example, domestic and family violence is a form of instrumental violence in that the goal of the aggressor is power and control over the family member(s) subjected to violence. Even though the perpetrator may assert that their actions were those of provocation or acts of passion, domestic and family violence is often preceded by deliberate actions to groom the victim and may include planned acts of violence.

Researchers point to different forms of aggressive behaviour (see Anderson, 2000; Monds-Watson, 2011). Aggressive behaviour differs by:

A) whether the aggression is expressed physically and/or verbally. Physical forms of violence involve the use of one's body or accessories to cause injury, while verbal aggression will use words, vocal tone and pitch to inflict discomfort or injury (or the lack thereof).

B) whether the aggression is expressed directly or indirectly towards the target. Direct aggression is where the aggressor directly attacks their target, such as yelling in anger at a person. By contrast indirect aggression involves concealing either the identity of the aggressor or the expression of aggression is indirect (Monds-Watson, 2011). For example, the circulation of malicious rumours about another person is a form of indirect aggression.

Our focus in this Chapter is on understanding and responding to anger that is expressed directly and which is verbal and/or physical in nature. The strategies we will outline are primarily for responding to affective aggression, that is aggression preceded by a heightened emotional state, usually anger. Nonetheless the strategies can also assist in responding to instrumental aggression in so far as a calm and thoughtful response communicates that the perpetrator's end goal will not be achieved through aggression.

What causes aggression?

There are many reasons why a person may behave aggressively. As we have indicated anger arises when a person perceives they are being: threatened; unfairly or unjustly treated; or frustrated in having their needs and wants met. There are factors that cause a person who is angry to behave aggressively. These factors include that the person:

1. has not learnt non-aggressive ways of articulating needs or negotiating challenging situations

2. experiences a loss of impulse control. Loss of impulse control can occur for a range of reasons including the impact of: alcohol use, some illicit drugs particularly methamphetamines, some prescription medications, some forms of brain injury, some developmental disabilities and some forms of mental illness (Forrester and Harwin, 2011; Manktelow, 2011; Price and Baker 2012; Sturmey and McDonnell, 2011)

3. is subject to environmental stressors. Stressors in the person's environment including chronic unmet needs, a highly restrictive or authoritarian environment, and an under or over stimulating environment can contribute to aggression (Ronan et al., 2013; Sturmey and McDonnell, 2011)

4. is rewarded for aggressive responses. A person may perceive that their needs or wants will only be recognised when expressed aggressively. This can occur because the family, community or organisational environment in which the person is located may lack norms or processes for recognising a person's needs or wants. The presence of an audience may also contribute to aggression in so far as a person who feels aggrieved may be encouraged by the presence of an audience to

express their anger in ways that they perceive to show strength and dominance. A key theme in the de-escalation literature is that of removing the need for a person to behave aggressively, to have needs or wants recognised, and further to remove, as far as possible, the audience for aggressive behaviour (Milner and Myers, 2007; Ronan et al., 2013; Price and Baker, 2012; Sturmey and McDonnell, 2011).

Understanding the experience of, and factors contributing to, anger and aggression can assist us to communicate in ways diffuse the emotional state of anger and reduce the likelihood of aggression.

The physiological experience of anger and aggression

Anger is an important human emotion and aggression is one expression of this emotion. Anger and aggression have important survival value and have been part of our evolution as a species. Because of the importance of this emotion and its expression as aggression, we are often highly attuned to anger and aggressive behaviours in others, though this recognition may not be conscious. To assist us to consciously recognise and respond to anger and aggression, it is helpful to articulate the features of anger and aggression.

The physiological experiences of anger and reactive or affective aggression are often, though not always, associated with the fight or flight states of heightened physiological alertness. The physiological changes associated with anger include: increased heart and breathing rates, pupils dilate to enable more acute sight, muscle tension increase as energy is released into the bloodstream (Monds-Watson, 2011, p. 3). As with other heightened emotional states, the angry person's capacity "for rational or logical thought becomes impaired." (Monds-Watson, 2011, p. 3). Anger and aggression are likely to be expressed also in our non-verbal behaviour. Facial expressions consistent with anger are bared teeth, widening of the eyes and staring, furrowed eyebrows and a hardening of the jaw (Monds-Watson, 2011).

The fight state, which is one way in which we respond to perceived threat, may influence communication in several ways including:

➤ focus on minutiae of the conversation with a focus on winning or domination of the interaction.

➤ heightened sensitivity to meaning of words or tone of voice used by others. The person who is angry may interpret words as further evidence of the perceived injustice or attack on them whether or not this was the intention of the speaker. For example, "There you go again," "That is offensive."

➤ change of vocal pitch, tone and pace. A person in a state of anger is likely to become louder, with a higher tone to their speech and the pace may increase. This can result in the person yelling or shouting.

➤ decreased sensitivity to the impact of their own words and tone. For example, the person may be unaware that vocal volume or pace has increased.

➤ may seek to emotionally harm the other person, through the use of words or tone that generate discomfort, fear or emotional injury in the other person.

While the flight state is also associated with heightened physiological sensitivity to their environment, in this state the person may withdraw physically or psychologically from the interaction. They may express themselves through passive-aggressiveness meaning "the intentional absence of activity with the intention to cause harm." (Monds-Watson, 2011, p. 10). Examples of this include refusing to speak or to make eye contact with the other.

It is important that social workers develop a conscious awareness of our own experience and expression of anger and aggression. By increasingly our conscious awareness of our experience of anger and aggression we improve our capacity to contain this emotion and behaviour and to understand and respond empathetically to anger and aggression in others.

Practice exercises

Reflect on your own experiences of anger and aggression. Consider a situation where you become angry:

a) What emotions and thoughts accompanied that experience?

b) What was your physiological experience?

c) How long did the state of anger last and what helped the emotion to pass?

Turning now to aggression. Consider a time when you behaved aggressively:

a) What thoughts or experiences led to the aggression?

b) What emotions and thoughts accompanied that experience?

c) What was your physiological experience?

d) How did the other person respond to the aggression?

e) What are your thoughts and feelings about that experience of aggression now?

Why are anger, aggression and risk of violence issues for social workers?

Many social workers report being exposed to anger, aggression and situations where there is the potential for violence. Schraer (2014) reported that of 446 social workers in the United Kingdom who participated in an online survey about workplace aggression, 85 per cent said they had been physically assaulted, verbally abused or harassed in the past year (see also see Criss, 2010; Robson, Cossar and Quayle, 2014). Savaya et al. (2011, p. 65) asked 130 experienced social workers in Israel to report on critical events that had shaped their social work practice, they found that:

> In more than half the critical events involving clients, social workers reported being the targets of hostility, anger, or aggression by clients, clients' family members, or others involved in the case. Broadly speaking, these instances fall into two types: actual, attempted, or threatened physical violence and verbal aggression."

There is substantial evidence then to suggest that anger and aggression are frequently encountered by social workers.

The risk of exposure to anger, aggression and violence arises because, as we have previously noted, service users often face life stressors that generate strong emotional responses. Monds-Watson (2011, p. 2) notes that these emotions may be difficult to contain and may be expressed in actions that are "threatening, intimidating, frightening or which present an actual risk of physical or emotional harm." Additional factors identified by OSHA (2015) that contribute to our increased exposure to anger, aggression and potentially violent situations include that as social workers we may:

➤ work with people in a variety of environments including people's homes.

➤ work irregular hours, particularly in crisis intervention settings where people may already be at risk.

➤ be involved in the exercise of power, such as statutory power, that can frustrate and enrage people.

➤ work with people who have histories of violence.

➤ work with people who have conditions, such as some mental health conditions, or substance that contribute to heightened emotional arousal.

Despite the prevalence of anger, aggression and the potential for violence in social work practice, many social workers are unprepared for responding to anger and its behavioural consequences (Savaya et al., 2011). In reviewing these findings, Schraer (2014, p. 1, online) observed: "part of the problem may be that half of social workers surveyed said they had never received any training on how to cope with violent individuals, despite most being required to enter high risk situations, often alone and without adequate support."

Remarkably, there is only a small body of literature on understanding and responding to anger and aggression towards social workers (see Taylor, 2011). The limited discussion on anger, aggression and violence contrasts with the frequent discussion of this topic in many other human services fields, such as mental health nursing (Price and Baker, 2012; Richter, 2006), emergency medicine (Sprigg, Armitage and Hollis, 2007) and policing (Compton et al., 2010). A small body of literature on anger, aggression and violence in some fields of social work particularly youth work (see Bowie, 1996; Epps, Moore and Hollin, 1999) and to a lesser extent child protection and mental health services. But the limited discussion of this topic should not lead us to under-estimate the possibility of anger and aggression and the importance of being able to respond when confronted with these emotions.

There are at least three reasons we need to develop our capacity to respond well to anger, aggression and the potential for violence. The first is, as we have indicated, we are likely to encounter these states in practice. Second, understanding and responding effectively to anger and aggression is important to building our professional competence and confidence and to reducing our risk being exposed to high levels of aggression. Savaya et al. (2011, p. 69) reported that workers who had been exposed to verbal or physical aggression by clients "felt angry at the client and guilty about it, as well as being wracked by self-blame and doubts about their personal and professional competence." As we become more confident and competent in responding to anger and aggression we can reduce our risk of exposure to high levels of aggression, though this risk can never be entirely eliminated (Richter, 2006).

The third reason is that by responding effectively to anger and aggressive we may further build the working alliance with the service user. We can demonstrate to those with whom we work that we can hear and respond to their anger without allowing the emotion to control or destroy the working alliance. In some situations, helping people through anger and aggression can also assist in their developing new communication skills relevant to improving their interpersonal relationships.

De-escalating anger and aggression

The process of de-escalating anger and aggression is similar to the process of de-escalating the range of heightened emotions discussion Chapter 4. However, the potential for anger and aggression to cause harm to the people involved and to the alliance between them means that developing our capacity to understand and respond in situations of anger and aggression are very important. Our focus is on preventing the escalation of anger and the expression of aggression and, if this is not possible, to containing this emotional state and to reduce the potential for harm arising from aggression (Figure 5.1).

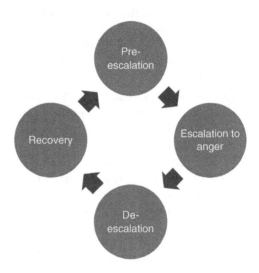

Figure 5.1   The Cycle of Anger and Aggression

Stage 1: Pre-escalation

Being aware of the potential risks of anger, aggression and violence is the first step towards preventing escalation. Prior to meeting with a person we can scan the environment and purpose of the meeting as well as factors in ourselves and the other that may pose a risk for escalation to anger and aggression.

First we need to consider the purpose of the meeting. We should review whether the purpose might trigger anger or aggression. As we have discussed, there is increased risk of anger or aggression in situations where people feel: threatened; unfairly or unjustly treated; or frustrated in having their needs and wants met. We need then to consider whether the purpose of the meeting is likely to give rise to any of these perceptions. The particular purpose of the meeting is important to take into account. This could include actions such as being involved in the removal of children, the issuing of a mental health order or a probation order. We need also to consider the person's situation and whether they are subject to the stressors that might give rise to heightened perception of threat. For example, a person with a prior history of emotional trauma may experience a heightened state of alertness in association with health and welfare services (Havig, 2008).

If the purpose of the meeting, or our presence as a representative of a health or welfare service, is one that is likely to trigger anger or aggression we can work to minimise the likelihood this response in several ways. These can include:

➤ reducing the perceived threat for the person by increasing their capacity to participate in the meeting on an equal footing. We can achieve this by providing a clear outline of the purpose of the meeting and the client's choices in relation to the meeting such as whether they have a choice not to meet with you and the benefits of doing so, as well as the consequences of not meeting.

➤ maximising opportunities for joint decision-making and involvement as far as is possible. For example, while the worker may be compelled to take actions that are intrusive, such as the removal of a child, we might also have be able to provide choices about visitation and processes for reunification.

➤ focusing the meeting on the present and the future rather than on the past. We can present the meeting as an opportunity for the worker and the client to work together on agreed goals.

Second, the risks within the physical context of the visit are important to consider (Koprowska, 2014). Social workers often meet people in situations other than a formal office environment. We meet people in their homes and public venues. This can carry additional risks. Taylor (2011, p. 40) notes that "many assaults on social workers occur in the client's home." In order to reduce the service user's sense of threat about the meeting we should provide choices about where the meeting is to occur, but we need to ensure that the location is a safe environment for all parties. If you need to meet in someone's home, try to meet in a part of the home from which you can easily exit if the situation deteriorates and you are at risk of exposure to aggression (Trotter, 2015). It is vital that workers have a safety plan for managing situations of heightened aggression. This plan should include others in the organisation knowing where the worker is at all times and particularly when entering situations where there is heightened risk of aggression and further that there is a protocol in place for immediate response to situations of heightened aggression.

Third, our approach as workers can substantially shape the chances of escalation. In their synthesis of research on de-escalation of aggression, Price and Baker (2012, p. 312) note that "Effective de-escalators are open, honest, supportive, self-aware, coherent, non-judgemental and confident without appearing arrogant (Delaney and Johnson, 2006; Duperouzel, 2008). Presenting oneself in a manner in that is calm, respectful, open and confident can reduce the likelihood of escalation to aggression. By demonstrating that we are interested in finding out the person's view of their situation and we are committed to collaborative solution seeking, we can reduce the person's perception of frustration and threat that often underpins escalation to anger and aggression. As mentioned in the previous Chapter, being able to maintain equanimity in the face of heightened emotions is important to responding to the cycle of emotional escalation. Being very aware of your own signs of increased escalation can help you contain your own emotional responses and remain calm in the face of hostility. Learning skills for managing your own emotional responses is important for reducing the risk of escalation and for responding to it.

We should also be mindful of the impact of our physical demeanour and appearance on perceptions of threat and vulnerability. We need to be aware that our appearance, particularly some forms of clothing and symbols, such as religious or political symbols may trigger or aggravate an already hyper-aroused person. In addition, some forms of clothing, such as scarves and ties or high-heeled shoes can increase our physical vulnerability by creating potential choke holds or by restricting our movement.

Fourth we can seek to understand and prepare for the likely response of the person. Prior to meeting a person it can be helpful to seek out information regarding the person's previous responses in similar situations. For example, is there evidence of a history of aggression or violence towards others? In some situations you may have the benefit of knowing of the person's current emotional state prior to meeting them. For example in services with reception staff or an intake officer, it is important to gather information about the person's situation and their emotional state.

Stage 2: Escalation

Being attuned and responsive to initial expressions of anger or aggression can reduce risk of escalation (Sturmey and McDonnell, 2011, p. 25). Signs of escalating, anger, and aggression may include changes in non-verbal behaviour such as facial cues of frowning and intense staring and postural changes towards a more aggressive stance and changes in vocal pitch, volume and pace.

At this point, the worker can act in ways that reduce further escalation. Actions we can take to reduce escalation include:

a) distraction or distancing from the trigger event or experience. For example, in a group work situation, the worker might ask a service user to assist with a task outside the group to provide time out and an alternative focus from the matter that is troubling the individual (Sturmey and McDonnell, 2011).

b) acknowledging, supporting and containing. It can help to acknowledge the person's frustration or sense of threat and provide a supportive response to their emotions. At this point, we can also articulate our commitment to working alongside the person in solution seeking. Containing involves helping the person to isolate the issue that is troubling them so that a solution can be sought together (Taylor, 2011).

c) reducing environmental stimuli that may be contributing to the escalation of the aggression. For example, an environment that is uncomfortable and highly stimulating, such as extreme temperatures, bright lights and lots of noise may escalate the distress of the person (Price and Baker, 2012; Sturmey and McDonnell, 2011).

d) reducing audience observation of the encounter. A person who is becoming angry and aggressive may be reluctant to back down if there is a fear that they will also lose face (Price and Baker, 2012).

e) providing a cooling off period. Encourage the person to take some time out before returning to the issue to be addressed.

f) avoiding touching the other person as they are likely to be in a hyper-aroused state and my find such touch to be intrusive.

Stage 3: De-escalating heightened emotions: staying engaged, protecting ourselves and others

A person in a heightened emotional state of anger expressed as aggression can be frightening to those around them including the workers. The exposure to aggression and potential violence is a threat that may cause our emotional response of fight or flight.

Our priorities should be to:

➤ ensure the safety of others and of ourselves.

➤ stay connected emotionally to the person.

➤ assist in the de-escalation of the heightened emotional state.

Turning first to ensuring the safety of others and of ourselves, we need to quickly assess the risks of harm in the environment. A checklist of physical safety issues includes:

➤ Does the person have a weapon or access to anything that could be used as a weapon?

➤ What is the means of leaving the situation quickly if it escalates to violence?

➤ Consideration needs to be given as to what type of support or back-up may be needed bearing in mind that this can escalate a person's sense of threat and thus may heightened the aggressive response (Price and Baker, 2012).

The next priority is to stay connected emotionally to the person who is expressing anger and behaving aggressively. Staying connected emotionally to the person helps to maintain the working alliance and to de-escalate the situation. In staying connected we recognise that the person expressing aggression is likely to be experiencing a level of hyperarousal that contributes to a state of sensitivity to others. Our behaviours such as facial cues, non-verbal behaviour and vocal tone must therefore convey a sense of calm. Sturmey and McDonnell (2012, p. 30) note that "raised voices should be avoided and gentle tone should be adopted." We need also to reduce the demands on the person at this time as they are likely to experience difficulty in processing information (Sturmey and McDonnell, 2011).

Demonstrating a calm and open demeanour, regardless of how we are actually feeling, is important to de-escalating anger and aggression (see Price and Baker, 2012; Taylor, 2011). Price and Baker (2012, p. 312) explain that by remaining calm, the worker communicates to the person expressing aggression that the worker is maintaining control of their emotions and further that "despite their anger, they [the service user] can be trusted not to be violent." This sense of the worker maintaining emotional control is important both for affective and instrumental aggression as it communicates that aggression is not needed nor will it help to achieve the end goal that the person may be seeking.

Practical strategies for demonstrating calmness even when we do not feel calm include:

➤ slowing our breathing to a relaxed breathing state.

➤ maintaining an open body posture.

➤ invoking a relaxed facial expression and an expression that demonstrates we are taking the other's emotion seriously. It is important to avoid smiling or frowning. Smiling may be misinterpreted as ridiculing or as minimising the seriousness of the person's view of their situation.

➤ our vocal tone and pace should be quiet, gentle and confident (Sturmey and McDonnell, 2011).

If possible we should reduce aggressive physical stances. It can help to move both parties to a seated position. However, it is important to note the tone and timing of a suggestion to sit is important (Taylor, 2011). We should not demand the other sits down, as in a heightened state of aggression any requests may further escalate the situation (Sturmey and McDonnell, 2011). Maintain an appropriate physical distance in order to reduce your risk of physical harm and also to avoid intruding on the personal space of the other as this too may lead to further emotional escalation.

De-escalation: What to say

De-escalation refers to action aimed at reducing aggressive behaviour and the risk of violence. The skills used in de-escalating anger and aggression are an extension of our foundational interpersonal skills (Koprowska, 2008 cited in Taylor, 2011, p. 43) and are based on the value of respect for all persons. By expressing respect we allow the other to regain dignity and we can reduce their perception of the need for aggression in order to have their needs met (Price and Baker, 2012).

To de-escalate anger and aggression we need to:

➤ engage the person as a communication partner. The worker needs to build on the working alliance by demonstrating that they understand and wish to respond to the person's concerns. Taylor (2011, p. 41) notes that: "Explaining calmly that you are there to help within your professional role, and that you are not there expressing a personal opinion" can help diffuse aggression.

➤ facilitate the person's expression of emotion and discuss their feelings of anger and frustration (Price and Baker, 2012, p. 313).

➤ seek the person's view of the problem and what needs to change. Seek to help them articulate and isolate the key areas of concern.

➤ demonstrate interest and helpfulness. Find out the person's perception of the situation that has invoked the aggression and what, from their perspective needs to change. In so doing we remove the need for aggression (Price and Baker, 2012).

➤ avoid making demands on the person, particularly requests that might be perceived as intrusive or complex. Some examples include requests to undertake: work tasks, social interaction or household chores (Sturmey and McDonnell, 2011).

➤ help the person to isolate the main areas of concern, and work with them to develop an agreed plan of action to address the issues raised. Remembering that a person in a heightened emotional state may find it difficult to prioritise and process information, and so whatever plan of action is developed it needs to be clear and readily implementable. To demonstrate our commitment to the change process, we should ensure that some of the actions we have agreed upon can be enacted immediately. For example, we might say to a person who is frustrated by their housing situation "Today we will sign off on your public housing application, and we will arrange for one week's accommodation at St Mary's hostel."

When to leave

Maintaining our own and others' physical safety must be a priority. Indeed staying and putting ourselves or others in harm's way in a deteriorating situation may damage the working alliance and may result in harm to ourselves and others. Taylor (2011, p. 44) observes "Do not forget that having the embarrassment of leaving is better than getting assaulted." We should consider leaving a situation if the aggression is continuing to escalate despite our attempts to de-escalate. We should leave when our physical safety becomes threatened particularly if there is a change in the situation to indicate escalation. Some examples of a deteriorating situation include: the person threatens your physical well-being and has the means to carry out the threat, where we become out-numbered, change to the safety of the physical environment such as one's pathway for exiting becomes blocked, or that the person grabs or reveals a weapon. We propose that if the situation deteriorates and if there is an option to leave, then the social worker should exercise that option. If the social worker is unable to leave the situation of escalating violence then a back-up should be called. Of course, if the risk of assault is imminent, there is no option of escape and back-up is yet to arrive, the worker must act in ways that reduce risk of harm to themselves or others by, for example, calling for help.

There is debate within the human service literature about health and human service professionals use of physical self-defence and restraints against those who pose a threat a violence to them (see Stewart et al., 2009; Taylor, 2011). Various training programmes on the use of physical self-defence and physical restraints are available in some residential and hospital settings (see Stewart et al., 2009). We urge caution on the use of physical self-defence and restraint in social work practice. Unless the social worker has the capacity to use these skills expertly they risk harm to themselves and others. Furthermore, the social worker may find themselves subject to criminal or civil legal action on the basis of whether their actions in self-defence were reasonable or not (Taylor, 2011). A poorly managed attempt at physical self-defence or restraint may escalate the other's aggression further and may contribute to the risk of violence.

Stage 4: Recovery and restoration

In this section, we refer to recovery after successful de-escalation and recovery where harm has occurred. We turn first to discussion of recovery after a "successful" de-escalation. By successful de-escalation we mean that together with the other we have managed to reduce the aggressive response and avoided harm to the self or other. Even successful de-escalation can have an emotional toll on those involved. Regardless of the outcome, we have been exposed to a heightened and possibly frightening emotional state in which our safety and or well-being was threatened. We may ourselves experience a fight or flight response to this and have a trauma response. Being exposed to anger, aggression and violence can be an overpowering experience that can deplete our emotional resources. The relationship based character of social work practice can contribute to workers' feeling exhausted and even harmed by the exposure to violence.

It is important to recognise our own emotional responses and to build our own personal and professional resilience. As mentioned in the previous Chapter, the opportunity to critically reflect upon challenging experiences can be important for recovery, and for drawing on your experience to develop your professional competence and confidence.

As workers we need to seek out safe places in which to review challenging experiences so that we can:

➤ recognise and learn about the impact and put in place further personal supports.

➤ evaluate actions taken in responding to the challenging situation and to consider future changes.

➤ minimise a sense of shame or personal responsibility for the actions of others towards us.

But what if you were harmed emotionally or physically? It is vital that you recognise "it is not your fault and you did not deserve it." (Taylor, 2011, p. 46). Emotional support is important to assist the person subjected to aggression or violence to recover. This includes access to supportive supervision and peer support. Some strategies that can assist you to manage the impact are:

➤ creating space from the work and its impact. Taking time to develop a fulfilling life outside of one's work including interests and sustaining personal relationships can help to put the challenging aspects of one's role into perspective and can assist in recover from traumatic events.

➤ developing effective peer supports. Bosly's (2007) qualitative study of practitioners' experiences of client anger identified the important role of peers in helping practitioners to maintain resilience in the face of encounters with people expressing anger and aggression.

➤ accessing supportive supervision. Supervision can provide a supportive place for worker's to critically reflect upon exposure to anger and aggression in practice. This reflection can assist in building workers' confidence and competence in responding to these challenging emotions.

➤ engaging in continuing professional development. Through professional development activities we can continue to develop our confidence in responding to anger and aggression, and to recognising and addressing the impact of these emotions and behaviours on ourselves and our peers.

➤ seeking therapeutic intervention. Exposure to anger and aggression can be experienced as traumatising and can trigger powerful memories of trauma in one's past. Insist on organisational safety supports. Working with our organisation to ensure that appropriate support systems are in place reduces worker's exposure to aggression, and provides supportive responses to enable the worker to develop resilience and to recover from aggression.

All incidents of aggression and violence that have, or could have, caused harm to the service user, the worker or others should be documented by the employing organisation. The details of what happened, what the response was and the outcomes, particularly in terms of harms caused and responses to that harm should be recorded. It can also help to note down any possible triggers or factors that seemed to either help reduce or inflame the situation. This information is important for preparing for any future encounters. It may also be required in the event of any further action arising from injuries to yourself or others.

Most people recover from traumatic experiences (Tuckey and Scott, 2014). However for some people the events will impact on their capacity to continue to maintain a working relationship with person who was the aggressor. Trauma can have negative effects on one's personal and professional life. Therapeutic interventions may be required to address the impact of exposure to aggression, particularly where this exposure has contributed to post-traumatic stress. In many human service workplaces, employers are now obliged to provide free access to employee assistance services to help employees to recover from psychological injuries arising from exposure to aggression and violence.

Conclusion

In this Chapter we defined the concepts of anger, aggression and violence. We considered the importance of social workers developing skills in identifying and responding to the emotional state of anger and its potential behavioural consequences, namely aggression and violence. We discussed strategies for responding to the risk of aggression and violence by early identification and response to anger and signs of aggression and then we outlined strategies for de-escalation. The process of recovery and continuing professional development following exposure to anger, aggression and violence were considered. While we have outlined strategies for reducing the risk of aggression and violence, we acknowledge that these behaviours frequently occur in many fields of social work and can be experienced as traumatising and may cause harm. Learning how to recognise and respond to anger and aggression are important to building our confidence and competence as social workers engaging with people who experience significant life challenges.

Practice exercises

Imagine you are a child protection worker who has received a notification for Jasmine Brown, a 35-year-old women who is a single parent to two girls, Holly, 8, and Sarah, 12. You have met Jasmine about two weeks ago when there had been a notification from a neighbour concerning possible physical abuse of the girls by Jasmine. At the time of that meeting, you felt you had built a rapport with Jasmine. She disclosed that she was struggling with bi-polar disorder and that pressures with money and her part-time work had led to behave aggressively to her children. At the time you met the children, both of whom seemed comfortable near their mother. Jasmine said that she regretted an incident where she had yelled at both girls and had hit Sarah across the face. Jasmine said she was seeing her psychiatrist in the next few weeks to assist with adjustments to her medication and that her doctor (general practitioner) was supporting her emotionally.

You are visiting Jasmine today following a notification from the school. You have interviewed the school guidance officer, who says that both girls are too afraid to go home as Jasmine is behaving very aggressively and is yelling and hitting them. You visit the home with another worker. When you arrive at the house, Jasmine is waiting on the balcony. She is shaking her fist angrily and shouting that she knows you have been to the school and you have humiliated her.

➤ How would you describe Jasmine's emotional state?

➤ What stage of the cycle of escalation and de-escalation does Jasmine appear to be experiencing?

➤ How would you respond to Jasmine and why would you respond this way?

➤ What are the safety issues for you, your co-worker, Jasmine and her girls, and how would you manage them?

➤ Are there any other people whose safety you may need to consider?

Chapter review points and questions

1. Define the terms "anger," "aggression" and "violence" and the differences between these concepts.

2. What factors may contribute to a person becoming aggressive?

3. Why is important for social workers to be confident and competent in responding to anger and aggression?

4. What can a social worker do to reduce the risk of aggression in others?

5. What are the components of verbal de-escalation?

Recommended further reading

Sturmey, P. & McDonnell, A. (2011) *Managing aggressive behaviour in care settings.* Hoboken, NJ: Wiley.
In this book, Sturmey and McDonnell outline a low arousal approach to preventing and responding to anger and aggression. This is an evidence based approach to reducing emotional arousal, particularly de-escalating anger and aggression, in care settings. Although primarily intended for practice in residential care settings and for practice with people living with developmental and learning disabilities, many of the components of the model are relevant to understanding, preventing and responding to anger and aggression.
Taylor, B. (ed) (2011). *Working with aggression and resistance in social work.* Exeter: Learning Matters.
This edited collection provides an accessible and evidence based approach to responding to aggression, ambivalence and resistance in a range of practice contexts including practice in child protection and with people experiencing mental health challenges.

PART 2

Communication and Diversity

In Part 2 we consider skilful communication, recognising diverse communication capacities and needs. The Chapters in this section align with the bottom line of our dynamic model of communication. Here we consider communication in the context of cultural and linguistic diversity, with children, young people and older adults, with people experiencing mental health challenges, and with people who face challenges with spoken communication, or who prefer to communicate in other modes (Figure P2.1).

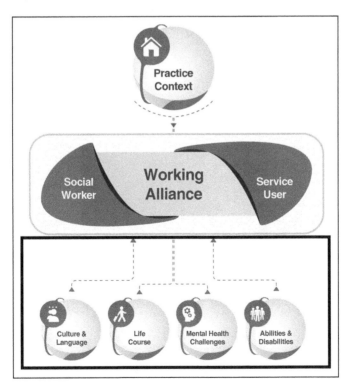

Figure P2.1   The Dynamic Model of Communication: Recognising Diversity

6

Communication and Cultural Diversity

Social workers frequently communicate with people from diverse cultures and linguistic groups. Social workers and the organisations in which we are located may include workers from diverse cultures. Intercultural communication skills then apply to communication with a range of people including colleagues, service users and community members. In this Chapter we define the concepts of culture, cultural diversity, and culturally competent practice. We outline an approach to culturally competent practice which includes three elements: understanding of context; intercultural awareness; and intercultural communication skills. We discuss the practical application of this approach to communication in social work practice.

Culture and cultural diversity in social work practice

The term "culture" is heavily debated. We adopt Liu, Volčič and Gallois' (2014, p. 55) definition of culture as "the particular way of a life of a group of people, comprising the deposit of knowledge, experience, beliefs, values, traditions, religion, notions of time, roles, spatial relations, worldviews, material objects, and geographic territory… culture is a process as well as product of communication." Culture shapes how we see the world; it guides our thinking, our experience and expressions of emotions, and our behaviour.

Cultural identity refers to "the identification with and perceived acceptance into a group that has a shared system of symbols and meanings as well as norms for conduct" (Jandt, 2016, p. 6). Jandt (2016) further notes that "ethnicity" includes both a shared heritage, such as a common history of migration, and culture. Our cultural identities have profound implications for how both we, as social workers, and the people with whom we communicate, perceive and respond to our world. Understanding our own and others cultural identities is important to building and maintaining the working alliance and to developing a shared understanding of the service user's situation and proposed responses or solutions (Rosenberger, 2014).

Acknowledgement of sub-cultures and sub-cultural identities is relevant, given that as social worker we often meet with people who experience social difference, discrimination or alienation within the dominant culture in which they live. A subculture exists "within dominant cultures and are often based on geographic region, ethnicity, or economic and social class" (Jandt, 2016, p. 13). Examples of sub-cultures include youth sub-cultures and groups that share a common sexual or gender identity such as members of the Lesbian/Gay/Bisexual/Transgender/Intersex (LGBTI) communities. It is important to be aware that not all of those "eligible" to identify with a sub-culture choose to do so.

The term "cultural diversity" refers to differences between people arising from their cultural and linguistic identities. While useful for appreciating differences, the term "cultural diversity" or "cultural and linguistic diversity" becomes problematic when it is taken to refer only to those who are "other" to the dominant culture, such as the European or Anglophone cultural groups. As Altman (2014, pp. 57–58) notes a "White" perspective dominates the social construction of cultural identities with the consequence that the term cultural diversity is often used to refer to the "non-White" and "non-English" speaking "other."

The concept of cultural diversity is useful to supporting culturally competent practice when based on a critical awareness that *all* cultural identities are constructed. There are several dimensions to this critical awareness. The first is to decentre "whiteness" as the normative category against which cultural diversity is assessed. "White" people no less than those who identify with any other "identity" category have cultural identifications and experiences and, further, cultural diversities exist within this identity category (Altman, 2014). For example, the category of "white" people includes people of different cultural and national identities and people with different histories of migration including forced migration, colonisation, and of class, gender, sexualities and so forth.

Second, a critical approach to cultural diversity recognises the provisional nature of all categories of cultural and linguistic diversity. Many of the categories change over time in response to the changing political and cultural contexts in which these categories have developed. For example, the term "culturally and linguistically diverse" (CALD) has replaced the term "Non-English Speaking Background" given that the latter is based on a "negative" view of an identity, that is a by a "lack of" English rather than a recognition of linguistic diversity. However, even the term CALD is problematic because it may continue to imply that diversity applies only to those who are other to a "white" "anglophone" norm.

The third dimension of a critical approach to cultural diversity is to recognise diversities *within* identity categories including local and regional variations. For example, there is considerable international variation in how Indigenous people are described by themselves and others. The term "Aboriginal" is often used to refer to people who are the original Inhabitants of Australia and Canada. The term First Nations is also used in the United States and Canada to refer to Indigenous peoples formerly known as "Indian" or "native American." The term however does not refer to other Indigenous people of the North America and Canada, such as Metis, nor does it refer to the Inuit who are the Indigenous people of Northern Canada, Russia and Greenland (Driedger et al., 2013, p. 1). Furthermore, considerable variations can occur within groups of Indigenous peoples. For example, the Aboriginal people of Australia comprise people of many Indigenous nations, each with its own cultural protocols (Eades, 2013).

Our communication practices are shaped by the cultures with which we identify and are identified. Cultural diversity is an important concept for social worker practice when it enables us to develop a critical awareness of the ways in which culture shapes how we and those with whom we communicate view the world. A critical appreciation of cultural differences underpins the development and maintenance of working relationships with people across cultural and linguistic differences.

Culturally competent practice

"Culturally competent practice" is a term that is often used in health care and social services to refer to "a set of congruent behaviors, attitudes, and policies that come together in a system, agency, or among professionals that enables effective work in cross-cultural situations" (Rose, 2013, p. 202; see also Briggs, 2009). This incorporates the notion of cultural sensitivity, that is "awareness of and respect for" the person's values and beliefs (Rose, 2013, p. 103) but also extends this concept to include behaviours, attitudes and policies that shape our interactions with people from cultures other than our own. Because we can never fully know a culture other than our own, it is perhaps best to understand cultural competence as a journey rather than a destination. We can strive to be culturally competent but it is likely that tensions and misunderstandings will occur along the way. Furthermore, in striving to become culturally competent, we must not overlook the unique experience and perspective of the individuals with whom we are communicating (Johnson and Munch, 2009).

Cultural competence is important in social work practice for promoting effective engagement with people whose cultural identities and language capacities differ from our own. Without cultural competence we risk alienating people from cultural and linguistic groups different from our own or different from the dominant culture of the society in which we practice. For example, should we uncritically apply the norms of the dominant cultural group regarding matters such as family and community responsibilities, we may alienate those who hold very different cultural values about these obligations.

Cultural competence is also important to enhancing the accuracy of our assessment, particularly in relation to the meaning others make of events and experiences. Referring to intercultural communication in mental health services, Altman (2014, p. 59) observes that "what is thought to be psychotic in one cultural context may be considered part of a normative spiritual experience in another." In addition, cultural competence can assist in improving our effectiveness as we need to engage clients in solutions that work for them in their cultural context. For example, individualistic solutions to problems may be unappealing and unworkable to a person who holds a collectivist worldview in which family and community ties have priority.

Elements of culturally competent practice

While culturally competent practice involves intercultural communication skills, it is much more than this. We propose culturally competent practice comprises three elements which we outline in Figure 6.1.

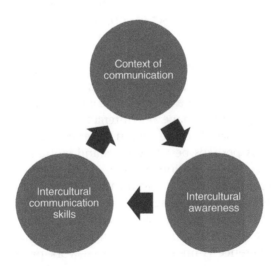

Figure 6.1   Elements of Culturally Competent Communication

We will now discuss each of these elements.

Contexts of communication

Culturally competent communication involves understanding the historical and political contexts of our communication and how these contexts shape how our services are organised and perceived by people from diverse cultural backgrounds. Historical and political processes, especially those associated with colonisation and globalisation, shape cultural identities and relations among people of different cultural and linguistic groups. These processes influence relations of power and shape people's perceptions of the trustworthiness (or otherwise) of health and human service professionals. Understood within its historical and political context, we can understand the valuation of cultural norms and practices is not neutral. The term "white privilege" is used by cultural theorists to explain how the cultural characteristics of white Europeans may come to be regarded as superior to those of some other cultural identities (Jandt, 2016, p. 11). Historical and political contexts also affect the nature and process of health and welfare service delivery.

Patterns of human migration have created the culturally diverse societies in which we live and in which we as social workers practice. Of course, human intercontinental migration has occurred over at least two million years. Over the past four centuries human migration has accelerated dramatically, often against a backdrop of social and economic struggles. These conflicts mean that intercultural communication is often infused with relations of power of which the social worker seeking to develop culturally competent approaches to practice must be aware.

The process of European colonisation has particular and ongoing effects that shape relations between governments, human service professionals and people who use our services today. Colonisation "involves the establishment of colonies for settlement or commercial purposes and historically has manifested in a diverse range of forms and practices in different countries" (Harrison and Melville, 2009, p. 18). European colonisation commenced in the fifteenth century and over the next four centuries led to dramatic population shifts. In many parts of the world, European settlement was associated with large scale violence, including murder, and displacement of Indigenous peoples in many countries and forced re-settlement of other populations such as African people who were transported to some colonies as slaves. Indigenous peoples throughout the world, and others who were exploited through the process of colonisation, continue to suffer the ongoing trauma and related health and social issues arising from this process.

Social workers and other health professionals are implicated in the ongoing trauma of colonisation. Driedger et al. (2013, pp. 1–2) note that "Aboriginal people have had a strong negative history concerning their health and accessing services in Canada" (see also Liaw et al., 2011). Indigenous people also have been the subject of racist child welfare policies throughout much of the nineteenth and twentieth century. In Australia, Canada, the United States and New Zealand, Indigenous children were removed by welfare authorities with the goal of promoting their assimilation. By cutting ties with the children's family and communities, colonialist governments sought to interrupt the transmission of cultural values in Indigenous communities. In the vast majority of cases, the children were removed to sub-standard care, almost always without the love and attention humans need to flourish and, often, into a highly brutalising environment (Barker et al., 2014; Bessarab and Crawford, 2013; HREOC, 1997). The trauma experienced those who were removed have been associated with increased risks of mental health and physical health issues, incarceration, homelessness, school dropout, unemployment, and child removal (Harrison and Melville, 2009; HREOC, 1997; Rose, 2013).

The historical legacy of colonialist expansion is not limited to Indigenous peoples. Many other peoples have also suffered economic and social disadvantage as a result of colonialist expansion and those people are disproportionately drawn from peoples whose cultural or ethnic identities are other to White Europeans. For example, the forced mass migration of African people to America as slaves for European settlers which commenced in the 1600s has ongoing legacies today. Despite the successes of the Civil Rights Movement, African American peoples continue to experience higher rates of economic and social disadvantage with attendant negative health, education and employment outcomes and over-representation in out of home care systems, youth justice and adult justice systems (Brulle and Pellow, 2006; Daining and DePanfilis, 2007).

Colonisation was associated with the devaluing of all aspects of Indigenous cultures (Jandt, 2016). This devaluing continues today with health and welfare policies that are discriminatory or unresponsive to the distinctive needs of Indigenous peoples (Barker et al., 2014; Tilbury, 2009). Indigenous social workers and their allies observe that Eurocentric notions of service provision such as assumptions about professional hierarchies and linear notions of time are alien to Indigenous ways of knowing and of forming and maintaining relationships (Bacon, 2013).

Developing culturally congruent practice requires social workers to appreciate how the history of colonisation and its aftermath impact on relations between our profession and the peoples who were harmed in this process (Green and Baldry, 2008). Indigenous people and people of diverse ethnicities who were exploited in the process of colonialist expansion have experienced considerable trauma at the hands of health and human service professionals and these experiences shape our relationships today. Social workers then should understand that relations of trust, that underpin the working alliance, may take substantial time and further that the worker needs to demonstrate openness to and respect for the cultural identities and practices of the peoples with whom they practice. Social workers, as a profession, need to work alongside Indigenous communities to ensure social justice in the formation of social and health policies, organisational protocol and in increasing the presence of Indigenous people and people of diverse ethnic groups as providers of health and welfare services (Green and Baldry, 2008).

The industrial era, commencing in the eighteenth century, also contributed to the cultural diversity of many societies today. The industrial era ushered in substantial increases in migration particularly from poorer to wealthier nations and this trend has intensified in the twentieth and twenty-first centuries as a result of global economic changes and migrations associated with global conflicts. The term "globalisation" refers to a process of intensified social and cultural interconnection across the world and the replacement of national and regional economic systems with a single global market (Dominelli, 2012). Globalisation has in part been fuelled by technological innovation that has made greater interconnectivity possible through increase opportunity for contact, such as through the internet, and reduced cost of travel (Czaika and Haas, 2014). When combined with other related political transitions in the late twentieth century, particularly the collapse of Communist states and the relaxation of prohibitions against intercountry migration in some regions, globalisation has contributed to dramatic shifts in migration. Czaika and Hass (2014) analysis of migration patterns shows that since 1980 the range of countries from which people are emigrating has increased, while the preferred countries of destination have become more concentrated. Increasingly then, the pattern of migration is from less economically developed regions to wealthier regions, particularly to and within Western and Northern Europe, North America and Canada, Australia and New Zealand, the Asian Tiger Economies and Japan, and the Persian gulf (Czaika and Haas, 2014). Vertovec (2007) created the term "super-diversity" to refer the unprecedented cultural diversity that now characterises these societies.

This movement of people from developing to developed countries is further intensified by global conflicts that have contributed to mass exoduses of people in conflict zones. Many of these people have been exposed to traumatic experiences in their country of origin and in the processes of seeking asylum in other countries. Consequently, social workers may work with people from diverse cultures and who may also have complex needs associated with exposure to trauma.

The intensification of migration patterns into and within some regions of the world, including the wealthy countries of Europe, Asia, Oceania and the Americas, means that social workers in those regions will inevitably communicate with people from cultures other than their own. Furthermore, it is likely that we will communicate with people from a diverse range of cultures rather than a singular or limited group of cultures. In addition, social work services are provided against a backdrop of colonisation that contributes to ongoing tensions in relations between social workers and some of the cultural and linguistically peoples with whom we communicate, particularly where we represent the dominant cultural group which initiated and benefited from colonisation.

Sensitivity to context means being aware of the political and historical context of intercultural communication. Some ways in which we demonstrate this awareness include creating a culturally inclusive practice environment wherein signs, posters, written material and equipment (such as children's play equipment) reflects Indigenous identities and cultural and linguistic diversity. We should continue to develop our understanding of the cultural protocols of the diverse communities with which we work and to incorporate this awareness into our communication with people from these communities. We should work to increase the cultural diversity of our workplaces to reflect the diversity of the societies in which we live. We should strive to ensure the people have access to a support person from their cultural group to be present during the course of our involvement with them should they request it.

Intercultural Awareness

The second element of culturally competent practice is intercultural awareness. Liu et al. (2015, p. 314) define intercultural awareness as involving:

> two qualities: one is awareness of one's own culture; the other is the awareness of another culture. Intercultural awareness means the ability of standing back from one's own point of view and to become aware also of the cultural values, beliefs, and perceptions of other cultures.

Awareness of the assumptions one brings from one's own culture as well as sensitivity to the cultural assumptions others bring to the relationship is vital to the development and maintenance of the working alliance. The cultural perspectives that we and the people with whom we communicate bring profoundly shapes direct practice as these views guide our "our day-to-day living, influencing how decisions are made and by whom and determine[s] what is perceived to be appropriate and inappropriate behaviour within any given context" (Connolly, Crichton-Hill and Ward, 2006, p. 17). By developing intercultural awareness we learn to value differences in cultural knowledge, values and behaviours, which then enables us to "adapt practice skills to fit the cultural context of the clients" (Rose, 2013, p. 50).

A failure to develop intercultural awareness can have significant consequences when overlaid with power differences that operate between social workers and the people who use of our services. Ethnocentric biases that lead us to assume our own cultural outlook and values are superior to others lead to errors of judgement which can have serious consequences for the people with whom we practice. For example, Eurocentric assumptions about child rearing practices have contributed to child protection workers failing to acknowledge protective and nurturing caregiving relationships outside the nuclear family unit (Connolly et al., 2006). Ethnocentricism can be reinforced through professional knowledge and education. For example, biomedical categorisations of mental health do not reflect culturally diverse understanding of mental health and illness which may include spiritual and social dimensions of mental health and illness (Altman, 2014; Ferrazzi and Krupa, 2016). Becoming culturally aware involves creating space in our practice to hear the alternative views people from cultures other than our own may hold about the challenges they face and the culturally appropriate responses to them.

Becoming culturally aware is challenging. As Jandt (2016, p. 6) observes: "we can have no direct knowledge of a culture other than our own. Our experience with and knowledge of other cultures is limited by the perceptual bias of our own culture." We propose three strategies for developing cultural awareness. The first is to actively seek out knowledge about cultural diversity about communication protocol and key concepts and phenomenon particularly as it relates to our field of practice (Rose, 2013). For example, social workers working in health services should become familiar with attitudes to health, ageing and disability across cultures. We can achieve this by engaging in continuing professional development activities focused on building intercultural awareness and in seeking out information about cultural knowledge, values and protocol from people who identify with cultures other than our own.

The second strategy is to critically examine our personal and professional beliefs (Rose, 2013). This critical examination requires us to examine our own belief systems in the light of other cultural viewpoints and to consider how different viewpoints may lead to alternative practice possibilities. For example, the dominant European cultures of "Western" often prize individual achievement over collective responsibilities and we should reflect on how these individualistic assumptions influence our approaches to engaging, assessing and intervening with service users.

Critical incident techniques provide a third strategy by which we can develop our intercultural awareness. Critical incident techniques require us to reflect on action so that we may learn from practice events (Fook, 2013). Critical incident techniques as a basis for preparation to communicate were discussed earlier in this book (see Chapter 2). In using critical incident techniques to develop cultural awareness in practice, we need to first to identify an incident or area of tension in our practice or proposed field of practice. For example, we might consider how we would engage (or have engaged) with a family from a culture other than our own in a child and family welfare scenario. The next step is to critically examine key personal and professional assumptions we hold that influence how we engage with the family and how we undertake assessment and intervention. In this critical examination, we should consider how our assumptions are in tension with, or possibly marginalise, the values and beliefs of the family. Third we should consider how we can re-work our assumptions to enable diverse cultural perspectives to be recognised. For example, a "western" individualistic view about caregiver relationships that often prioritises the role of the mother as primary caregiver, might be expanded to consider how the kinship network of a child can be assessed and supported to promote the health and well-being of the child.

Intercultural communication skills

Culturally competent practice requires social workers to develop skills in "intercultural communication." This concept refers to the skills associated with "the ability to communicate effectively and appropriately with people of other cultures" (Jandt, 2016, p. 53). Significant cultural differences exist in communication norms, and selecting the appropriate behaviour in circumstances where we are working with people from many and varied cultural groups other than our own can be challenging. Furthermore, while we can learn of the "typical" norms associated with various cultures, it is important that we encourage the person with whom we are communicating to "express themselves in their uniqueness" (Jandt, 2016, p. 60). It is important to take time to observe and learn about the communication norms of the people with whom we are communicating.

On first meeting a person we recommend that one seeks to demonstrate non-possessive warmth, genuineness, accurate empathy and a desire and capacity to be helpful discussed earlier in this book (see Chapter 2, see also Sheldon and Macdonald, 2009; see also Healy and Darlington, 2009; Trotter, 2013, 2015). It is important also to introduce oneself and inquire as to the person's preferences about the name they wish us to refer to them by. Within some cultural groups formal approaches are preferred, with the use of formal titles being normative, whereas in other cultural groups the use of the first name is preferred. In addition, cultural variations exist around what information should be shared about in relationship building. Whereas many of the dominant cultural traditions of the West place a high value on formal and bounded professional relationships, in many other cultural traditions greater expectations of mutual sharing may exist (Zubrzycki and Crawford, 2013). For example, Indigenous Australians use the term "yarning" to refer to the process of getting to know a person and this is "not a one way process but a dialogical process that is reciprocal and mutual" (Bessarab and Ng'andu, 2010, p. 38). Contravening culturally bound rules around names and about the sharing of self can start the interaction off badly and so it is important to inquire about the person's preferences in this regard and to also provide the person with information about how they should refer to us.

In the remainder of this Chapter, we will discuss intercultural communication skills. We will first focus on non-verbal communication. We will turn then to outline verbal communication skills including recognising and responding to diversity of language use among people who use the same language and the processes of communication with people where we do not share a common language. We will outline the process of engaging an interpreter in communication with people who speak a language other than one's own.

Cultural differences and nonverbal communication

It is important to be aware of cultural differences in non-verbal communication. Chen and Han (2001, p. 118) observe that as "nonverbal communication is more culturally bound than verbal communication, it can quickly elicit confusion and irritation, leading to ethnic stereotyping." Communication theorist Jandt (2016) identifies nine dimensions of non-verbal communication. These elements are: kinesics, proxemics, paralinguistics, silence, chronemics, haptics, artifactual communication, territoriality and olfactics. The intercultural communication literature in the health and human services literature has tended to place greater emphasis on a narrow range of non-verbal communication. While there is extensive discussion of bodily gestures and paralinguistics, far less consideration has been given to perceptions of time, touch and smell. Yet, as we shall demonstrate these are all important dimensions of communication and can have a strong influence on intercultural communication and misunderstanding. In this section, we will discuss nine dimensions referred to by Jandt (2016) and, in addition, we will also discuss gender differences and inter-cultural communication.

We turn first to "kinesics." This term refers to facial, gestures and body movements that can be intentional but are often also unconscious (Jandt, 2016). The human services communication literature places great emphasis on kinesics particularly eye contact and facial expressions (see Egan, 2010). Furthermore, the human services communication literature often reflects Eurocentric kinesic norms. For example, it is frequently assumed that high levels of eye contact are important for effective engagement in casework contexts. Yet, cultural norms about the use of eye contact vary considerably. In many Asian and Indigenous cultures, high levels of eye contact can be viewed as impolite, invasive or intimidating (Chen and Han, 2001). If the service user appears uncomfortable with eye contact, we should take steps to reduce the level of eye contact in the interaction. Some ways of doing this include: changing the seating arrangements into a V shape, that we are more side on, rather than facing the service users squarely; being conscious of increasing our visual focus in other directions, such as looking down at our notes, or outwards in the same direction as the service user's visual gaze, rather than directly at the service user; and mirroring the non-verbal behaviour of the service user.

Cultural norms in relation to facial expression, like the norms governing eye contact, vary markedly by culture. Drawing on a large body of research, Butler, Lee and Gross (2007, p. 31) assert that, "Western European values such as independence and self-assertion encourage open emotion expression in most situations" and, by contrast, "Asian values such as interdependence and relationship harmony might encourage suppression equally." In many Western cultures, an open, highly expressive face is regarded as engaging and, hence, many counselling and casework texts emphasise the importance of open facial expressions, such as smiling, in building rapport. However, in some cultures, such as some Asian cultures, there is much emphasis on the containment of facial expression. Like all other forms of non-verbal expression, it is important that we are aware of the nature and impact of our facial expression. Being able to adapt our facial expression to more closely mirror that of the client is an important dimension of all communication but appears to be especially important in culturally sensitive practice.

A second dimension of nonverbal communication is "proxemics" which refers to "our use of personal space" (Jandt, 2016, p. 106). Proxemics vary between cultural groups. Sue and Sue (1977) suggest that people from the dominant cultures of "Western" nations, tend to expect greater interpersonal distance than those from some African and Asian cultures. Again, the issue is that we are able to moderate our behaviour to more closely mirror that with which the service user feels comfortable. At the same time, the worker should not compromise themselves to the point that they become uncomfortable in the interaction.

A third area of non-verbal communication is "paralanguage." These are vocal but not verbal cues that shape communication and can include tone, pitch of voice or continuers (Jandt, 2016, p. 112). Considerable cultural variation exists in the use and interpretation of paralinguistic cues. For example, an increasingly loud volume can indicate anger in Anglophone groups such as among British, American and "white" Australians, while this same increasing volume can indicate engagement and interest in some other cultures (Lago, 2006).

A fourth area of non-verbal communication is the use of silence. Expectations regarding the presence of silence in conversation vary considerably. In many dominant cultures of western societies, silence may be regarded as an absence of communication, as uncomfortable or as invitation for the other person to speak. By contrast, intercultural researchers observe that silence appears to play an important role in communication in many cultures. Reflecting on group work practice, Chen and Han (2001, p. 118) assert that Asian participants may remain silent to avoid disagreement or keep a low profile in the group. Further, Chen and Han (2001, p. 118) assert: "In these cases, silence is not necessarily a signal inviting others to take over the conversation." Similarly, Indigenous social workers urge practitioners to allow for space for silence in their interaction with Indigenous people (Skuse, 2007). Silence can be important for participants in any interaction. However, for people from some cultural groups silences have significant cultural importance that should be recognised and valued in our communication.

A fifth dimension of nonverbal communication is chrometics which refers to perceptions about time (Jandt, 2016, p. 110). Dominant cultures of Western societies adopt a adopt a linear view of time, while people of many other cultures, particularly Indigenous cultures and many cultures within the global South hold a cyclical view of time. A cyclical view of time does not recognise concepts such as yesterday, today, tomorrow, as time is viewed as part of repeated cycles such as the cycle of day and night or seasonal variations. Referring to Australian Aboriginal peoples' use of time, Eades (2013, pp. 50–51) notes:

> Aboriginal people operate with different notions of time from whites [*sic*]. In pre-contact time, the passing of time was marked by seasonal, geographical and social events. Chronological, seriated time marking and reference were not used. [This] way of viewing time persists [in some ways] today, so that, for example, people talk about events which happened when Johnny was as big as this little one now, or in the winter time, or last time Auntie Daisy was in town, or less specifically, a long time ago. ... future time reference is frequently either vague or tied to some seasonal or social event, such as ... when it's a bit cooler, or ... after Billy comes home.

This non-linear approach to time can create confusion and frustration between Indigenous and non-Indigenous peoples in negotiating shared understandings of social phenomena and events. A cyclical view of time does not readily fit with "Western" human service approaches involving structured interviews and time limited problem solving. Further, these different perceptions of time can be invested with meaning that can create tensions in the working alliance. For example, Altman (2014) observes that a service user being late for an appointment may be misread by a practitioner from a Western cultural tradition as resistance to service.

A sixth dimension of non-verbal communication is "haptics" which refers to "our use of touch to communicate" (Jandt, 2016 p. 114). There is considerable cultural variation in the use of touch. Jandt (2016) observes that the dominant cultures of the United States and Britain have very low rates of casual touch among adults compared to European or Asian nations. In many cultures, extensive use of touch is incorporated into greetings and everyday gestures. Nicholls (2012, p. 191) different gestures involving touch "betray deep roots that relate directly to collective histories, beliefs and values." The use of touch in professional practice with people from cultures other than one's own is a complex terrain. In striving to be culturally competent we need to be responsive to cultural differences about touch and its importance in a supportive working alliance. Yet, at the same time, we need to be aware of the potential for touch to be experienced as inappropriate, intrusive or potentially triggering of traumatic memories (see Havig, 2008). We need then to observe how the person with whom we are communicating uses touch as well as reflecting on what forms of touch are appropriate and helpful to reflecting and maintaining the working alliance (Green, 2017).

A seventh dimension is "artifactual communication" which refers to "how we decorate our homes and offices as well as what we wear and our physical appearance with jewelry, tattoos and body piercings." (Jandt, 2016, p. 116). Our presentation of self, our work environment and accessories to our work (such as play equipment) is imbued with culturally meaning. Our self-presentation in terms of attire and demeanour profoundly shapes the initial engagement process and how we present ourselves visually can have lasting effects on the working relationship. As recommended in Chapter 3, the worker should strive for a neutral clean appearance without signs or symbols that might be a distraction for the service user. Similarly our workplaces should reflect respect for cultural diversity. As mentioned earlier in this Chapter, we should ensure that accessories to our practice, for example, books, brochures and play equipment reflect a culturally inclusive worldview. Visual aspects of our work environment should reflect respect for cultural diversity. Possible sources of distraction for people from culturally and linguistic backgrounds include images that reference specific religious, spiritual or political affiliations that may conflict with their own. As one illustration, posters and reading material in the waiting rooms and workspaces should be drawn a diverse range of cultures and should reflect the major cultural groups who access our services.

Territoriality refers to the use of space to communicate (Jandt, 2016). When visiting people's homes and places of gathering, we should be attuned to how others use space. For example, in some cultural contexts, wearing shoes or hats within the house is not acceptable and to avoid offence we should remove our shoes or hats before entering a home. Our office spaces should be designed to facilitate non-hierarchical communication exchange. We should be mindful of our location and that of others in a meeting space. For example, we should avoid people sitting in hierarchical formations such as a person at the head of the table and, where possible, arrange furniture in a circular formation. In many cultures, the presence of refreshments is a sign of welcome and significant meetings may begin with a drink or meal and a short ceremony (see Briggs, 2009). Where conducting significant decision-making meetings, such as family group conferences, with people from cultures other than one's own, we should consult with those present prior to the meeting about any cultural protocol that they would expect or prefer for the meeting.

A final dimension of non-verbal communication is olfactory communication, that is communication via smell (Jandt, 2016, p. 120). The influence of smell has not received significant attention in the study of non-verbal communication in human service settings and, indeed, is an underdeveloped area of investigation about non-verbal communication more generally (Levitan et al., 2014). Yet smells and aromas can evoke powerful memories and emotional responses both of which may be culturally bound (Ferdenzi et al., 2013; Levitan et al., 2014). Jandt (2016, p. 120) notes that "Smell is the only sense linked directly into the limbic system, which may be evidence to its being our most basic, primitive sense."

Cultural variations in the interpretation of different odours and aromas can be direct or indirect. Direct cultural variations relate primarily to habituation to particular smells within specific cultural contexts. For example certain strong food smells can provoke disgust among people from some cultural groups while other groups may evaluate these smells and aromas positively (Ferdenzi et al., 2013). Indirect cultural variations in emotional responses to smell reflect the association of the smell with a cultural practice. For example, in many Indigenous cultures, smoking ceremonies are associated with significant life events and spiritual processes and hence the strong aroma of smoke may evoke powerful memories for a person with a recent or enduring memory associated with such a ceremony.

Turning now to norms about gender and cultural differences, we note that all cultures have rules that govern the norms of interaction within and across genders. Interactions among people of the same gender are also governed by rules which are often unacknowledged. For example, in many Western societies, physical touch among women is relatively common but among men is may be regarded as inappropriate. In some Indigenous cultures there are strict rules about issues that might be regarded as "women's business" and "men's business" and it would be considered inappropriate, for instance, for a male social worker to discuss some aspects of "women's business" (Corporal, 2007, p. 14).

When we are working regularly with a cultural group other than our own, it is vital that we become knowledgeable about, and demonstrate respect for, the norms governing interaction within and across genders. If, by contrast, our work brings us into contact with people from a wide variety of cultural backgrounds, it may be difficult to be aware of the all the cultural variations concerning appropriate forms of interaction within and between genders. In these cases, it is important that we are alert to cultural differences in interaction between and within genders and to ensure that, as far as possible, we avoid contravening cultural protocol. Until we are certain of these protocols, it is advisable to err on the side of caution by maintaining a polite and respectful distance in our contact with service users of a different gender. It is helpful to be especially alert and responsive to signs of discomfort in others. For example, if we offer to shake the hand of a person of a different gender and that person appears reluctant to do so, be ready to withdraw that offer in a low-key way so as to avoid embarrassment to the other.

Communication and linguistic diversity

Working with people from culturally diverse group also involves responding to linguistic diversity. In this section we first consider linguistic diversity among people who share a common language. We then consider communication with people who speak a different language and the involvement of interpreters in facilitating communication in these circumstances.

Language diversity within the same language group

Language diversity can exist even among people who speak the same language. Often these variations reflect differences of class, region or ethnicity. The differences can be at the level of word use, such as words having different meanings, and also in patterns of language use. We will consider both of these differences here.

The term "dialect" is used to refer to distinct patterns of language use such as differences in sounds, grammar, words and their meanings (Eades, 2013). Dialects often reflect regional, cultural, or national differences in the development of the same or similar languages. Dialects are mutually intelligible for people within the same language group. One example of within language variation is international variations in language use among people from countries in which English is the dominant language. Among these countries variation in people's accents and use of terminology exists and can be sources of confusion errors in communication. For example, in Australia, New Zealand and the United Kingdom the term "torch" refers to a flashlight, while in the United States the term "torch" refers to an open-flamed instrument like that required to light the flame at the Olympic Games. A health or welfare professional who requests a torch may receive a very different instrument (and reception!) depending on the context in which they make the request.

"Within" language variations often reflect social differentials, such as class differences. Class based language differences can be a source of tension and frustration in social work practice given that the often different class positions of the social worker and the service user. In building and maintaining the working alliance, social workers need to be sensitive to how class based language variations can be a barrier to effective communication and as such be willing to adapt our language use to be more congruent with those with whom we communicate.

Language use also reflects cultural norms that can vary substantially among people from different cultures but who share a common language. Cultural variations exist around many dimensions of language use including: the level of formality in titles and interaction particularly between people of different social groups; rules around turn-taking, such as who can initiate turn taking and when; politeness; and the levels of directness that are considered desired or acceptable. In her analysis of differences in the use of "please" and "thank-you" between people living in Britain and America, Murphy (2016, p. 49) notes:

> "polite words" like please, thanks, sorry and pardon are a particular challenge for transatlantic communication. The differences are hard to pin down, and they have implications for whether we're considered polite in a conversation or not. From there they have the potential to affect stereotypes of whether people from one country or another are "polite" or "rude", "obsequious" or "brusque", "attentive" or "oblivious".

Different rules around language exchange, even among people who share a common language but a different cultural background, can be sources of misunderstanding and tension that have the potential to undermine the working alliance.

Within language variation and Indigenous peoples

An important area of within language variation pertains to the interactions between Indigenous and non-Indigenous Peoples in post-colonial countries such as Australia, New Zealand, the Americas, Canada, Africa and Scandinavia. For some Indigenous people, particularly those living in traditional communities, the dominant language of the society (such as English) may be their second language. Indigenous peoples who speak the dominant language of the society may speak in a different dialect of that language. These Indigenous dialects, like all languages, may vary from region to region (Fadden and LaFrance, 2010). The forms of Aboriginal English spoken by Indigenous peoples in countries where English is the dominant language are not simply lesser versions of Standard English, but rather have their own separate rule-governed dialects (Eades, 2013). Studies of Aboriginal English in Australia and Canada have suggested these dialectics merge "English vocabulary with elements of Indigenous sound systems and grammars" and the dialects also reflect cultural world-views such as the emphasis on avoidance of confrontation (Fadden and LaFrance, 2010, p. 145; see also Eades, 2013). These dialectics are often unrecognised or devalued by non-Aboriginal people (Eades, 2013).

Confusion arises where common terms between Aboriginal forms of English and Standard English hold different meanings between the two dialects. For example, in Australia the terms "aunty" and "uncle" are commonly used in both dialects, however, in Aboriginal English the terms "aunty" and "uncle" are used to respectfully refer to any older woman or man in one's social network, whereas in Australian English the term tends to be confined to a relative by blood or marriage. This different meaning of a common term may create confusion for a non-Aboriginal social worker who is seeking formation about the immediate family network of the person.

Aboriginal English, like all languages and dialects, is governed by a variety of rules that determines matters such as: how individuals should be addressed and the order in which they should be addressed; what information should be sought and how it should be sought. Differences around language use may contribute not only to tensions between non-Aboriginal and Aboriginal people but also to social injustices (Fadden and LaFrance, 2010). Liberman (1981 cited in Eades, 2013, pp. 100–101) coined the term "gratuitous concurrence" to refer to the tendency of Australian Aboriginal people to "agree with whatever is being asked by a non-Aboriginal questioner, even if they do understand the question." This practice both reflects Aboriginal cultural norms that prioritise relationship maintenance and avoidance of confrontation, and it is also a strategy used by Aboriginal people to protect themselves from the perceived intrusive use of questioning by non-Aboriginal people (Eades, 2008). When linked to other features of Australian Aboriginal English, particularly the deflection of direct questions and the use of silence, gratuitous concurrence can place Aboriginal people at a distinct disadvantage in legal contexts. These linguistic features often found within Indigenous people's use of English have been shown to contribute to injustice towards Indigenous people both in Australia and elsewhere (Eades, 2013; see also Fadden and LaFrance, 2010).

"Within language" variations can lead to misunderstanding, tension and social injustice. The likelihood of injustice is greatest where one cultural group has the power to impose its dialect on another, that is where one dialect and its assumptions are the norm. At a minimum, as social workers we need to be alert to the possibility of within language variations and to observe and, where appropriate, adapt our language use. For example, when class based differences in language use create difficulties in achieving shared understanding we may negotiate either a common term or use the terms of the person with whom are communicating. Where systematic disadvantage is associated with "within language" variations the presence of their party mediators or liaison officers may help to address the power imbalance. For example, in Australia, Aboriginal liaison officers often practice in legal settings to assist the development of mutual understanding between non-Indigenous legal personnel and Indigenous people using these services (Bartels, 2015).

Working with interpreters

Communication with people can be very challenging where we do not share a common language. Linguistic differences can result in frustration and perceptions of disrespect between professionals and people who do not speak the dominant language in which society where the service occurs (Chand, 2005; Hadziabdic and Hjelm, 2013).

Communication with people with whom we do not share a common language will usually involve a third party providing translation and/or interpretation services. Translation refers to the written word, while interpretation refers to the spoken word. As this book is primarily about face to face communication in social work we will not focus on translation except to point to the importance of all important written material being made available in a range of languages, particularly people from the language groups who use our services (Rose, 2013).

Interpretation can, and does, happen by a variety of means: including the involvement of family; bilingual workers; and professional interpreters. The role of the interpreter is to improve accessibility of health and human services through addressing language barriers to service access (Brisset, Leanza and Laforest, 2011). There are numerous considerations as to who to involve as an interpreter, which we will discuss later in this Chapter, but for matters requiring the disclosure of highly sensitive information is it widely acknowledged that a professional interpreter is best practice. (Hadziabdic and Hjelm, 2013; Rose, 2013).

We turn now to the process of involving an interpreter in communication in social work practice. We have adapted the framework described by Hadziabdic and Hjelm (2013) in their review of the evidence for interpreter mediated health services. We have added a first stage to their framework, that of "Identifying the need for an interpreter."

Phase 1: Identifying the need for an interpreter

When we are seeking to communicate with a person with whom we do not share a common language, we need to assess whether the person has sufficient language proficiency to fully utilise our service. In some situations this will be obvious, such as where the referrer or the person seeking our service or their support person requests an interpreter. In other situations it may be less apparent. For example, the person may have developed some language proficiency for general language use but may be more limited in their capacity to engage in language concepts required for the clinical or emotional content of the issue (Miletic et al., 2006). In addition, the person may seek to conceal challenges they experience in communicating in the language in which the service is provided. There are a variety of reasons for this, and can include the person's fear of stigmatisation or wish to maintain their privacy.

A key way of assessing a person's language proficiency is through "concept checking." This involves exploring the person's understanding of the content of the communication in which you are engaged. We "concept check" by asking open questions and seeking responses that enable us to assess whether the person has sufficient proficiency in the language in which the service is provided to participate in further stages of assessment and intervention independently. Closed questions are generally not useful for concept checking as these may be more easily responded to in a way that fails to clarify the person's level of relevant language comprehension. Some examples of concept checking questions include:

➤ What do you understand to be the reason for our meeting?

➤ What are the outcomes you would like from our meeting today?

➤ What are your main concerns for yourself/your children?

➤ From your viewpoint, what are the main things we have agreed to today?

Other ways of assessing include observation of the person's responsiveness to our questions. For example, if the person is unable to respond spontaneously to our initial questions or appears to require another person's support to do so, we should consider involving an interpreter.

Phase 2: Choosing the interpreter

The role of the interpreter is to provide the flow of communication between people who speak different languages and to do so in a way that is confidential, accurate and impartial (AUSIT, 2007, p. 1; Hadziabdic and Hjelm, 2013, p. 22). Once we have decided that an interpreter is required, there are several options available to us and the person with whom we are communicating.

One option is for a family member or friend to interpret the communication between the worker and the person receiving social work services. This can have several advantages, including that the person receiving services may trust the interpreter and the interpreter is likely to have a good understanding of the person's context and needs. However, Hadziabdic and Hjelm (2013, p. 74) note that "The use of relatives [and friends] as interpreters entails a risk that important information will not be interpreted because of limitations on language ability, cultural barriers and social ties to next of kin." These barriers can lead to errors in interpretation and to the withholding of important information due to cultural barriers or relationships that preclude the sharing of certain information that might be regarded as private or embarrassing. For example, a person may find it deeply embarrassing or dangerous to reveal private information regarding domestic violence in the presence of a member of their kinship network.

A second option is to engage bilingual staff member to assist with interpretation (Hadziabdic and Hjelm, 2013). There are many advantages to this such as possible enhanced sense of relationship and trust between the social worker and service user. However, there are many problems with this as well. The first being a common language does not necessarily create a common understanding of the situation. Furthermore, the worker knowledge and skill set might not be the most appropriate the service user's needs and concerns. For example, the bilingual staff member may have an opinion about the form of service or outcome required by the service user and this may influence the interpretation process. A second issue is that in our multi-cultural societies, it is highly unlikely that a social worker (or indeed any other human service professional) would work only with one other language group. Hence a bilingual staff member may be of assistance with one linguistically diverse service user population only.

The third option is the involvement a professional interpreter. A professional interpreter is a person who is proficient in the language of both parties to the communication and who is employed to facilitate the two way flow of verbal communication between two (or more) parties. Professional interpreters may be qualified in interpretation and, ideally, should have specialist knowledge of the domain in which the interpretation is to occur (Chand, 2005). For example, medical interpreters need understanding of medical terminology, while interpreters working with community services require a sound understanding of the issues arising in these services such as child protection, mental health and homelessness. Professional interpreters may be bound by a Code of Ethics. Professional interpreters are not cultural guides nor are they advocates for either party (Smith, 2012).

The involvement of professional interpreters may be required by law or recommended by our ethical codes in circumstances where a person lacks proficiency in the language in which the service is provided. Hadziabdic and Hjelm (2013) note significant international variation in the extent to which a person's right to interpreters is recognised. In some countries, such as Sweden, these rights are stipulated in law, whereas in other countries, such as the United States and Australia the provision of interpreter services in health and welfare services is not a legally enshrined right (Hadziabdic and Hjelm, 2013). Nonetheless, the professional practice codes of social workers may emphasise our obligation to provide such services wherever possible. For example, the Australian Association of Social Workers Code of Ethics states that "Social Workers will endeavour to provide accessible services to clients in languages or modalities they understand using an independent, qualified interpreter and/or translator where feasible and appropriate" (AASW, 2010, p. 18).

Involving a professional interpreter has many benefits particularly increased accuracy of interpretation services. Systematic reviews of the research indicate the superiority of professional interpreter services, specifically trained in the domain where the interpretation is to take place

(Bird, 2010; Brisset, Leanza and Laforest, 2011; Hadziabdic and Hjelm, 2013). In their systematic literature review, Karliner, Jacobs, Chen, Mutha (2007) concluded that in health care services the involvement of professional interpreters compared to "ad hoc" interpreters was associated with: fewer errors in interpretation; greater satisfaction among patients and practitioners than was the case with informal interpreters; and better use of relevant health services and better health outcomes.

Phase 3: The process of engaging a professional interpreter

We turn now to the process of engaging a professional interpreter. Steps in engaging an interpreter service are, firstly to seek out a service where the interpreters are formally qualified, are accountable to a professional code of ethics and, preferably, have expertise in the domain in which the interpretation is to occur. For example, if the interpretation is to occur in a medical context then an interpreter with expertise in this domain should be engaged. Other issues to raise include:

➢ language proficiency of the interpreter. Wherever possible that the interpreter should use *both* the same language and dialect as the individual or family who will participate in the communication (Smith, 2012).

➢ consideration of specific intra-cultural identities such as ethnic, religious, regional, class identities that may affect the acceptability of the interpreter to the service user (Miletic et al., 2006). Hadziabdic and Hjelm (2013) note that conflicts between different groups in the person's country of origin need to be recognised as shaping who may be engaged in interpretation services.

➢ checking that the participants do not know each other socially (Miletic et al., 2006).

➢ cultural expectations regarding age, gender or other identity characteristics of the person. For example, in some cultures strict rules exist about conditions under which men and women may interact and accordingly it may be very challenging to involve a person of one gender in interpreting sensitive personal matters with a person of another gender.

The interpreter should be made aware of the nature and purpose of the communication they are engaged to interpret, including any sensitive issues that might arise and they should be provided with brief information on the person's circumstance and likely emotional or other state during the meeting (e.g., "This will be a tense meeting"). The process of selecting an interpreting is a mutual one in which the social worker, service user and the interpreter need to assess the suitability and availability of the interpreter for the role. AUSIT (2007, p. 2) notes that: "The interpreter may need to withdraw from the interview if interpreting performance is likely to be adversely affected for any reason, such as conflict of interest, potential compromising of impartiality (religious beliefs) or other reasons."

The social worker should ensure that the person using the social work service is aware of the interpreter's name and other relevant information, such as the agency from which the interpreter is sourced and country and region of origin. This is to assess whether the proposed interpreter is suitable from the perspective of the person to whom social work services is provided. If the person is deemed unsuitable an alternative should be offered.

Phase 4: Preparing for the meeting

Preparation for the meeting should involve ensuring all parties are comfortable with the proposed process. Given likely challenges around direct spoken communication between the worker and the person who is using services, written material about the interpretation service should be provided in the person's language.

The social worker should contact the interpreter prior to the meeting with the service user. The purpose of this contact is to establish basic ground rules and expectations, such as expectations regarding confidentiality, any possible ongoing implications of the interpreter's involvement such as possible legal implications, and the basic situation that is to be interpreted. This is also an important opportunity to outline any sensitive and potentially taboo topics that might be discussed, such as sexuality or family relationships (AUSIT, 2007). Prior to the commencement of the meeting, the interpreter may ask for a few minutes alone with the person to "accustom themselves to any regional variation" in the accent of the speaker (AUSIT, 2016, p. 1).

Phase 5: Communication with the support of an interpreter

We should recognise the service user as the primary focus and the person with whom we are seeking to build and maintain a working alliance. The interpreter supports the communication but they are not the primary focus of the communication.

Synthesising the recommendations of the Australian Institute of Interpreters and Translators (AUSIT, 2007), Miletic et al. (2006) and

Hadziabdic and Hjelm (2013, p. 73) review on best practice in the use of interpreters in health care, we propose the following tips and techniques for social work communication involving an interpreter:

➢ place yourself in direct eye contact with the person with whom you are working, but make sure that you can both see the interpreter.

➢ introduce all parties and invite discussion of each of your roles in the communication and any agreed signals for communication problems. For example, "Mrs Barthes, the interpreter will raise her hand like this (provide a hand gesture) if there is a problem such as she needs us to slow down." Explain that both you, as the worker, and the interpreter are bound by Codes of Ethics that obliges you both to maintain the confidentiality of the communication.

➢ always speak directly to the person and avoid both side conversations with the interpreter by you or by the other party.

➢ avoid jargon and specialist terminology.

➢ avoid lengthy speech segments as these can be difficult to interpret accurately.

➢ speak slowly and clearly and allow the interpreter sufficient time to interpret your words. Remember that languages vary considerably in the amount of words needed to convey the same message.

➢ avoid interrupting the other person.

➢ respect the professional boundaries and roles of the interpreter. The interpreter is not there as an expert in the field of social work practice and accordingly we should avoid asking their opinion on matters of our professional assessment.

As part of supporting the two way flow of communication between the social worker and the person using social work services, the interpreter may become aware of a cultural issue that is influencing the communication. These might include cultural differences around family relationships, the nature and causes of illness and expectations of professional workers. AUSIT (2007, p. 4) notes that in these circumstances, the practitioner "should allow the interpreter to briefly indicate what may be causing a cultural misunderstanding if this is impeding good communication with the patient [person]." For example, when speaking with a couple, the interpreter may need to inform that social worker of the need to address both parties in a particular order according to cultural expectations related to age or gender.

Phase 6: After the interpretation

At the conclusion of the meeting we should invite both parties to make any observations they wish to about the communication. The interpreter should leave the meeting first so as to avoid any perception of further involvement of the interpreter in the professional assessment process (AUSIT, 2016). If post-meeting communication occurs between ourselves and the interpreter, we should not ask them to provide cultural guidance nor to contribute to our professional assessment. Nonetheless we could provide the interpreter with our contact details should any issues arise from the communication. Miletic et al. (2006) also note the social worker should ask the interpreter to de-brief with them in relation to the emotional content of the meeting and also the worker should provide feedback about the interpretation process.

Conclusion

In culturally diverse societies, social workers must be competent in building and maintaining relationships with people from diverse cultures, and who use languages other than their own. In this Chapter we have considered three dimensions of culturally competent practice. We have emphasised the importance of social workers understanding the historical and contemporary contexts in which we engage in intercultural communication, and also the significance of self-awareness to achieving culturally competent practice. We considered skills in intercultural communication including the processes of involving interpreters in social work communication.

Review questions

1. What does the term "culturally congruent" communication mean?

2. Why is it important for social workers to be aware of the historical and political contexts of communication with people from cultures other than their own?

3. What were the nine dimensions of non-verbal intercultural communication discussed in this Chapter?

4. What does the term "dialect" mean?

5. What are the steps in involving an interpreter in communication discussed in this Chapter?

Practice exercises

Practice exercise 1

Imagine you are in a local government authority that provides supported housing to people experiencing a range of life challenges. The government authority is located in a culturally diverse area and your role will involve communicating with people from diverse cultural and linguistic groups often at a time of great personal crisis.

Define the term "cultural competence", and identify and discuss how you will develop your capacity to engage in a culturally competent way with the people from diverse cultures who you will meet in this role.

Practice exercise 2

Imagine you work at a children's hospital in the child protection team. The Clinical Nurse Consultant from the accident and emergency unit called you to meet with the Wasem family. They are the family of a seven year old boy, Karam, who has been brought into the hospital by ambulance with injuries consistent with being beaten. The injuries are serious, but not life-threatening, and include multiple severe bruises to the arms, back, bottom and legs, the child may have a fractured arm. The parents, Farid (father, who is 34 years old) and Iman (mother, who is 32 years old) state that their son was set upon by a group of older boys at the park. The police have been called, and a formal interview of the family will occur. In addition, the medical team would like you to meet with the family to provide support, and seek information about the circumstances of the family and the child's injuries while the child undergoes emergency medical treatment and is transferred to a ward for ongoing medical care.

The Clinical Nurse Consultant (CNC) states that the family is from Syria and arrived three years ago. It is noted that both parents are distressed: the father appears angry while the mother is sobbing. They have their 12-year-old daughter (Jamal) with them. CNC is uncertain of their English comprehension though she notes that the Jamal has excellent English and has helped to explain what happened to Karam to the medical team. The CNC is unsure whether the daughter is speaking to her because of the parents' distress or whether the parents' English comprehension is poor.

1. What are the pros and cons of involving Jamal in interpreting between you as the social worker and her parents?

2. What are the grounds for involving a professional interpreter to facilitate communication between you as the social worker and her parents?

3. Discuss the steps you would use to engage a professional interpreter in this situation?

Recommended readings

Eades, D. (2013). *Aboriginal ways of using English*. Canberra: Aboriginal Studies Press.

Diana Eades is a linguist who has studied Aboriginal English and the tensions between these dialects and Standard English in Australian institutional settings, particularly legal contexts. Her work incorporates discussion of the linguistic features of Indigenous languages with a critical analysis of the interpersonal and institutional tensions and injustices that arise when these differences overlay social power differences as exist between non-Aboriginal and Aboriginal people in post-colonial societies. The book provides insights into the rules and norms associated with Aboriginal English dialects in Australia which also have relevance for understanding Aboriginal dialectics in other countries.

Fadden, L. & Lafrance, J. (2010). Advancing Aboriginal English. *Canadian Journal of Native Education*, *32*, 143–155.

In a similar vein to Diana Eades' book, this article provides an excellent overview of Aboriginal English dialects in Canada and the importance of their recognition in facilitating education opportunities for Aboriginal Canadians:

Hadziabdic, E. & Hjelm, K. (2013). Working with interpreters: Practical advice for use of an interpreter in healthcare. *International Journal of Evidence-Based Healthcare*, *11*(1), 69–76.

This article provides a synthesis of the empirical evidence of best practice in the use of interpreters in health care settings. Because the evidence reviewed refers to communicating with people in human service settings at a time of life challenge and often involving the negotiation of professional power relations, the findings are relevant to many human service environments. The paper provides a staged process for engaging interpreters including the initial preparation, practical strategies for conducting an interpreter mediated session and follow up from the session.

Jandt, F. (2016). *An introduction to intercultural communication: Identities in a global community* (8th edition). Los Angeles, CA: Sage.

Fred Jandt is a communications specialist who has written extensively on intercultural communication. In this book, Jandt offers a succinct introduction to the theory, evidence and practice of effective intercultural communication. There is a strong focus on the development of intercultural communication skills. Case studies from diverse cultural contexts and related to contemporary events and issues are included.

Recommended websites

The International Medical Interpreters website

http://www.imiaweb.org/

The International Medical Interpreters Association is a US-based international organisation committed to the advancement of professional medical interpreters as the best practice to equitable language access to health care for linguistically diverse patients. The website includes an excellent range of resources related to working with interpreters and with language diversity. The resource by Miletic and her colleagues (2006) from the Victorian Transcultural Psychiatry Unit provides an informative guide to incorporating interpreters in communication with people experiencing mental health crises.

The Australian Institute of Interpreters and Translators

https://www.ausit.org/

The Australian Institute of Interpreters and Translators' website provides a range of resources for professionals, community members and interpreters and translators to use language in practice. The website includes many useful discussion papers and reports on engaging interpreters relevant to human services contexts.

Minority Rights Group International

http://minorityrights.org/

Minority Rights Group International campaigns internationally to ensure that disadvantaged minorities and Indigenous peoples across the world can make their voices heard. The website includes numerous resources such as reports on a diverse range of matters related to protecting Indigenous cultural and linguistic diversity including languages rights, rights to education and employment.

7

Communication with Children and Young People

Social workers communicate with children and young people in a variety of practice contexts and for a broad range of professional purposes. All social workers, then, need foundation knowledge and skills in communication with children and young people. In this Chapter, we outline a child-centred approach to communication with children and young people. Munro (2011, p. 16) draws on the United Nations Convention on the Rights of the Child (UNCRC, 1989) to describe child-centred practice as supporting "the basic human rights all children have including the right to survival; to develop to the fullest; to protection from harmful influences, abuse and exploitation, and to participate fully in family, social and cultural life." By child-centred communication we refer to communication that respects children's rights to information and to participate in decision making affecting them and which is responsive to individual differences and to changing communication needs of the child at different stages of human development.

Who are children and young people?

Consistent with the United Nations Convention on the Rights of the Child (UNCRC), we define children and young people as people from birth to 18 years. We note that even among signatories to the UNCRC, inter-country variations exist in the point at which children and young people gain rights to make some decisions about themselves and their well-being. For example, in some countries, the concept of the "Gillick" principle allows for children much younger than 18 years to independently seek out health care treatments. We will discuss this principle in more detail later. Yet even so, the State may also continue to limit the young person's right to exercise decision-making power beyond their 18th birthday. For example, in some contexts, young people are not legally allowed to consume alcohol or to vote until the age of 21 years. In many countries, the State continues to assume responsibility for young people beyond the age of 18 years. For example, in many jurisdictions across the world, child protection authorities recognise the need to support young people in out of home care beyond the age of 18 years. This recognises that young people often continue to require emotional and financial support to continue education or to successfully transition to employment and to independence (Daining and DePanfilis, 2007).

Social workers communicate with children and young people in a variety of practice contexts. In some domains the child or young person may be the primary client. For example, social workers are often responsible for implementing legislation related to the care and protection of children and the youth justice system. In addition, the social worker may be an advocate for the child, representing the child's viewpoint in various decision-making forums such as to Courts and in family group meetings. In other contexts, the child may be part of the primary client group, such as in families receiving family support services, or as a secondary client, such as when a social worker is working with the parents or caregiver of the child. For example, social workers in adult mental health services may also communicate with children of parents receiving these services for a variety of reasons including explaining their parents' care plan, and to assess whether the child or young person requires referral for family support or alternative caregiving arrangements when the parent is unwell.

What is child centred communication?

A child-centred approach to communication refers to "a commitment to meeting children's rights as well as their needs, including the right to have a voice in decisions that affect them" (Lefevre, 2010, p. 69). A child-centred approach is informed by recognition that the period from birth to 18 years is typically one of rapid development in cognitive, emotional, social and physical capacities. A child-centred approach incorporates "developmentally appropriate" communication techniques which take account of the developmental phase of the child or young person. Although age is usually an important factor in determining developmental phase, it is not the only factor. Daniel et al. (2010, p. 145) note that "The sequencing of developmental milestones is much more consistent than is the actual *age* at which they are attained" (see also Bywater et al., 2012).

A child-centred approach acknowledges that children and young people are diverse. Children and young people, like adults, vary individually and also have a variety of identities and experiences related to class, ethnicity, ability and disability, gender and sexual orientation. Bywater et al. (2012, p. 94) note that "the practitioner will need to engage the young person by taking account of the young person's: particular vocabulary; communication skills/abilities; culture; emotional and behavioural needs; strengths and difficulties."

The children and young people with whom we communicate may experience trauma, social and economic disadvantage and may be vulnerable to social exclusion (Daniel et al., 2010) Social workers need to be particularly skilled at creating a positive and engaging relationship with children and young people who may be facing adverse life circumstances (Daniel et al., 2010).

From a child-centred perspective, we need to be aware that children and young people we meet come from a variety of cultural backgrounds. Cultural identity formation is an integral part of the child's identity development. From at least middle childhood, children are increasingly conscious of their own and others cultural identities (Corenblum and Armstrong, 2012). Research evidence suggests that children raised in collectivist cultures, such as Indigenous cultures, may develop awareness of their cultural identity even earlier than children from individualist cultures. In their innovative study of Canadian Aboriginal children, aged 7–10 years, Corenblum and Armstrong (2012, p. 135) found that "being an Aboriginal was ranked as more important to them than their own gender identity, and their community membership was rated as only somewhat less important than being a good family member or being a good son/daughter." While children from middle school years onwards are often able to articulate the importance of cultural identity, it is very likely that earlier representations of cultural identity will have an influence on the child's developing sense of self from early childhood. For this reason, it is important that social workers are cognizant of promoting cultural diversity and positive cultural identity affiliations in our communication with children of all ages. We can achieve this in part by ensuring that props for engaging children include items that reflect diverse cultures and experiences such as dolls with a range of skin colours and clothing, picture books that reflect diverse cultures, and through the inclusion of culturally appropriate play and creative activities.

In a variety of social work practice contexts, we may encounter children and young people with communication differences that create difficulties in their capacity to receive, interpret or respond to communication. This can be due to a range of causes including: birth or later injury, disease or disability. The needs of children and young people who have difficulty in communication should be identified as soon as possible so that they receive relevant support and interventions to enable their full inclusion in society. In some instances, a delay in receiving this support can have enduring negative consequences for the development of the child.

In Chapter 10 we focus on strategies for communication with people who experience communication differences. In that Chapter we outline the Total Communication Approach which was an approach initially developed for the education of Deaf children. Bywater et al. (2012, p. 87) note the relevance of a total communication approach for communication with children who experience a range of communication differences. This involves supplementing verbal communication with other forms of communication, such as the use of pictures and gestures and through the use of Augmentative and Assistive Technologies.

Why child-centred communication matters

Building our capacity for child-centred communication is important for several reasons. First, child-centred communication matters to children and young people. In her review of the Child Protection System in the United Kingdom, Munro (2011, p. 24) noted that "Evidence provided by children to this review gives a mixed view of what they [children] experience in practice, but it also conveys what a positive impact professionals can have when they find time to spend with children they are helping and have a clear focus on their needs."

Second, as members of a profession that promotes human rights, we have a responsibility to communicate in ways that recognise and facilitate the human rights of children and young people. The UN Convention on the Rights of the Child (1989) enshrines children's rights to non-discrimination and their rights to: information as long as that information is not damaging to the child; a right to freedom of expression in the language and format of the child's choice; and the child's right to have his or her opinions taken into account.

Third, in many practice contexts, social workers are obliged by statutory law and organisational policy to communicate with children and young people in ways that promote the child or young person's contribution to assessment and decision making. Lefevre (2010, p. 125) remarks that:

> Social workers and other professionals in children's services are required by policy, legislation and practice guidance to seek out and listen to children's thoughts and feelings about their lives and experiences and, while balancing them with assessment of their needs and any risks, take their opinion into account.

Legislative and policy reforms aimed at increased recognition of children's voices have emerged in part to respond to critical analyses of child protection systems failures (Munro, 2011). For example, in the tragic case of Victoria Climbie, a child who died as a result of child abuse and neglect, it was found that the failure of the authorities to provide Victoria with an interpreter was a factor in the poor understanding of the gravity of her situation (Laming, 2002).

Fourth, we are required by our ethical codes to demonstrate respect, promote self-determination and social justice. While these obligations pertain to all people, when communicating with children and young people we need also to be cognisant of their developmental stage. As we shall discuss further, social workers need to develop skills in communication that is responsive the changing needs of the developing child and young person as well as respectful of their individual, social and cultural differences (Lefevre, 2010).

Fifth, by modelling confidence and capacity in communicating with children and young people in their care, we can contribute to caregivers' capacity to do the same. It is well established that the quality of interaction between the child and their caregivers is important for the achieving cognitive, emotional, physical and social developmental outcomes (Neven, 2010). Insights from neuroscience have also identified that the quality of caregiving relationships and the child's physical environment shapes the emerging architecture of the brain (Daniel et al., 2010). Yet, parents and caregivers may experience challenges in their capacity to communicate confidently with children. Low confidence may emerge from a lack of quality parenting, current challenges in the caregivers' environment or mistaken beliefs that prevent parents seeing the opportunities for play with children, such as a belief that children need expensive equipment to engage in play. By demonstrating effective communication with children and young people we provide opportunities for caregivers to build communication skills and to strengthen the caregiving relationship.

What we communicate

Our communication with children and young people, as with people of all age groups, should be grounded in a clear sense of professional purpose. Conradie and Golding (2013, p. 7) assert that professionals should communicate the formal nature of their role, noting that: "children and young people need you to be their youth worker, teacher or social worker, not their friend or parent." In introducing ourselves to the child or young person we should explain and negotiate our purpose in ways that are meaningful to them. We negotiate our purpose in part by communicating our obligations, such as legal or organisational obligations and ethical responsibilities and, also, by clarifying and where possible accommodating client hopes and expectations. Bywater et al. (2012, p. 90) note that children from three years of age upwards should be provided with developmentally appropriate explanation of our professional purpose. For preschool and middle school aged children this would involve explanations that are linked to their experiences of other professionals in their lives. For example, we might explain how our role is similar or different to their teacher. With older children and teenagers, we may also discuss their previous experiences with social workers and their hopes for our work together.

A child-centred approach also involves providing information to children and young people about matters that concern them. Lefevre (2010, p. 131) states that "Professionals need to explain clearly to children and young people what is going on and what is to happen during assessments in a way that makes sense to them." Under the UNCRC, children and young people have a right to information as long as that information is not harmful to them. Forms of information that could be harmful might include detailed information about a parent's reasons for being unable to care for the child particularly where this could expose a young child to information they may have trouble making sense of such as details about substance abuse, severe mental health challenges or criminal activity. The worker needs also to inform children and young people about the nature of assessment and intervention processes. Such information needs to be presented in a developmentally appropriate manner. For example, a picture book might be used to help a child understand a judge's decision to place them with a foster family.

Similarly a child-centred approach requires a commitment to involving children and young people in decision making. The degree of involvement can vary from the fundamental right of the child to express their views and have those heard by decision makers through to the child or young person making decisions on their own behalf. Social workers need to balance the child's rights to participate with an understanding of the individual child's capacity to do so. We need to take into account the developmental phase of the child and young person as well as their individual circumstances and the circumstances in which the decision is be made. The worker needs to work alongside the child and those who know and care for the child in determining the nature and level of involvement in decision making that is appropriate for the child. Where we deem that the child cannot directly participate in decision-making activities due to either a limited capacity to fully comprehend that situation or the risk of exposure to harmful information or dynamics, we need still to represent their views. We can incorporate creative techniques such as images of the child, the presence of the child's favourite toy, or creative works produced by the child to focus the meeting on the needs of the child (Healy et al., 2011, 2016). As child advocates, we can also use creative techniques to assist the child or young person to develop our understanding of the child's experience and wishes, and to articulate their opinions to decision makers. Later in this Chapter we discuss the use of play and creative techniques to aid communication with children and young people.

When working with older children and teenagers, the concept of Gillick competency is also relevant to consider. The term "Gillick competency" refers to the legally enshrined right of children and young people to take responsibility for decision-making when it can be demonstrated they have sufficient maturity to understand the nature of the decision and its consequences. Harris and White (2014) explain that the concept of "Gillick competency" emerged case of *Gillick v. West Norfolk Area Health Authority* (1986), where a parent, Victoria Gillick sued her local health authority "in an attempt to make it illegal for doctors to give contraceptive advice or treatment to her under-16-year-old daughter without parental consent." After a series of rulings and appeals, the House of Lords ultimately determined that child under 16 years could seek and consent to medical treatment provided she/he had "sufficient understanding to make informed decisions" (Harris and White, 2014). The notion of Gillick competency is now referred to more widely by health, social care and legal professionals in assessing whether a child or young person has "sufficient understanding and intelligence to comprehend what is being proposed and to make a choice in their own best interests"(Lefevre, 2010, 199). Where this is the case, the professional can decide to refer to the young person's instructions and wishes rather than those of their caregiver or guardian.

Observation of how family members, particularly primary caregivers communicate with the child or young person can provide important information that we may use in developing the working alliance with the child. Observation can also yield information about the quality of caregiving and other family relationships. For instance, a toddler with a secure relationship with their primary caregivers is likely to become distressed on their caregivers leaving their proximity but will usually be readily soothed by the caregivers' return. In family work with older children and adolescents, observation of communication may assist in supporting children and family members to develop strategies for addressing challenges they face. For example, a social worker may assist a parent and young person to develop skills to negotiate expectations about responsible behaviour in order to support the young person's transition to increasing independence. Later in this Chapter, we will discuss how to engage children and young people in family decision-making processes.

Developmentally sensitive communication techniques

Children and young people share many similar communication needs with adults. Children and young people need to be listened to and have their concerns taken seriously (Neven, 2010). Our core communication skills, discussed in Chapter 3, remain relevant, including listening, demonstrating empathy, appropriate use of questions, and open non-verbal communication. Yet, we need also to adapt these communication skills to respond to the developmental phase and the diversity of the child or young person with whom we are communicating. We refer to this adaption as developmentally sensitive communication. Conradie and Golding (2013, p. 100) observe:

> It is important not to alienate the children through language and communication that is too difficult or complex but also not to patronise the child or young person through language that is too simplistic. It is important to incorporate visual aids and other alternative methods of communication to ensure clarity of message, for example by using pictures or diagrams and actions that reinforce the message communication.

We need to tailor our communication to the developmental phase of the child or young person. This involves consideration of vocabulary, the pace of communication, and the topics of discussion (Chalmers, 2016; Petrie, 2011).

Developmentally appropriate communication often involves the integration of play and creative techniques (see Bywater et al., 2012; Lefevre, 2010; Neven, 2010). These techniques can aid with all aspects of the social work process including engaging, assessment and intervention. Our main focus here is on the use of play and creative techniques to aid the development and maintenance of the working alliance.

A wide variety of play equipment and creative activities can be incorporated into communication with children and young people. Social workers who are regularly in contact with children or young people should consider developing a toolkit of items and activities relevant to the developmental phases and individual diversity of the children and young people with whom they work. Where workers are typically working away from an office, they may need to develop a mobile toolkit of such items and activities. Some examples of the items and equipment that can be incorporated into our communication include:

➤ soft toys and rattles in bright colours, especially for babies.

➤ picture books including books with textures and sounds.

➤ story books and novels featuring children and young people facing life challenges.

➤ dolls, remember to include dolls that represent diversity of gender and ethnicity.

➤ building blocks and puzzles.

➤ computers with a range of games and activities.

➤ creative writing and stimulus materials such as visual images of different emotional states.

➤ paints, crayons and colouring pencils.

While syndicated toys and equipment associated with films and other media are readily recognised by children, they are often much more expensive than other toys or equipment. A reliance on these can limit recognition by children, young people and their families of the opportunities for play and creative activity all around them.

Later in this Chapter we will discuss how some of the items and activities discussed here can be incorporated into communication with children and young people at different phases of their development. There are a large number of books, handbooks and videos on the use of play and creative activities with children and young people, some references to these are provided at the end of the Chapter. We need to ensure that the play and creative communication props we offer reflect the broad range of interests and capacities of the child or young person. This can be challenging as we have our own biases and strengths. In integrating these activities we should aim to learn of the range of tools and equipment available, including the use of emerging technologies so as to enhance our capacity to meet the different needs of the children and young people with whom we practice.

Play is a familiar medium for children and its integration into our work can help to create a relaxed and fun atmosphere. Bywater et al. (2012, p. 93) note that "Young children will engage spontaneously with any play material." This can be important as, at least initially, children may feel intimidated by our presence as strangers in their lives. The use of play allows us time and a context to build rapport with the child. Play is also important to understanding the emotional states and the life experiences of the child. Chalmers (2016, p. 29) observes that children may demonstrate their understanding through their actions, long before they are able to verbalise what they are doing or thinking (see also Bywater et al., 2012; Neven, 2010).

For older children and teenagers, the integration of creative techniques can assist communication in a range of ways. As with younger children, the use of creative techniques with this group can provide a useful distraction, enabling workers and young people to be together without having to focus on an "issue" or concern. The skilful use of creative techniques can also assist those who feel uncomfortable with spoken language to express themselves or for whom the issue are too difficult to put into words, at least initially. Creative techniques can be integrated into community education strategies with young people and may be especially useful for engaging those who are alienated by more didactic educational processes. Creative techniques have been used in youth health campaigns on a variety of topics such as: safe sex; alcohol and drug education; and parenting education for young parents.

Some common themes apply to the application of developmentally sensitive communication techniques across the age span from birth to 18 years. First, is it important to create a relaxed and welcoming space for the child or young person (Lefevre, 2010). We need to create an environment in which the child is physically and emotionally safe. We should be aware of the power dynamics of the child's social environment and aim to create opportunities for children to express themselves in their own way and at their own pace. We should never pressure a child to express themselves as this may add to the trauma the child may have already experienced. Furthermore, creative activities should not be used to avoid discussion of matters of concern to the child or young people. Lefevre (2010, p. 136) observes that: "While play and activities can be an extremely helpful way of building rapport and gathering information more creatively, this does not mean there is no place for direct dialogue, particularly with older children and young people."

When communicating for the purpose of assessment or investigation of child protection concerns, we should be alert to the potential for children to seek to comply with our views or other powerful adults in their lives (Daniel et al., 2010). We should avoid leading the child in any way and we must ensure that the child has opportunities to express themselves freely and openly (see Leferve, 2010).

It is important that we provide the child or young person choice in what and how they communicate with us. When integrating props or creative activities in our communication we should ensure that a variety of options are available reflecting the diverse identities, abilities and interests of the children and young people with whom we practice. For example, playboxes for young children should include toys and activities that are of interest to both boys and girls and for children with different abilities and disabilities, and for children from a range of cultural backgrounds.

We should be non-directive in engaging children and young people in creative activities. Aside from providing an introduction to, or basic instruction in, a play or creative activity, we should encourage children and young people to choose how they will engage with it. Lefevre (2010, p. 173) observes that:

> non-directive play and interactions with children are purposeful activities at the centre of the social work role, not added extras. They can help to engage children who are particularly wary, distant or angry in a safe and trusting relationship where difficult issues can be worked through.

A non-directive approach can also help us to get to understand the child or young person's strengths, capacities and preferences. We should also avoid exposing the child or young person to judgement or criticism from themselves or others. Encouraging children to choose activities rather than forcing an activity is one way of minimising this risk. We need to be careful also to avoid any judgement in interpreting the child or young person's play or creative expression. For example, we might observe that the child has drawn a lot of sad faces and ask them about this, but we should avoid creating any sense of critical judgement of these representations.

A final consideration is how we recognise and support the role of the family in our communication with children and young people. Article 7 of the UNCRC recognises that children "have a right to know their parents and, as far as possible, to be cared for by them." In circumstances where is it not possible for the child's family of origin to care for them, the UNCRC (1989) requires maintenance of the connection between the child and their family. The Convention is consistent with practice evidence suggesting that families and care-providers remain important in the lives of many children and young people as they develop, though the role of caregivers will change over time (Daniel et al., 2010).

In some contexts, we may need the permission of parents and caregivers in order to communicate with children or young people in their care. Even where we are not legally bound to engage parents or caregivers, children and young people may feel more comfortable if their parents are involved at least initially in the communication with us. For young and securely attached children, from around 10 months to at least 2 years, the infant is likely to become distressed by the absence of a primary caregiver. With young children, we may require the parent or caregivers' involvement in explaining our presence to the child and encouraging the child to communicate with us, despite our being strangers in the child's life. Even for older children and teenagers, family members can provide an important part of their supportive environment and their involvement in the communication may be helpful (Daniels et al., 2010). In some cultural contexts, the involvement of extended families may be expected and important to the development of culturally appropriate responses to the concerns of the child and young person (see Slater, Lambie and McDowell, 2015).

Communication across developmental phases

We turn now to a discussion of developmentally sensitive communication techniques at key phases of the child's development. We have divided this into to four periods that align with Piaget's phases of cognitive development in children. These phases are: infancy (0–2 years); early childhood (2–6 years); middle childhood (7–11 years); and early to mid-adolescence (12–18 years).

Infancy (0–2 years)

Social workers may engage with babies and infants for a variety of reasons. These include in the assessment of children's safety and well-being, providing family support and parenting education to families. We need to be comfortable with communicating with children at these earliest stages of development.

The first two years of life are typically a period of phenomenal development. At birth, the newborn is entirely dependent on their caregiver to meet all of their needs and over the course of the next two years the infant will usually rapidly acquire the capacity to interact physically and socially with their environment. Piaget developed the term "sensory motor stage" to refer to the cognitive development of infants in the first two years of life. As Daniels et al. (2010, p. 153) observe "During this stage the baby knows the world through actions and sensory information." A baby is responsive to sensations and images in his or her environment. It is important that the worker is alert to creating an emotionally warm and calm atmosphere for the child. Sudden loud noises and silence should be avoided as both can be frightening to babies and infants (Chalmers, 2016).

From birth onwards, the baby is learning to communicate. Within the first weeks of life, the baby will seek out familiar faces and will observe the world around them. The baby will usually respond to the attentiveness and comfort of others. For example, a newborn may snuggle into the body of the person holding him/her. Within the first few weeks of life the baby makes eye contact and at around 4–6 weeks, the baby begins to smile in response to pleasant stimulation. Around 4–5 months the baby will begin to babble which is the beginning of learning to speak (Chalmers, 2016). By the age of 6 months, most babies will be able to sit unaided and show preference for toys or objects.

From age 6 months onwards the baby begins to communicate vocally. Initially this occurs through the expression of vocal sounds, known as "vocalisation," and in the second six months of life, through the formation of words. Between one and two years, the infants' vocabulary rapidly develops, which according to Piaget, reflects growth in the infant's capacity for symbolic thought (Daniel et al., 2010, p. 193). At around 10 months, babies may have the capacity to engage in simple games, such as pick-a-boo or activities that involve a pincer movement, such as picking up objects and placing them from one place to the next. Chalmers (2016, p. 31) observes that:

> Between twelve and eighteen months, toddlers gradually become more skilled at naming the people, animals and objects they point to and at requesting more information from those around them, which they absorb rapidly and easily. During this period they also learn to understand simple instructions, such as: "Find your shoes" or "Give this to Granny", and to carry them out.

The rapidly developing capacities of the child from birth to infancy require considerable flexibility in our communication capacities. Our communication with babies requires us to interpret the babies' signals, and as the infant develops he/she becomes more able to actively interact with us.

Generally, babies and young children respond well to people who are warm, friendly and playful (Petrie, 2011). In speaking with the baby and infant we should adopt patterns of language that engages them. Chalmers (2016, p. 12) uses the term "parentese" to refer to language that is "simplified, repeated and exaggerated and [in] a higher pitched tone" (see Petrie, 2011). This approach is useful for attracting and holding the newborn and infant's attention. As the baby develops his/her capacity to communicate non-verbally we can assist in promoting interaction with them through interpreting their non-verbal cues into words. For example, when a three month old baby smiles, we might say "You're a happy girl/boy." As the child develops simple words, we can incorporate those words into our interaction with them. It is important too to reward the baby and infant's "attempts to communicate with smiles and responses" (Chalmers, 2016, p. 20).

Just as we respond to the child's language development, so too we can incorporate the child's changing capacities to interact with their physical environment in our communication with them. In the second six months of life, the baby is likely to be able to sit unaided and to begin to point to familiar objects. Between 1 and 2 years the infant's capacity for physical movement and dexterity will usually develop as well. We can include these developments into play activities, such as involving the infant in identifying different objects and textures in picture books and in working on simple puzzles.

Workers who are in frequent contact with newborns and infants should consider creating a playbox to assist in their communication with these children. Because babies and infants are prone to putting objects in their mouths, it is vital to ensure that items in our playbox are free of toxins and choking hazards and do not include toys with removable batteries. Some items we may include in a playbox for babies and infants:

➢ toys that incorporate the use of sound – rattles, squeaky toys.

➢ soft toys.

➢ simple books with interactive aspects, such as books with different textures.

➢ for children over one year, we can incorporate basic puzzles such as three- to five-piece jigsaws and simple music instruments that do not require advanced dexterity, such as hand-drums and tambourines.

Early childhood (2–6 years)

At two years, the child's capacity to actively interact with others is developing quickly. Usually, the child's vocabulary and speech fluency is developing rapidly. By age three, the child will often become increasingly sociable and also interested in exploring the world around them. The three year old will often question "Why?" (Chalmers, 2016).

Piaget refers to development at this stage as the "pre-operational stage." He uses this term to refer to the child's ability to understand symbols, such as language symbols, but without the capacity to use logic to develop ideas or to understand connections between ideas. During this phase, the child is often highly imaginative and will enjoy activities that involve role playing. As the child advances they increasingly understand the difference between reality and imagination even though they will continue to enjoy imaginative play.

During the phase, the child is egocentric. Daniels et al. (2010, p. 154) note that, in the pre-operational phase, the child's "thinking is still very centred on the child's own perspective and he [sic] finds it difficult to understand that other people can see things differently." One consequence of this is that the child may imagine they are responsible for events in their world, such as a parent's illness. The egocentricism that characterises the earliest phases of development begins to decline thus allowing children to be aware of and increasingly interactive with others.

As with babies and infants, young children will generally respond well to people who are warm and welcoming. In addition, the child is likely to be curious about us and we should offer explanations about who we are and our role in a manner the child can understand. Chalmers (2016, p. 73) states that people communicating with children at this developmental phase should:

> Aim to be friendly and welcoming, confident and interesting and speak to the children at an appropriate level. This means squatting down to achieve eye contact, greeting the children by name and introducing themselves.

Parentese-type language in which the adult speaks in simple terms, and slightly exaggerated changes of pitch is appreciated by children in this age group as well as for younger children. We need to carefully match our vocabulary to the child's range, or they may resent being spoken to as they were a "baby."

Child will be able to engage in self-directive play. In this phase, children are becoming increasingly aware of their identity, particularly gender identity, and this needs to be considered when creating a playbox for work with children of this age. Children's imaginative play at this age is likely to reflect their life experiences and to involve mimicking of the behaviour of people around them (Chalmers, 2016). This role-playing can provide insights into the home life of the child and, as such, may be a useful part of our assessment of the child's situation.

Children in this age group are highly inquisitive about the world and appreciate explanations delivered in words and using concepts they can understand. Chalmers (2016, p. 83) states that in providing explanations:

> Adults must offer reasons for rules and actions, speaking honestly and pointing out facts that the children may not have thought of. Small details appeal to them and allow them to make new connections and progress in understanding.

So for example if we are working with a young child who has been temporarily removed to a kinship care placement while her mother is receiving medical treatment, it is important to take the time to explain this to the child. We should also encourage and assist other significant people in the child's life to help the child understand their changed situation.

As recommended for newborns and infants, we also suggest that workers regularly engaging with children in early childhood should create a playbox. While the risk of accidental ingestion of objects lessens as the child grows older, it is still important in this age group to avoid items with toxins or choking hazards, such as removable batteries. Suggested items to keep a playbox for children at this developmental stage include:

➤ items for dress ups.

➤ story books, particularly books that reflect the diverse life experiences and cultural identifications of the children with whom we communicate.

➤ basic musical instruments.

➤ play houses (including mobile play houses).

➤ building blocks.

➤ playdough.

➤ paints and crayons.

Middle to late childhood (7–11 years)

During the middle to late childhood period, children typically become increasingly interested in and engaged with the broader world outside their immediate home and family. According to Piaget's development theory, between 7 and 11 years children through the "concrete operational phase" As Daniel et al. (2010, p. 179) assert in this phase, children "become less egocentric. Their mental functions involve the use of logic and they can think ideas through in order to work out the properties of objects in the world and to make deductive inferences." In this phase, children become increasingly aware of their social identities, such as their class, gender and cultural identities, including the positive and negative social attributes associated with those identities (Corenblum and Armstrong, 2012). This can contribute to strong rules about in-groups and out-groups. Children may for example, seek to play only with other children with whom they have shared characteristics, such as similarities of gender or culture.

An important feature of this developmental phase is the child's developing capacity to use logic to make sense of their world. They can make inferences from rules, principles and symbols. We can use this developing capacity for logical thought to explain events and changes in the child's life. For example, in communicating with a child the decision to remove them from their family while their caregiver seeks medical treatment, we could first begin with a discussion of the notion of safety and what it means and feels like to the child. We could then explain why it is not "safe" to stay where they are now and why it is important to be "safe." We could then use the child's own concepts of time to address issues about: how and when they will see their caregiver; who will decide this and how they will decide. We should also explain how the child will contribute to the decisions which will vary on the circumstance and the child's abilities to understand the consequences of decisions.

By the age of seven, children will have developed the ability to "reflect on their own mental processes and to engage in a form of inner speech" (Daniel et al., 2010, p. 180). They can increasingly understand and describe their emotional states and how others' states may differ from their own. We can incorporate this developing emotional maturity and increasing capacity for logic thought to promote mutual respect and pro-social behaviour in our communication with the child (Daniel et al., 2010). For example, at this age we can begin to agree on some ground rules for communication based on the child's own experience of how different forms of communication affect them.

In this phase, children typically will have an extensive vocabulary and capacity to "see that language can have multiple meanings and can therefore understand pun" (Daniel et al., 2010, p. 174). Children's increasing facility with language and growing emotional maturity can be incorporated into our communication with them. At this stage, children can begin to apply the fictional and non-fictional stories to their own lives as well as to begin to express their feelings and experiences in words and images.

Activities and props that can assist in engaging children at this age include:

> structured and free form drawing and painting.

> stimulus material to assist in expressing their own life experiences.

> rule-based games, e.g., card or board games.

> creative writing – life stories.

> life stories of children and young people with similar experiences.

Early to mid-adolescence (12–18 years)

Adolescence is a time of growing independence for the young person. For the majority of young people, adolescence is a period of "increasing social competence, autonomy and self-control" (Daniel et al., 2010, p. 231). The family continues to play an important role of the lives of many young people, yet the role of the peer group will also gain significance during this time. However, for young people who have experienced trauma, developmental or health challenges, or social exclusion, this can be a time of increasing difficulty. For young people who have been separated from family or kinship networks, for whatever reasons, the absence of family and kinship support can intensify challenges at this time.

Adolescence is an important time for identity exploration and development. The young person will have already established the foundations of their social identity in earlier developmental phases, such as gender, ethnic and family identity. Adolescence is often a time of sexuality identity exploration and of the commencement of sexual activity. Daniel et al., (2010) observe that young people may become egocentric with an increasing emphasis on their thoughts, body image, and emerging social identity.

Typically, young people have developed advanced reasoning capacity at this stage. Piaget referred this phase of cognitive development as the formal operational state. As Daniel et al. (2010, p. 230) outline "Formal operational thinking involves the consideration of a number of possible solutions to a problem. When they have reached this stage, young people can construct hypotheses and check them out with reality before coming to a conclusion." Yet the young person's advancing capacity for logical thinking can be in tension with aspects of their cognitive and social development.

In recent years, an extensive literature has emerged on the neuroscience of the teenage brain. This research can assist our understanding of some challenges that may emerge in communication with teenagers. This research has highlighted that "during adolescence there is a tremendous change in the organization of the brain, though not all regions of the brain develop at the same pace" (Crone, 2015, p. 15). One consequence is that adolescence may appear to think in apparently contradictory ways. This is particularly evident in the evaluation of risk. On the one hand, the young person typically develops the capacity to think through consequences associated with actions. However, the capacity to identify dangerous situations takes longer to develop. Crone (2015, p. 59) proposes that "This warning system matures slowly and doesn't get going until late adolescence." In part this is because the young person is often highly motivated by social rewards, particularly recognition by their peers. On implication is that the social context in which a decision occurs has a considerable influence on how the young person interprets and acts on perceived risk. A young person is much less likely to accurately evaluate risk when they are in a situation of potential social reward, such as the endorsement of their peers.

While the young person typically has developed the cognitive, linguistic and social capacities to engage in spoken communication with the social worker, communication can be enhanced by the incorporation of developmentally appropriate creative techniques. Creative techniques that can be used to support communication include:

➤ group-based activities, particularly those that assist the young person to reflect on their identity and experiences and to develop knowledge and skills relevant to their emerging identity. For example, peer based education on health issues.

➤ creative writing including song writing, story writing and video production.

➤ free form art work, including art work that makes a public statement such as preparation of posters or painting of public spaces.

➤ electronic media activities, such as website development and use.

Conclusion

In this Chapter we have outlined a child-centred approach to communication. We have considered why all social workers need foundational knowledge and skills in communicating with children and young people. Throughout this Chapter we have emphasised the rights of children and young people to communication that recognises their developmental phases as well as social, cultural and individual differences in their life experiences. We have outlined strategies for engaging with children and young people that recognise their changing communication needs during this time of rapid of development.

Review questions and exercises

1. What is child-centred communication and why does it matter?

2. Why is it important to incorporate developmentally appropriate play and creative techniques in our communication with children and young people?

3. In what circumstances might a social worker need to communicate with a child under two years of age and what strategies might the social worker use to engage with a baby or infant?

4. Imagine that you are a family support social worker working primarily with babies, infants and children 0–5 years. Identify the items and activities you would include in a playbox for children of this age range and discuss how these items and activities match the developmental phase of the children with whom you are communicating.

5. What are the key differences in the communication needs of children and young people in middle childhood and in adolescence?

Practice exercises

Exercise 1

Imagine you are a student on a placement involving family support work with young parents. Many of the young parents who use this service have poor experiences of being parented and are unconfident in caring for their babies and children. In your first week of placement, you accompany your supervisor to a visit to the home a young single mother, Nancy, who is 17 years of age. Nancy was removed from her family at 5 years of age due to extreme neglect. She experienced numerous foster care placements, with the longest period of stability being one year. Nancy left school at 15 years of age and was unemployed prior to becoming pregnant with Obe, her baby who is now 8 weeks old. Nancy is no longer with Sam, who is Obe's father. Nancy lives alone in a public housing apartment. She told the hospital social worker that she is struggling emotionally and feels very unsure of herself as a parent. Nancy was referred to your service by the hospital social worker for follow up support. Your supervisor has had one phone contact with Nancy, but this is the first time you and your supervisor are meeting Nancy and her baby. Nancy is sitting in the lounge when you and your supervisor arrive and her 8-week-old baby, Obe, is lying on the blanket beside her.

Identify and discuss how you would engage with Nancy and Obe on this home visit.

Exercise 2

Imagine you work in a children's hospital. Nine-year-old Jake has been hospitalised due to medical neglect. Jake has Diabetes Type 1 and his parents have refused to provide him with medication. Three days ago, Jake fainted at school as a result of his symptoms and was rushed to hospital. The health care team suspect that Jake's mother, Susan, is a subject to domestic violence by his father, Paul. Paul is adamant that Jake does not need medication and Susan appears compliant with Paul's wishes. The health care team have referred the matter to the child protection authority which has made a decision to temporarily remove Jake to a foster family while the situation is investigated.

Identify and discuss how you could use creative techniques to engage with Jake and explore his family situation and attitudes towards his health condition with him.

▶

◀

Identify and discuss what and how you would communicate with Jake about the decision to remove him temporarily from his parents' care.

Exercise 3

Imagine you work in a youth support and advocacy service. Jamaal is a 14-year-old who was recently charged for shoplifting camera equipment from an electrical goods store. Jamaal has been brought to your office by his distraught parents who say this this is the second time Jamaal has been in trouble with the law. Jamaal was previously caught shoplifting two mobile phone chargers from a computer store. He was cautioned by the police and this time he will go to the Children's Court. With his parents' permission, you speak with Jamaal alone. Although apparently quiet and withdrawn in his parents' presence, once alone with you he is more forthcoming. Jamaal regrets upsetting his parents. He also is concerned about attending Court. He is a high-performing student and has ambitions to be an engineer. He says that his friends at school are interested in technology and that there is some buying and selling of technologies among his friends at school. He had intended to sell the equipment he had shoplifted. Jamaal says that he does not want to get into any more trouble and would like to make amends with his parents. He said he plans to make a full disclosure to the Court. He says he is not sure how to communicate his regret to his parents and to the Court.

Identify and discuss how Jamaal's shoplifting behaviours might be explained in human development terms.

Identify and discuss what, if any, creative techniques might be used to assist Jamaal to communicate his regret to his parents and to the Court.

Recommended further reading

Chalmers, D. (2016). *Communication with children from Birth to Four Years.* London: Routledge.

This book provides a highly accessible guide to the developmental phases from birth to four years and the implications of this for effective communication between adults and children. Written primarily with parents, care givers and teachers in mind, this book nonetheless provides a range of practical strategies for engaging babies, infants and young children.

Crone, E. (2015). *The adolescent brain: Changes in learning, decision-making and social relations.* London: Routledge.

In this book, neuropsychologist Eveline Crone, outlines recent neuroscientific research regarding adolescent brain development and the implications of these findings for understanding how young people see themselves and their world. Professor Crone emphasises the developmental variations and individual differences among adolescents including some reference to the impact of disadvantage on brain development. The book is accessible and uses a good variety of case studies.

Daniel, B., Wassell, S. & Gilligan, R. (2010). *Child development for child care and protection workers* (2nd edition). London: Jessica Kingsley Publishers.

This book provides an excellent introduction to child development with a focus on children and young people facing life challenges.

Lefevre, M. (2010). *Communicating with children and young people: Making a difference.* Bristol: The Policy Press.

This book provides a practical overview of the theory and practice of communication with children and young people. The book introduces a framework of being, knowing and doing emphasising that techniques of communication must be linked to a commitment to child-centred practice and knowledge of human development and of social contexts of the lives of children and young people. Numerous case vignettes ground theory, knowledge and skills in examples relevant to social work practice.

Websites

The Communication Trust

https://www.thecommunicationtrust.org.uk/

The Communication Trust is a UK peak body concerned with improving communication with children and young people, especially those with communication differences and disabilities. The website include a large range of resources, tips sheets and games including guides on the use of Assistive and Augmented Communication with children and young people.

Create

https://www.create.org.au

Create is an Australian advocacy organisation dedicated to creating a better life for children and young people in out of home care. The website includes a range of resources including information about, and resources for, children and young people in the care system. The resources include videos about young people's transition from care and an online workbook to assist young people to prepare for transition from care.

Activities books and websites

There are large range of activity books and websites that provide ideas for creative exercises for practice with children and young people. Here are some books that may inspire you to develop your own creative ideas in practice.

Cornish, U. & Ross, F. (2004). *Social skills training for adolescents with moderate learning difficulties.* London: Jessica Kingsley Publishers.

This book outlines a social skills training package targeted at young people with learning difficulties. The book presents an overview of a group work program approach to social skill development. Even if you do not work with young people with learning difficulties, the book provides useful practical tips up setting up an interactive group work program with young people.

Lowenstein, L. (1999) *Creative interventions for troubled children and youth.* Toronto: Hignell Book Printing.
... (2002). *More creative interventions for troubled children and youth.*
... (2006). *Creative interventions for bereaved children.*

Liane Lowenstein is a social worker specialising in therapeutic practice with children and young people. She has published a range of activity books for therapeutic practice with children and young people facing a variety of life challenges. Her exercises can be easily adapted to communication with children and young people in a range of social work practice settings.

UK Youth

http://www.ukyouth.org/activities.html

This webpage of the UK Youth organisation outlines a range of creative activities for engaging young people.

8

Communication and Older Adults

In many societies, people are living longer and many older people continue live independently in their communities. The World Health Organisation (2016, p. 1) states that the proportion of world's population of people over 60 years will nearly double from 12 to 22 per cent between 2015 and 2050. Like people at other points in the life course, older people are a diverse population with a variety of roles, concerns and needs. Regardless of the contexts in which we practice, social workers are likely to communicate with older people who occupy a variety of roles, as community members, as caregivers and as service receivers. In this Chapter, we focus on developing skills for communicating confidently and respectfully with older people. We will define whom we refer to as older adults and the communication needs of older adults. We then discuss challenges with communicating with older adults and how these challenges can be addressed. We conclude with a discussion of practical strategies for communicating respectfully and building the working alliance with older adults.

Who are older adults?

In this Chapter we define older adults as those 65 years and over (Storlie, 2015, p. 1). The age group of 65+ is itself inherently diverse, covering more than five decades from the "young old" to the "super-centenarians," people who are 110 years and older. Like people of all ages, each older person has their own unique personality and characteristics as well as different life experiences shaped by social factors such as gender, education, geographical location, health, sexuality, disability and functional level (Kampfe, 2015). Older people are culturally diverse and are likely to become more so as the current increasingly diverse younger populations of many societies grows older. Drawing on the data from the US Department of Health and Human Services (2007), Kampfe (2015, p. 4) notes that in the United States, "The fastest growing subgroup of older people is composed of those from minority backgrounds. In 2000, the minority subgroup represented 16.4 per cent of the older population, but this proportion is projected to rise to 23.6 per cent by 2020." Similar trends have been noted in other increasingly diverse, also referred to as "superdiverse" societies of Western and Northern Europe, Australia, New Zealand and the United Kingdom (Peace, Dittmann-Kohli, Gerben, Westerhof and Bond, 2007; Rao, Warburton and Bartlett, 2006).

Older adults are an important group of citizens, care providers and service users. Older people may play significant roles as informal care-providers to family members such as other ageing family members and as kinship care to young family members (see Hayslip, Blumenthal and Garner, 2015). Older adults are also largest population segment seeking regular health care, often to address complex health needs and they are significant users of social services including community-based home care services (Nussbaum and Fisher, 2009). Despite the importance as older adults as providers and receivers of informal and formal care, human service professionals often lack the education, training and support needed to communicate confidently and competently with older adults (Nussbaum and Fisher, 2009; Storlie, 2015).

Older people, like people of all ages, want to be treated with respect and for their uniqueness to be recognised. As Storlie (2015, p. 13), a social worker with extensive experience in working with older people states:

> In every encounter, the older adult wants to be seen for who she or he is—a person, heard and listened to, respected, and appreciated. In each encounter, the older adult is listening, not only to the content of what is being communicated, but to how he or she is being treated.

In this next section we consider barriers to effective communication with older people and how these might be addressed in practice.

Ageism and communication

A key barrier to effective communication is ageism. Responses to advancing age vary among cultures. In some cultures, advancing age is associated with wisdom and maturity. In Indigenous cultures, for example, the older person is respected as an "elder" of the community and protocols may exist that demonstrate respect for the person's status within the community (see Coffin, 2007; Warburton and Chambers, 2007). However in many cultures, particularly the dominant cultures of the West, advancing age is often regarded negatively (Gendron et al., 2016). This negative view gives rise to ageism. Storlie (2015, p. 73) states:

> Ageism is the tendency to negatively stereotype older adults, to display prejudice against the elderly, and discriminate against people simply because they

are older. Founded in myths, stereotypes, and language that conjures up negative images, ageist beliefs can significantly interfere with a provider's ability to communicate effectively and respectfully.

Ageism is reflected in negative attitudes about older people including views of older people's lives as less valuable or worthwhile than those of younger people, and of older people as a burden on society. Ageism can have profound and negative effects on the quality of life of older people.

Ageism can prevent the social worker from seeing and responding to the older person as a unique individual (Kampfe, 2015). Ageism can contribute to older people's exclusion from decisions that affect them. It can lead to unsatisfying professional and personal relationships. Professionals may disregard the physical and personal losses experienced by an older person as a "normal" part of the ageing process and thus fail to provide the older person with access to the services that may assist them to manage or adapt to life changes. For example, the professional who assumes sensory impairments are a normal part of ageing which the older person must accept may neglect to provide the older person with information about assistive technologies that can assist them to adjust to losses. Similarly, the grief experienced by older people even in relation to their own or another older person's impending death may be ignored or downplayed. Hence, the grief experienced by older people is often disenfranchised grief, meaning that person experiences a loss that "is not, or cannot be, openly acknowledged or publicly mourned or socially supported" (Doka, 1989, p. 4 cited in Moss and Moss, 2003, p. 4). This disenfranchisement can be further intensified where the older person's grief relates to a socially devalued relationship, such as the loss of a lesbian or gay partner.

Internalised ageism, in which the older person accepts the negative valuation of older people, is associated with negative health outcomes (Gendron et al., 2016). At its most extreme, ageism can contribute to elder abuse by providing a rationale for harmful treatment of older people. This can include physical, verbal, emotional, financial and spiritual abuse of older people.

Where a person holds ageist views, these are likely to shape their approach to communication with older people. Gendron et al., (2016, p. 997) note that:

> Ageism, or discrimination based on age, is extraordinarily complex and is often covert. In fact, many ageist sentiments are very subtle in nature, and are often missed or overlooked. To add to the confusion, ageist remarks may be well-intentioned.

The subtle and often unrecognised influence of ageism on communication is a substantial threat to effective communication with older people.

Communication adaption theory posits that we adapt our communication to accommodate the perceived communication needs of the people with whom we are communicating (Nussbaum and Fisher, 2009). "Elderspeak" is an example of how communication adaption underpinned by ageism results in inappropriate communication with older people. Elderspeak refers to infantalising communication towards older people that "implicitly questions the competence of older adults" (Gendron et al., 2016). As Williams et al. (2009, p. 12, brackets in original) define it:

> Elderspeak (ie, infantilization or secondary baby talk) features simplistic vocabulary and grammar, shortened sentences, slowed speech, elevated pitch and volume, and inappropriately intimate terms of endearment. Features of elderspeak include diminutives, inappropriately intimate nominal references, such as "honey" and "good girl." Collective (plural) pronouns substitute the plural reference when a singular form is grammatically correct and imply that the older adult cannot act independently.

Elderspeak is threatening to older person's self-concept and can precipitate communication breakdown (Storlie, 2015; Williams et al., 2009).

Ageism is widespread in many societies. It can be internalised by us and by the people with whom we communicate with, including older people themselves. We can challenge ageism by promoting positive attitudes towards ageing, including an acceptance of the gains and losses that come with every age and encouraging older people to utilise emerging technologies to support them to effectively communicate despite age-related losses. We should model positive attitudes to people who are older to our peers and their families by ensuring that older people are included in decisions that affect them and by challenging language and processes that undermine older people's dignity and personhood (Kampfe, 2015). In the context of widespread ageism, it is important that we reflect on, and seek to eliminate ageist attitudes that shape how we communicate with older people. The following exercise is intended to assist the reader to reflect on their communication with older people.

Practice reflection: reflection and discussion questions

We suggest you consider these questions on your own or as part of a discussion group.

1. What experience do you have communicating with older people (people over 65 years)?

2. How comfortable are you in speaking with older people?

▶

1_____3_____5

Not comfortable   neither   very comfortable

Discuss why you have given this rating.

3. In your everyday life, what examples have you observed of ageism?

4. How might you, as a social worker, prevent ageism in your own communication with older people?

Cohort effects and communication

A second barrier to effective communication with older people relates to the impact of age cohort effects on the expectations of the partners to the communication. People of specific age groups have shared experiences arising from the time period into which they were born and in which they were socialised that may differ from people of other age cohorts. As Kampfe (2015, p. 2) observes:

> Age cohort is much different than chronological age and often reflects the experiences that a group of people have in common. People who were born in 1925 will have very different experiential backgrounds than people who were born in 1945.

Cohort effects are associated with often unconscious rules and expectations about informal and formal relationships, such as the level and nature of formality between professionals and services users, and about communication protocols. These cohort effects can give rise to tensions between people of different age cohorts.

In seeking to communicate effectively with older adults, it is important to be mindful of cohort effects on communication protocol. Indeed, differences that are unacknowledged can lead to communication breakdown. In a study with older adults aged 73–96 years (Froemming and Penington, 2011), participants identified certain communication practices they perceived to be common among younger people that were offensive or annoying. Communication practices identified as offensive by the older participants in the study were those that inferred "false familiarity," such as the use of first names without the expressed permission of the older person to do so and "inappropriate assumptions," such as assuming an understanding of the older person's personal experience (Froemming and Penington, 2011). In the same study, older people reported "tuning out" speakers who used poor grammar and who chose uninteresting or irrelevant topics. Of course, substantial differences exist among people within age cohorts and no generalisations can be made. However, in communicating with people of different age cohorts, we need to be sensitive and responsive to the possibility that age cohort effects may have an impact on the communication partners' expectations and on the quality of the communication.

Acknowledging age cohort effects does not always mean accepting them. Indeed, some assumptions that people have become accustomed to can be unhelpful or disempowering and inconsistent with a person-centred approach to care. For example, Sales (cited in Kampfe, 2015; see also Harwood, 2007) notes that some older people may have been socialised into an unquestioning acceptance of medical authority that in turn contributes to their disempowerment in health care situations. This notion of unquestioned professional authority is less common among younger adults as a result of increasing levels of education and access to information, as well as increased awareness of the fallibility of professionals and of the human rights of all people to participate in decisions affecting them. Kampfe (2015, p. 73) proposes that human service professionals have an important role to play in assisting older people to seek greater control over decisions made about them.

Reflective exercise

Write the down the time period in which you were born. Now list up to 5 unwritten rules or expectations that you believe many people of your age cohort have about communication between professionals and service users/patients. For example, how do you expect to be addressed by a professional person and you to them? What information should the professional person share with you about your health and well-being? What information should the professional share about themselves?

Now discuss these questions with someone of a different age cohort to you, such as a person at least 20 years older or younger than you. What similarities and differences did you discover and to what extent were the differences attributable to age cohort effects?

Finally, consider how you would negotiate age cohort related differences in expectations about communication.

Ageing and communication difficulties

A third barrier to communication with older people is age-related communication difficulties. We refer here to age-related processes that contribute to difficulties in a person's capacity to receive or process communication and to express themselves. In this section, we will consider three major areas of communication difficulties often associated with ageing these are: sensory loss; cognitive losses and impairments; and challenges with expression that can accompany some age-related conditions. We emphasise at the outset that while these communication difficulties are more common as we age, they do not affect all older adults.

We turn first to sensory losses. The ageing process is associated with sensory loss in all five senses (Kampfe, 2015). As with other aspects of human experience, individuals are diverse and some may experience little or no change in any of their senses. Significant age-related sensory losses can present different challenges compared to when these losses are experienced at an earlier age. Ageist attitudes can lead health professionals and family members to downplay the impact of these losses as "normal ageing" and something which the person must accept. These attitudes can lead professionals and older people to overlook opportunities, such as technological solutions, to adapt to age-related sensory losses. Furthermore, the older person may conceal the sensory loss due to fear of the stigma associated with ageing processes. While, as mentioned, some sensory loss across all five senses occurs as we age, in this section we will focus on the two areas of sensory loss most crucial to interpersonal communication – hearing and visual losses.

Hearing loss is common as people age (Froemming and Penington, 2011). Hearing loss is more frequently experienced by men than women and often has profound effects on communication (Storlie, 2015, p. 92). Age-related hearing loss has a distinctive pathway and impact. As Kampfe (2015, p. 153) observes:

> Regardless of the cause, late-onset hearing loss typically involves a slow degeneration of the nerve cells (sensorineural) in the cochlea and the eighth cranial nerve that connects the inner ear to the brain. Hence, hearing loss is sensorineural and results in the distortion of or inability to hear high-frequency sounds, especially those associated with speech (e.g., the letters m, l, and p). Because of this distortion of sound, increased volume does not usually help.

Hearing loss can be frustrating for communication partners as it can interfere with mutual comprehension of the conversation. Speakers trying to accommodate the hearing loss of the older person may engage in behaviours that are unhelpful and experienced as patronising by the older person, such speaking too loudly or speaking on behalf of the person. It can also contribute to increased social isolation and loss of confidence by the older person. The person experiencing hearing loss may become anxious due to exposure to risks associated with hearing loss such as loss of capacity to hear warning sounds or not being able to hear important instructions from health or social care professionals (Kampfe, 2015).

Hearing loss can have a range of impacts on the communication behaviour of the older person. It can lead to emotional distress and to behaviours that may be "inaccurately perceived by others as a deterioration of intellectual abilities and may even result in a misdiagnosis of cognitive or behavioral [sic] issues" (Kampfe, 2015, p. 156). For example, the older person may become cranky or evasive as a result of hearing challenges and the perceived inadequate response of communication partners to those challenges.

If hearing loss is recognised, it is possible for others to make appropriate and helpful accommodations to support the communication. Yet it can be difficult to assess whether a person experiences hearing loss. A person with age-related hearing loss may have limited awareness of the loss as it occurs within a specific range of sound and the person may hear well at the lower ranges. In addition, the person may conceal the level of hearing loss due to the stigma associated with age-related conditions. We can assess a person's level of hearing loss by using concept checking (discussed in Chapter 6) or "teach back" methods discussed later in this Chapter. These methods involve assessing whether the person has received the message we intended.

Because age-related hearing loss occurs within a specific range of sound, the upper register, it is not helpful to raise your voice to a heightened pitch. Drawing on the work of Kampfe (2015) and Storlie (2015), we identify the following practical strategies for improving communication with people experiencing age-related hearing loss:

➢ make sure you have the person's attention from the outset. If the person misses the first part of the conversation, it can be difficult for them to comprehend the remainder. If necessary, or if requested, be ready to start again.

➢ face the person so they can read your facial cues.

➢ slightly lower your vocal pitch, speak more clearly and a little more slowly.

➢ where a person appears not to have understood you or asks you to repeat yourself, it can help to "rephrase the sentence rather than repeat it exactly as said the first time. This rephrasing is helpful because some words are more difficult to hear or lip read, and rephrasing may provide words and sounds that are easier to see and hear than the ones that were not understood" (Kampfe, 2015, pp. 159–160).

➢ use non-verbal cues and written information to supplement spoken communication.

> avoid quick changes of topic.

> avoid specialist jargon.

> create a supportive physical environment by eliminating ambient sound and by ensuring there is adequate lighting (so that the person can read facial or other non-verbal cues).

Deterioration of vision, including substantial vision loss and blindness, is more common among older adults than younger people. As we age, most people encounter changes to their vision. In middle age, many people experience decreased flexibility of visual lens (also known as Presbyopia), resulting in short or long sightedness (Heiting, 2016). Older adults typically experience additional changes including increased sensitivity to sudden changes in lighting and reduction in their peripheral vision (Heiting, 2016). Many age-related visual changes, particularly presbyopia, can be easily accommodated, such as through wearing glasses.

Some visual changes can significantly impact on a person's capacity to engage in daily living activities. The American Foundation for the Blind (2008, p. 1) states that visual impairments or low vision "refers to a loss of vision that may be severe enough to hinder an individual's ability to complete daily activities such as reading, cooking, or walking outside safely, while still retaining some degree of useable vision." The incidence of visual impairment increases with age, particularly over 60 years and affects almost 25 per cent of people by age 85 years (Kampfe, 2015). Cataracts are a cause of age-related vision loss but are correctable with surgery. Other age-related diseases particularly age-related macular degeneration, glaucoma and diabetic retinopathy can cause irreversible vision impairment and, in some cases, may lead to blindness (Heiting, 2016). Some age-related diseases processes and conditions, particularly stroke, can also lead to vision impairment or blindness.

Late onset visual loss can have a range of devastating physical, emotional and social impacts. Visual impairment is associated with a decline in economic participation and increased social isolation (Köberlein, et al., 2013). Kampfe (2015, pp. 147–148) notes that:

Acquiring low vision as an older adult can be very difficult and may result in frustration, dependency, anger, fear, isolation, loneliness, depression, and reduced quality of life. These outcomes can occur because individuals may be unable to accomplish routine tasks or perform lifelong leisure activities.

Decline in visual capacity can also influence a person's capacity to communicate. For example, the person may also be unsure of who is present in the conversation and may lose access to the visual cues that support conversation.

Age-related visual loss can affect how others respond to the older person (National Federation of the Blind, 2016). Well-meaning family members and professional carers may assume the person with visual loss is unable to participate in everyday living tasks. Yet, as the National Federation of the Blind (2016, p. 1) points out that "By learning to use some alternative techniques that employ senses of touch or hearing rather than sight, low-vision seniors continue to do almost everything they wish." Adaptions to one's physical environment including for example, increased lighting, the use of assistive technologies and access to written material to large print or Braille can also assist the person with vision impairment to negotiate their environment.

Drawing on information from the National Federation of the Blind (2016) and Kampfe (2015), we offer the following tips for communicating with a person with age-related vision loss:

➤ maintain your voice at its usual pitch and tone (don't raise your voice!).

➤ provide an environment that supports use of limited vision. This can be achieved through bright lighting and by providing material in accessible format for people with low vision, such as large print and braille can assist.

➤ avoid physical intrusion. For example, do not touch the person, such as touching their arm, cane or guide dog without their permission.

➤ introduce yourself and anyone else in the room.

➤ ensure that any written material, such as service information and forms, is in accessible form, such as in large print format or braille.

Cognitive losses and impairment

Cognitive loss and impairment refers to the decline in our ability to store, retrieve and process information. Cognitive losses, such as some decline in short term memory, are encountered by up to 90 per cent of older adults (Levy, 2011). However, these age-related cognitive losses do not infer a decline in intellectual capacity. Rather, it means that as we age we may require more time to retrieve and process information, solve problems or learn new skills. Furthermore as we age, we bring more experience to various cognitive tasks leading potentially to greater creativity and ingenuity in our approach to cognitive tasks such as solving problems (Kampfe, 2015; Nussbaum and Fisher, 2009; Underwood, 2010).

Cognitive impairment, by contrast to cognitive loss, refers to impairments in one's capacity to: "attend to and filter stimuli, store and recall information, communicate, make decisions, self-correct behaviour, and use judgment" (Wolf and Baum, 2011, p. 41). These cognitive impairments can range from mild to severe. People with mild cognitive impairment (MCI) "do not have pronounced impairments in daily function" and as such are able to live independently (Levy, 2011, p. 127). People with MCI nonetheless report that the condition can have profound and distressing impacts for them and often results in maintaining work, hobbies or social activities (Wolf and Baum, 2011). More advanced cognitive impairment, that is moderate to severe age-related cognitive impairment, has even greater enduring and substantial impact on many aspects of a person's life. This level of cognitive impairment is often referred to as dementia. As Levy (2011, p. 130) states: "Dementia can be broadly defined as a syndrome of progressive cognitive impairment severe enough to affect daily function. This term is reserved for chronic, progressive, irreversible, global cognitive impairment." People living with dementias will often encounter significant challenges in negotiating the demands of daily living and may, for example, have trouble in decision-making, in maintaining hobbies and interests and in communicating with others (Levy, 2011).

Cognitive impairments can affect communication in a myriad of ways with the impact becoming more significant as the severity of the impairment increases. Cognitive impairments can contribute to confusion as the person is unable to differentiate those aspects of communication requiring attention versus those that do not. The person may have difficulty in recalling recent information including information discussed in the course of the conversation. The person may experience difficulty in recalling names or key terms. These changes occur because age-related cognitive impairments are often associated with a decline in the short-term memory affecting the person's capacity to store and process information and the information required for speaking and understanding language (Storlie, 2015). Cognitive impairments can be linked to loss of inhibitions and the inability to correct one's behaviour in response to social cues. For example, the person may continue to talk after others have lost interest. Cognitive impairments can affect one's ability to make judgements in a range of areas of life including impairments in spatial ability, loss of judgement about social relationships and financial concerns. The person may lose the capacity to follow a logical sequence of ideas thus compromising their capacity to solve everyday problems.

A range of age-related conditions can result in temporary cognitive impairments. For example, severe urinary tract infections (UTI), more common among older people than younger adults, can lead to significant cognitive impairments that resolve once the UTI is treated. Because a host of health conditions can result in dementia type symptoms, which are reversible with appropriate treatment, it is important to encourage those displaying possible signs of cognitive impairment to undergo a medical assessment of their conditions (Kampfe, 2015).

Other age-related neurological conditions are associated with permanent cognitive impairments. These cognitive impairments may be sudden, such as following a stroke. Cognitive impairment following traumatic brain injuries can range from mild to severe. Or the cognitive impairments may be progressive with the impairments becoming more extensive over time. There are a range of age-related neurological conditions associated with progressive and severe cognitive impairments and these include Parkinson's disease, vascular disorders and Alzheimer's disease (Palmer, Newsom and Rook, 2016).

Age-related cognitive impairments are often very distressing for those who experience these impairments. In reflecting on biographical material written by people experiencing dementias and those who care for them, Kampfe (2015, p. 81) observes: "the riveting fear and worry associated with losing contact with reality, losing the sense of time, having difficulty finding words, being confused about what one is doing and where one is, and the feeling of losing oneself." This emotional distress can influence communication. The person may become socially withdrawn because their impairments become obvious in social interactions. Well-meaning family members and professionals may also communicate in ways that reinforce the person's sense of loss of autonomy and confusion. For example, family members and professionals may refer to the person as a third party even in their presence or make decisions about them without adequate consultation.

Practice exercises

Imagine for a moment that you are unsure of what day or time it is, you are finding it difficult to recall the names of those closest to you and you feel confused about where you are. What emotions does this image evoke for you? Imagine now you are meeting with a social worker who has been asked to conduct an assessment of your home situation. What could that person say to you to help build a sense of trust and confidence in them?

Age-related cognitive impairments or dementias become more common with age but are not part of the "normal" ageing process. Rather they are signs of underlying injury or disease (Pachana, 2016). It is important that a person who presents with age-related cognitive impairments receives a medical assessment as some forms of impairment can entirely resolve with appropriate treatment. In any case, understanding the underlying health contributors to cognitive impairment can assist the person in managing the disease or injury and its effects. As cognitive impairments become more frequent with age, social workers need to develop skills in communicating with people experiencing age-related cognitive losses and impairments. This applies to communicating with people with relatively minor cognitive losses and mild cognitive impairments through to those with severe impairments. As Storlie (2015 p. 98) notes, "Appearances to the contrary, even in late-stage dementia, the individual may understand more than is apparent and can still benefit from the provider's caring, compassionate communication."

Strategies for effective communication with people experiencing age-related cognitive loss and impairment include:

➣ allowing more time for the older person to process information and to respond (Kampfe, 2015).

➣ avoiding sudden changes of terminology or topic that may contribute to confusion. For example, if you refer to the nurse visiting as Nurse Maria, do not use other names as well, such as Nurse Smith, to refer to the same person.

➣ using direct language, avoiding the use of metaphors or jargon.

➣ encouraging the use of written and other visual supports to verbal communication, such as the use of lists, providing material in written as well as spoken form.

➣ being patient with repetitive story-telling or restatement of information. Repetition can be a common communication feature among people with dementias (Kampfe, 2015; Levy, 2011). We might gently point out that the person has already provided the information to let them know we have heard them, but we should not stop them from re-telling their story if they need to do so.

A range of age-related illness, some forms of age-related motor neurone diseases (such as Amyotropic Lateral Schlerosis [ALS]), strokes and some dementias can affect a person's speech capacity. In the case of ALS and strokes, muscle weaknesses can affect a person's speech in ways that may make it difficult for others to understand. The condition known as "dysarthria", which may accompany brain injury, and ALS is associated with slowed or slurred speech. People who have a stroke or other traumatic brain injury may experience "aphasia" which refers to a range of problems in language comprehension and expression including difficulties in expressing more than one word or phrase at a time or retrieving the correct word and placing "it in the correct order in a sentence" (Evans and Shaw, 2012, p. 127). Some forms of dementia also result in language difficulties, particularly that the person is unable to find the right words or terms. In late stages of motor neurone disease and advanced dementias and in some forms of severe brain trauma, the person may entirely lose the capacity for oral communication.

We can support communication with the person experiencing problems with spoken expression in several ways. One way is to spend time listening to the person. As we become accustomed to their pattern of speech our comprehension may improve. A second way is through use of "total communication" strategies. These strategies involve "different modalities, including speech, gesture, drawing, writing, and pointing to pictures" to supplement spoken communication (Johansson et al., 2012, p. 145). We discuss these strategies further in Chapter 10. A third option is the use of assistive technologies to support communication. A range of augmentative and alternative communication (AAC) devices are available that can enable a person with significant impairment to their capacity for oral expression to communicate through touch and eye gaze. As these technologies are rapidly evolving, it is important that the older person experiencing problems in spoken communication and their family or support person has access to up-to-date information about relevant AAC.

What about the family and carers?

Older people often involve family or other support people in health and personal care decisions. Nussbaum and Fisher (2009) note that many older people have a support person with them to health care home appointments. Health and community service providers should view older adults' companions as an integral part to the older person's care and well-being (Nussbaum and Fisher, 2009). The family of the older person may play an important role in the effectiveness of social work and heath care intervention. The family have the potential to support or undermine the care plans developed with the older person (Nussbaum and Fisher, 2009). In addition, the family may be called upon to facilitate aspects of the plan. For example, a family member may be willing to provide support with transport or to attend an information session on augmentative and assistive technology with the older person. The social worker can also use meetings with family members to model behaviours of respect for the older person's personhood, particularly their right to be involved in decisions that affect them. For example, "When a client is present but someone speaks about that client rather than to that client, the counselor [sic] can face the client and speak directly to him or her about the topic" (Kampfe, 2015, p. 8).

Tips for involving family and other support persons in meetings include:

- ➤ the older person must remain the focus and their wishes, desires and needs should be our primary concern.

- ➤ the older person should be adequately prepared for the meeting, with their wishes for meeting protocol and processes acknowledged. For example, the older person may have concerns about being spoken over by a particular family member and so the meeting may begin with a statement of ground rules that include those earlier identified by the older person.

- ➤ all communication should involve the older person. The older person should never be discussed as a third party.

- ➤ the physical environment should support the older person's equal participation. For example, ambient noise should be kept to a minimum, any written material should be in accessible format and lighting should be bright to allow clear visibility of facial and non-verbal cues. We should seat the older person and ourselves in a way that enables them and us to have eye contact with all meeting participants.

- ➤ consistent with the Total Communication approach, it can help to have all key spoken points and agreements written down in a manner that is visible to all participants, such as through the use of a white board. Having writing material available to all participants can also help all parties to keep track of the conversation.

- ➤ allow time for information to be processed and be aware that fatigue may be an issue for the older person. Thus do not try to cover too much in one meeting.

- ➤ any agreements should be provided in writing at the end of the meeting and provided to all participants.

Putting it all together

Older people share many of the same desires and expectations as people at other points on the life course in relation to effective communication. When communicating with older people, service providers need to demonstrate respect, non-possessive warmth, genuineness, accurate empathy and a desire and capacity to be helpful as discussed earlier in this book (see Chapter 2). As we have discussed, the key barriers to effective communication with older people are ageism and, to a lesser extent, insensitivity to possible age cohort differences.

We note that older adults are more likely than young adults to experience loss or impairments in capacities for "hearing, vision, and information processes – losses that may impede the communicative experiences" (Nussbaum and Fisher, 2009, p. 199). Yet we also take heed of Harwood's (2007, p. 222) observation that "Obsessively linking aging with ill health can mean that we forget about the positive aspects of old age and ignore the potential of older people." Older people with, and without, physical and cognitive losses are important members of our society whose inherent worth and dignity should be recognised in our communication with them.

When communicating with older adult, we propose the core communication skills discussed in Chapter 3 should be supplemented with the following strategies:

➤ self-reflection on our attitudes towards ageing and older adults. We need to understand any biases against older people that we hold and strive to overcome them. We should reflect on critical incidents with older people, particularly where the incident may reflect a breakdown in communication. We should use these incidents as opportunities to understand how our communication with older people can be improved.

➤ be formal in our initial meeting with the older adult. Consistent with the importance of sensitivity to possible age cohort effects, Storlie (2015, p. 78) recommends that "During the initial encounter, providers are advised to call the older adult by his or her surname. After that, ask the older adult how he or she wants to be addressed. Unless an older adult prefers to be called by something other than his or her given name, doing so could be construed as an expression of ageism and a sign of disrespect." It is important also to inform the person about how you would like to be addressed. The use of the person's name during the interaction is vital to personalising the communication. In addition, when working with people of other cultures, learning something of their linguistic or cultural norms can assist in building rapport (Small et al., 2015).

➤ provide information about our role and contact details. Older adults often encounter a myriad of professionals, particularly where the older person has complex health needs. Upon meeting the older adult, it can help to provide the person with written information, such as a card with your name, role and contact details on it. This is relevant to all people, but can be especially important where a person is experiencing age-related cognitive decline and resulting limited capacity to process and retain new information.

➤ ensure that our physical environment supports communication for people who may have experienced hearing, visual or cognitive impairments. This means the environment should be free of ambient sound, have adequate lighting, have comfortable chairs and include provision of written materials (such as forms and service information) in visually accessible formats, such as large print and in braille.

➤ make sure that sensory aids (such as eye glasses, hearing aids, communication devices, memory aids) are available and used (Yorkston et al., 2010).

➤ make time for communication including allowing extra time for the older person to retrieve and process information and to respond. We should also ensure we speak clearly and at a pace that is accessible to the older adult with whom we are communicating.

➤ use language that is direct and accessible to the older person (Kampfe, 2015; Yorkston et al., 2010).

➤ adopt an empowering approach. This means enabling the person to take as much control as possible over their environment. According to Kampfe (2015, p. 15) this "involves respecting and honoring [sic] clients' autonomy. It might also involve supporting older people as they identify, evaluate, and make decisions about their options. Furthermore, it may involve advocacy for client choice and independence among significant others and institutions." (Kampfe, 2015, p. 15).

➤ a Total Communication approach means that spoken information should be supplemented with accessible written material and pictures if useful (Yorkston et al., 2010). We discuss the Total Communication approach further in Chapter 10.

➤ if the person is from a cultural or linguistic background other than our own, we should assess the extent to which the person's communication needs are limited by our cultural or linguistic differences. If necessary, consultation with a cultural advisor or involvement of an interpreter may be required (see Chapter 6). In addition, it is important to be sensitive to how cultural and linguistic differences may be positively incorporated into our communication. For example, in many cultures the provision of food is an important part of social interaction and so accepting a refreshment may help to facilitate communication flow.

➤ provide take-home information or educational material "in the preferred format and at the appropriate reading level" (Yorkston et al., 2010, p. 314).

The teach back approach

Yorkston et al. (2010) recommend that health and social service professionals use the "teach back approach" to reinforce any information or agreements reached in the communication. This approach is commonly used by some health professionals usually in relation to the physical aspects of maintaining a health care regime without direct professional supervision. However, the method has potential for supporting communication in relation to the psycho-social issues discussed by social workers and other allied health professionals. The term "teach back approach" refers to clarifying the learner's (person's) understanding of instructions or information:

> through an approach that identifies learning gaps and provides an opportunity for healthcare providers to address misunderstandings and target individual learning needs. Also known as "tell back" or "show me," teach back works best when healthcare providers preface their evaluation by placing accountability for poor understanding on themselves rather than the [person]." (Peter et al, year).

Teach back involves a similar approach to "concept checking" discussed in Chapter 6. The approach, as developed in health care, requires that we not only check the person has understood the concepts discussed but also that we take responsibility for addressing gaps in understanding and communication. For example the social worker may ask an older person to "tell back" the content of their communication with a statement such as "I want to make sure that that I did a good job in explaining the next steps in your care plan, so can you tell me what you understand to be the next step in the plan for you?"

Conclusion

Older adults are diverse, with a variety of communication strengths and needs. In this Chapter, we have considered key barriers to effective communication with older people, particularly barriers associated with ageism, age-related cohort effects and challenges associated with age-related conditions that can contribute to communication difficulties. We have emphasised that older adults deserve our respect, support and advocacy as do people at other points in the life course. We have outlined strategies to support effective communication with older adults.

Practice exercise 1

Imagine you are a social worker who is part of an aged care assessment team. The team is responsible for supporting older people to remain in the community, and where this is not possible in assessing their need for supported residential care. In this role you are planning a meeting.

Helen Christopoulos is an 81-year-old woman who was widowed 12 years ago. Mrs Christopoulos was born in Greece and left there in the 1960s shortly after she married. Her late husband, Con, was also Greek. Until her retirement at the age of 65 years, Mrs Christopoulos worked a part-time cleaner for the government. She owns her home. Mrs Christopoulos is bilingual, having command of both English and Greek. She lives alone, she has four adult children who live in the same city, two daughters and two sons. Her adult children have developed a roster system to ensure that she has regular family contact including a visit from one family member each week and at least one phone call from one of them on a weekly basis. The opinion of Mrs Christopoulos' doctor and family members is that Mrs Christopoulos appears to be developing some signs of dementia. For example, she appears at times to confuse her children's names and has trouble recalling her activities over the last day. The referral to you from the doctor indicates that while Mrs Christopoulos acknowledges she is becoming forgetful, she is offended by the suggestion that she may have some signs of dementia. Mrs Christopoulos also recently fell down the stairs, resulting in some bruising to her left leg and arm. Her adult children report that Mrs Christopoulos is becoming more isolated, as many of her friends from the neighbourhood have either passed away or are in nursing home care. Mrs Christopoulos has said to her children that she hopes she dies before she needs nursing home care.

In consultation with Mrs Christopoulos doctor, the adult children have arranged for the aged care assessment team to visit Mrs Christopoulos to assess her home environment. As the social worker in the aged care assessment team, you have been tasked with making the initial home visit to conduct an assessment of Mrs Christopoulos home and social environment and to assess what further professional opinion is needed in relation to Mrs Christopoulos' situation. On phoning Mrs Christopoulos to make a time to meet, she says she is only meeting with you to "keep the children happy." She says she likes living in her own home and doesn't need any support. The appointment is made for tomorrow.

What do you see as the possible challenges to developing a working alliance with Mrs Christopoulos?

How would you manage the initial meeting with Mrs Christopoulos? How would you refer to her? How would you introduce yourself and your purpose?

How would you demonstrate respect for Mrs Christopoulos and seek to develop a collaborative relationship with her?

Practice exercise 2

Seventy-five-year-old Harold Newman is a carer for his wife Delia who has advanced breast cancer and has less than three months to live. Mr Newman is devastated by the impending death of his wife and is finding it hard to sleep and has lost interest in his usual hobbies. He is disappointed and angered by the responses of his adult children and his local doctor who imply to him that Delia's illness and impending death are a normal part of the ageing process. His doctor recently said that Newman and his wife were "lucky" to have had such a good long life together.

How might the responses of those around Mr Newman reflect an ageist attitude?

How would engage in Mr Newman in a way that demonstrates respect for his wishes and his loss?

Recommended readings

Kampfe, C. M. (2015) *Counseling older people.* Alexandria, VA: American Counseling Association. doi: 10.1002/9781119222767

The book provides an excellent introduction to human service provision with older adults. Kampfe covers a broad range of topics related to counselling older adults, including successful ageing as well as detailed information about health and social challenges that confront many people as they age. The book includes many practical exercises for deepening our understanding of the discrimination and losses many older people face. Kampfe provides many useful practical tips for communicating effectively in a helping relationship with older people and for advocating for social justice for older adults.

Pachana, N.A. (2016). *Ageing: A very short introduction.* South Melbourne: Oxford University Press.

This book provides a succinct introduction to the history of social attitudes to ageing. It explores the biological, psychological, and social changes humans undergo as they age and outlines contemporary scientific research into these changes. The book provides strategies for promoting positive and successful ageing.

Storlie T. (2015). *Person-centered communication with older adults: The professional provider's guide.* Burlington, MA: Academic Press.

Tim Storlie is a social worker with extensive experience in working with older people. In this book, he outlines an evidence informed, person centred approach to communication with older people. The book is structured around nine "c"s of effective communication with older people, which he describes as: care; compassion; courtesy; clarity; conciseness; congruence; completeness;

calmness; coherent; and connectedness. The book includes practical exercises for reflecting on and eliminating ageing in our practice and also for addressing common aging-related communication challenges.

Websites

The International Federation on Ageing

https://www.ifa-fiv.org/

The International Federation on Ageing (IFA) aims to be a global point of connection to experts and expertise as a means to help influence and shape policy related to older people and population ageing. The website includes resources related to policy, research and practice in fields associated with population ageing. There is also information on forthcoming conferences and webinars.

The National Federation of the Blind

https://nfb.org/about-the-nfb

This is a US-based support and advocacy network for people experiencing vision loss and blindness. There is a Chapter of the organisation dedicated to older people experiencing vision loss.

National Support and Advocacy Networks

In many countries, there are organisations dedicated to advocacy for, and empowerment of, older people. Here are the websites of some of these organisations. We encourage you to explore these and other websites for useful resources on support and advocacy for and with older people.

http://opaal.org.uk/ (The Older People's Advocacy Alliance, UK)
http://www.cota.org.au (The Council on the Aged, Australia)

9

Communicating with People Experiencing Mental Health Challenges

Many people experience mental health challenges at some point in their life. In this Chapter we focus on communication with people experiencing mental health disorders. The term "mental health disorder" refers to mental health challenges which are defined by a "clinically significant" disturbance of a person's thinking, emotions or behaviours (American Psychiatric Association, 2013). Some of these disorders are common such as depression, while others are not, such as schizophrenia.

We begin this Chapter by defining the term "mental health disorder" and outlining some of the major mental health disorders. We discuss the wide variety of circumstances where social workers are likely to communicate with people experiencing mental health disorders. We aim to assist the reader to develop a foundation of knowledge and skill to communicate with a person experiencing a mental health disorder. Our focus is not on assessment or intervention in mental health, which we recognise as requiring a depth of mental health expertise. We then consider how mental health disorders can affect a person's thinking, emotions and behaviours and the subsequent implications for communication. We turn finally to a discussion of how the principles of communication in response to heightened emotions discussed earlier in this book (see Chapter 4) can be applied and extended when communicating with people experiencing mental health disorders.

Mental health disorders: What are they?

According to the American Psychiatric Association, Diagnostic and Statistical Manual, hereafter DSMV, (2013, p. 20):

> A mental disorder is a syndrome characterized by clinically significant disturbance in an individual's cognition, emotion regulation, or behavior that reflects a dysfunction in the psychological, biological, or developmental

processes underlying mental functioning. Mental disorders are usually associated with significant distress or disability in social, occupational, or other important activities. An expectable or culturally approved response to a common stressor or loss, such as the death of a loved one, is not a mental disorder. Socially deviant behavior (e.g., political, religious, or sexual) and conflicts that are primarily between the individual and society are not mental disorders unless the deviance or conflict results from a dysfunction in the individual, as described above.

We note that this definition includes the requirement that a mental health disorder is characterised by "clinically significant" disturbances of thought, emotions or behaviour. This means that the wide range of human variation in "ways of being" in the world, such as differences in personality and temperament, are not, of themselves, considered mental health disorders. When these differences in thoughts, emotions or behaviour produce significant distress to the person or impair in their person's capacity to engage with work or study, to maintain relationships or to participate in other important activities it may be that the person is experiencing a mental health disorder (Maxmen, Ward and Kilgus, 2009). Our focus in this Chapter is on communication with people who are experiencing a mental health disorder and not simply a variation or difference in personality, emotional expression or behaviour.

The identification and categorisations of, and responses to, mental illness are culturally variable (Altman, 2014). As noted in the DSM-V (American Psychiatric Association, 2013, p. 14) the "Thresholds for tolerance of specific symptoms and behaviors differ across cultures, social settings, and families. Hence, the level at which an experience becomes problematic or pathological will differ." Similarly how a mental health condition is interpreted and expressed is culturally variable. It is vital then that when communicating with a person who may be experiencing a mental health disorder, we seek to understand the person's cultural context and the meaning of their thoughts, emotions and behaviour within its cultural context. For example, in some cultural contexts it may be expected that the widow or widower withdraws from social contact for a period of time following the death of her/his spouse. Yet social withdrawal is a also feature of some mental health disorders such as major depression or schizophrenia. It is important then that we seek to understand a person's behaviours in terms of the individual's own sense of meaning and the cultural expectations that shape their response.

Mental health disorders often have their onset in the teenage or early adult years. However, some conditions can be triggered by a traumatic life event, such as being in a serious accident, being attacked, or the death or injury of a loved one. In these situations people's capacity to cope may be overwhelmed resulting in a number of possible adverse mental health outcomes.

Considerable variation exists in the course and impact of mental health conditions. Kitchener, Jorm and Kelly (2013, p. 4) note that: "Some people may only have one episode of mental illness in their life-time, while others have multiple episodes and periods of wellness in between. Only a small minority have ongoing mental health problems." Where a person experiences multiple episodes of a mental health issue, it is likely that there will be variations in the experience of mental health condition over time. For example, a person with schizophrenia is likely to experience periods of illness in which distressing symptoms such as delu-sions and hallucinations may occur, while at other times these symptoms may be absent or reduced.

A controversial term

Both the term "mental health disorder" and the biomedical construction of mental health and illness the term connotes are controversial. This construction is evident in the Diagnostic and Statistical Manual (DSM), which is a publication of the American Psychiatric Association. The DSM provides a biomedical categorisation of "mental disorders" and lists the symptoms and signs of a large range of mental health disorders. The first edition was published in 1952. The most recent edition, the fifth edition (DSM-V), was published in 2013 and includes twenty broad categories of mental disorder and numerous sub-categories within each of these. For example, the Chapter on personality disorders includes twelve forms of personality disorder.

A variety of controversies surround the dominant biomedical constructions of mental health disorders. Maxmen et al. (2009) note criticisms about the opaqueness of signs and symptoms of these con-ditions leading to potential misuse of the diagnostic criteria. Concern exists that human diversity in personality and in ways of thinking, being and acting can be pathologised through the categorisation of some aspects of human difference being judged as "abnormal" (Brown, 2003; Drescher, 2015).

Critics of the dominant biomedical conceptualisations of mental health disorders also point to social, cultural and historical variations in what is considered to be a "disorder" (Altman, 2014; Brown, 2003). For example, the first version of the DSM published in 1952 referred to homosexuality as a mental health disorder (Drescher, 2015). Furthermore, critics observe that the focus on individual pathology may overlook, yet also reinforce, discriminatory assumptions associated with gender, cultural identities, sexualities and class (Altman, 2014). For instance, there is a strong relationship between schizophrenia and social class with the condition being more commonly diagnosed among people who were raised in circumstances of low social economic status and/or who currently live in these circumstances (Gallagher, Jones, McFalls and Pisa, 2006). Gallagher et al. (2006, p. 236) propose that the environmental stressors children in poor families may experience including "poor nutrition, inadequate housing and limited health care" may contribute to increased risk of the condition. The important implication of this finding is that it challenges an exclusive focus on individual symptoms and causal factors and points to the importance of economic and social contexts of mental health disorders.

We recognise the continuing controversy surrounding the term "mental health disorder" and the biomedical constructions of this phenomenon. We also acknowledge the provisional nature of the categories. Nonetheless, we also recognise that the biomedical categorisation of mental health disorder, as exemplified in the DSM-V, provides "clinicians and researchers with a common language for research, and for the treatment of people with mental disorders" (Bland, Renouf and Tullgren, 2015, p. 106). In addition, this understanding can assist communication with people experiencing mental health disorders as we can recognise and adapt our communication to recognised patterns of thinking, emotional (dys)regulation and behaviour that often (though not always) accompany particular categories of disorder.

Major mental health disorders

There are a large range of mental disorders and various ways of categorising them. As we have acknowledged, the categorisations change over time and, to an extent, reflect social and cultural understandings of mental health and disorder. There is an extensive range of disorders recognised in the mental health literature. Here we will briefly outline some mental health disorders that are highly prevalent and also some disorders that are less prevalent but which have highly significant and enduring health and well-being impacts, and which are associated with high levels of hospitalisation and risk of ongoing disability or social exclusion. We acknowledge that these mental health categories are provisional and further that they are not necessarily distinct. A person can experience a range of co-occurring mental health challenges. For example, a person can be depressed and have schizophrenia. We intend that this brief overview will provide a foundation for understanding the challenges of communication with people experiencing a mental health disorder.

Anxiety

Bland et al. (2015, p. 109) note that "Anxiety and depression are among the most commonly diagnosed mental health disorders." These disorders can occur separately or simultaneously. Maxmen et al. (2009, p. 374) outlines the symptoms of anxiety disorder as primarily characterised by "a subjective sense of apprehension, worry, tension and uneasiness without a known object or event, or out of proportion to the specific event." This is often accompanied by hypervigilance, as the person seeks to contain their anxious feelings or protect themselves from anxiety provoking situations. Physiological symptoms including muscular tension and "autonomic hyperactivity (sweating, heart racing, frequent urination, diarrhea, dizziness, hot or cold spells)" may be present also (Maxmen et al., 2009, p. 374). Anxiety disorders are linked to other mental health conditions particularly phobias, such as social phobia and obsessive compulsive disorders (Beyondblue 2013b, p. 2). The impact of anxiety on communication is varied but can include: increased perceptions of threat which is linked to increased emotional reactivity and liability and to distrust of others; increased speech pace and elevated pitch; confusion or distraction thus impacting on the person's capacity to engage in logically ordered information processing.

Depression

Major depression is a common condition that often causes significant distress for people subject to it and those around them. Major depression is also associated with increased suicide risk. Maxmen et al. (2009, p. 332) note that "the first essential feature of major depression is either a depressed mood or anhedonia – that is, a pervasive loss of interest or ability to experience pleasure in normally enjoyable activities." According to the DSM-V (American Psychiatric Association, 2013), this depressed or disengaged mood is accompanied by a combination of the majority of following symptoms: significant unexplained weight change; insomnia or hypersomnia; slowing of physical movement or physical restlessness; unexplained loss of energy; feelings of worthlessness or excessive or inappropriate guilt; diminished ability to think, concentrate or making decisions; recurrent thoughts of death which may include thoughts of suicide. The World Health Organisation (2014, p. 1) states that: "Depression is a common mental disorder and one of the main causes of disability worldwide. Globally, an estimated 350 million people are affected by depression. More women are affected than men."

Post Traumatic Stress Disorder

Post-traumatic Stress Disorder (PTSD) refers to distinct pattern of response to exposure to psychologically traumatic experience(s). Whereas anxiety disorders may arise without a specific environmental trigger, in PTSD a specific event or series of events are associated with a trauma response in the individual. For a person to be considered to have developed PTSD, they must first have been exposed to a traumatic event(s) either directly as the victim of the event, or witnessing a trauma to others, or be exposed indirectly by learning of trauma to someone to whom they are deeply attached or through involvement in investigating or in other ways intervening after a traumatic event (American Psychiatric Association, 2013). Examples of traumatic events can include: accidents that are life threatening or which produce serious injury; being subject to attack and abuse where one's life or sense of self is threatened; being involved in investigating or intervening after a traumatic event. For instance, a child protection worker involved in repeated investigation of child sexual abuse may experience PTSD as a result of exposure to deeply distressing information.

According to the DSM-V (American Psychiatric Association, 2013, p. 271) signs of a post-traumatic stress response to a traumatic event(s) include "recurrent, involuntary, and intrusive distressing memories of the traumatic event(s)." This may also include dreams or flashbacks related to the events and marked physiological reactions such as increased heart rate and sweating, when exposed to reminders of the traumatic events. Behavioural signs of PTSD can include: social withdrawal, hypervigilance, and misuse of substances as a strategy to avoid memories associated with the traumatic event (American Psychiatric Association, 2013).

As discussed in Chapter 4, the concept of trauma-informed care is increasingly recognised in many fields of health and human service provision. Trauma-informed care incorporates awareness of the ongoing impact of previous trauma on the person's current experience of health and human service provision. In general the approach encourages health and human service professionals to be cognizant of the potential triggers of traumatic memories that may accompany current communications or interventions. For example, in a group work setting, a social worker may work with group members to establish protocol for managing triggers that may arise as part of the group process. Such strategies usually involve increasing the person's sense of control of their environment such as encouraging people to exercise their right to leave the group if a trigger occurs or to engage in physiological de-arousal strategies such as focused breathing and visualisation.

The concept of PTSD is criticised for its focus on individual pathology rather than on the social and structural conditions that give rise to trauma and to the signs and symptoms of PTSD. The psychiatrist Jonathan Shay (2014) draws on his work with war veterans to reject the term PTSD. Instead Shay (2014, p. 183) use the term "moral injury" to describe the traumatic psychological injuries suffered by soldiers and others who have been subject to "betrayal of what's right by someone who holds legitimate authority (e.g. the military – a leader) in a high stakes situation." The concept of moral injury draws attention to psychological trauma suffered in contexts where leaders, such as political or institutional leaders, have established conditions or in other ways commissioned or permitted harm. This concept has also been deployed to explain the trauma experienced by survivors of institutional abuse in various health, welfare and faith-based institutions (Dombo, Gray and Early, 2013).

Schizophrenia

We turn now to some disorders which, though relatively uncommon, often impact substantially on a person's quality of life particularly their capacity to maintain work, education, as well as intimate and other social relationships. As social workers meet with people facing life challenges, we can anticipate that we may encounter people experiencing mental health disorders that have serious and ongoing impact on a person's life.

We turn first to schizophrenia. This term refers to a set of disorders that involve significant disturbance of thought and emotions over a substantial period, of at least six months, which may be coupled with bizarre behaviours. Schizophrenia is characterised by a combination of: delusions (false beliefs), hallucinations (false perceptions), disorganised thinking, grossly disorganised or abnormal motor behaviour, and emotional symptoms particularly diminished emotional expression or loss of motivation to participate in everyday activities (American Psychiatric Association, 2013). Schizophrenia is also often associated with unusual or blunted emotional responses. Kitchener et al. (2013, p. 57) note: "The person does not react to the things around them or reacts inappropriately. Examples include speaking in a monotone voice, lack of facial expressions or gestures, lack of eye contact, or reacting with anger or laughter when these are not appropriate." These responses can be distressing for both the person experiencing schizophrenia and those around them. This can contribute to social isolation of people with this condition.

Schizophrenia is relatively rare, with a rate of between 0.3 and 0.7 per cent in the population (McGrath et al., 2008 cited in DSM-V) but its consequences are far reaching. Maxmen et al. (2009, p. 290) state: "Of all the psychiatric disorders, schizophrenia arguably devastates like no other, for no other disorder causes more pervasive and profound an impact – socially, economically and personally." Schizophrenia is often a chronic condition that remains over the life course, though the intensity of episodes of unwellness may reduce as one ages (American Psychiatric Association, 2013). The risk of suicide is very high and may, in part, be related to the "depressed or hopeless thoughts which may be associated with the losses and dysfunction caused by the illness" (Bland et al., 2015, p. 125).

Bipolar disorders

DSM 5 notes three forms of bipolar which are: bipolar 1 disorder; bipolar 2 disorder; and cyclothymic disorder. All forms of bipolar disorder involve significant mood changes. As Kitchener et al. (2013, p. 23) note that person experiencing a bipolar disorder "will experience periods of depression, periods of mania and long periods of normal mood in between."

The bipolar disorders can be differentiated by severity of mood swings and to the presence or absence of psychotic experiences. People who are diagnosed with bipolar 1 or bipolar 2 disorder have experienced at least one major hypomanic and one major depressive episode. Features of a hypomanic episode include: "a distinct period of abnormally and persistently elevated, expansive, or irritable mood and abnormally and persistently increased activity or energy ..." The person may express "inflated self-esteem or grandiosity" and changes of behaviour including decreased need for sleep, increased talkativeness, distractibility and excessive involvement in high risk or impulsive activities, such as spending sprees (American Psychiatric Association, 2013, p. 133). By contrast, a major depressive episode is characterised by a significant change in outlook and behaviour which includes significant depressed mood most of the day every day; marked diminished interest or pleasure in all or almost all activities. The depressed mood is often accompanied by a range of concerning signs including: unexplained significant weight changes, sleep disturbances, difficulty concentrating and recurrent thoughts of death, self-harm or suicide (American Psychiatric Association, 2013, p. 133).

People who experience bipolar disorder 1 are likely to experience psychotic episodes including delusions and hallucinations, whereas these symptoms are not typically present in other bipolar disorders (Bland et al., 2015, p. 129). People with "cyclothymic disorder" may demonstrate hypomanic or depressive symptoms but do not meet the criteria for either a major hypomanic or depressive episode. Bipolar disorders often have significant consequences for the person's life and can significantly disrupt their capacity to sustain work and relationships. Bipolar disorder is associated with increased lifetime risk of suicide estimated to be "at least 15 times that of the general population" (American Psychiatric Association, 2013, p. 131).

Personality disorders

The American Psychiatric Association (2013, p. 645) defines a personality disorder as "an enduring pattern of inner experience and behavior that deviates markedly from the expectations of the individual's culture, is pervasive and inflexible, has an onset in adolescence or early adulthood, is stable over time, and leads to distress or impairment." In the American Psychiatric Association (2013) it is noted that the enduring patterns of inner experience and behaviour associated with personality disorders include: disorders of cognition that impact on the way the person perceives themselves, others, or events; unusual or disturbing emotional responses that vary from those expected within their specific cultural context; challenges in interpersonal relationships; difficulties in controlling impulses leading to behaviours they may place the person or those around them at risk of harm.

People with personality disorders may experience challenges in maintaining close interpersonal relationships, social networks and employment. However, Maxmen et al. (2009, p. 547) note that "People with personality disorders are not always in significant emotional distress. Often the people they are living or working with are more distressed." This appears to be true for some forms of personality disorder, such as anti-social or narcissistic personality problems. Yet, some forms of personality disorder appear to create significant distress for the person involved. People with borderline personality disorders (BPD) experience "chronic feelings of emptiness" and may demonstrate "recurrent suicidal behavior … and self-mutilating behavior" (American Psychiatric Association, 2013, p. 663; see also Brown, Comtois and Lineham, 2002).

Common effects on communication

In our short overview of some high prevalence and high impact mental health disorders we have attempted to show some of diversity of these disorders. We note that despite this variation, all forms of significant mental health disorder involve disturbance in at least three domains that impact on communication. These domains are:

➤ thinking

➤ emotions

➤ behaviour

We will now consider how disturbances in each of these domains may impact on communication.

Thinking disturbances and communication

Mental health disorders involve differences in patterns of thinking. The nature of this difference varies and may include "cognitive distortions." This term refers to ways of seeing the world that are inconsistent with external stimuli (such as events or experiences). Lefebvre (1981, p. 518) observes that cognitive distortions lead the individual to "systematically misinterpret or distort the meaning of events so as to consistently construe themselves, and their world, and their experiences" in ways that are exaggerated or irrational. Some mental health professionals propose that cognitive distortions contribute to some of the most common mental health disorders – depression disorders and anxiety disorders. For example, Maxmen et al. (2009, p. 333) note that: "Individuals with depression view the world through gray-tinted glasses. To them, everything is bleak – their life, their world, their future, and their treatment." The presence of cognitive distortions can interfere with the working alliance. For example, a person with major depression may distrust the social worker's attempts to communicate their strengths or to provide hope about the future and may instead see this as the social worker's misunderstanding of their situation or a failure to empathise with him/her.

Whereas cognitive distortions involve systematically different interpretation of events or situations, some mental health conditions cause people to think in ways that bear no apparent relationship to the realities around them. Psychosis refers to significant disturbances of thought "where a person loses some contact with reality. There are severe disturbances in thinking, emotion and behaviour" (Kitchener et al., 2013, p. 56).

Two key types of thought disturbance associated with psychosis are delusions and hallucinations. Delusions are unfounded or false beliefs, such as that one has special powers, or a special identity, or that one is being subject to special treatment such as persecution. For example, a person may experience a delusion that he or she is God, or that that he or she is being spied upon by secret police.

Hallucinations, refer to "perceptual experiences in the absence of the corresponding appropriate stimuli" (Bland et al., 2015, p. 121). Hallucinations can affect all senses including sight, smell, hearing, taste or touch (Maxmen et al., 2009). Bland et al. (2015) note that hearing voices is one of the most common forms of hallucinations. Hallucinations can be uncomfortable and may lead to harm of self or others. For instance, a person may cut their skin to seek release from the sensations of movement under their skin.

We acknowledge that the diverse opinions about the nature of "delusions" and "hallucinations." An international movement of researchers and citizens propose that these phenomenon are not pathological but rather part of the diversity of human experiences (see Leudar and Thomas, 2000; Watkins, 2008). Intervoice (2017, p. 1) states that: "Whilst it is the case that some people define hearing voices as a symptom of medical illness, other voice hearers are able to live with their voices and consider them as a positive (or at least manageable) part of their lives." Blackman (2001) proposes that when people who hear voices develop non-pathological understandings of this experience, they may integrate this experience into their lives without the need for psychiatric intervention.

We acknowledge that people's experience of seeing visions or hearing voices may be understood in ways other than as evidence of mental health disorder. Even so, these experiences are also associated with several major mental health disorders including:

➤ schizophrenia

➤ psychotic disorders similar to schizophrenia such as schizoaffective disorder

➤ bipolar 1 disorder

➤ drug-induced psychoses

Conditions involving psychoses are often episodic. This means that the person does not permanently experience the psychosis. Indeed, once the psychosis has resolved the person may experience substantial problems associated with coming to terms with the impact of the state on themselves or others. For example, a person may feel guilt or shame associated with how they behaved towards others when affected by psychosis.

People experiencing mental health challenges can also experience changes to their capacity to process information. People may find that their capacity to process information is limited because they are distracted by anxious or depressive thoughts, that they find it hard to slow down their thoughts, as can happen when a person is highly anxious, or alternatively that the time it takes to process information slows substantially, such as can happen when a person experiences major depression.

As this summary indicates, thought disturbances associated with mental health disorders can have substantial and varied impacts on communication. Turning to communication between social workers and people experiencing mental health challenges, we consider the impact of these challenges on developing and maintaining a working alliance. One challenge is that significant thought disturbances can make it difficult for the parties to achieve a congruent understanding of a situation. This can result in frustration and confusion for both parties and undermine the developing of a working alliance. For example, a person experiencing a delusion that they are God may find it frustrating and confusing that the social worker does not appear to recognise them as such (McCabe and Priebe, 2008).

A second issue is that thought disturbance may be directed towards the social worker in ways that are deeply challenging to the establishment and maintenance of the working alliance. Some forms of thought disturbance may lead a person to systematically distort or misunderstand the role and authority of the social worker. For example, a highly anxious person may be concerned about the integrity and confidentiality of the social worker without due reason. In some circumstances, the worker may be incorporated into the psychosis the person is experiencing. For instance, if a person holds a false belief that they are being persecuted, they look for or perceive signs of the social worker as a persecutor.

Emotional dysregulation and communication

Mental health disorders are often associated with challenges to emotional regulation (Howe, 2008). The term "emotional dysregulation" or "emotional lability" is used to refer to difficulties people may encounter in containing emotional responses in ways that are appropriate to the situation and to the social and cultural contexts. Examples of emotional dysregulation associated with various mental health disorders include:

➤ heightened emotional responses that seem incongruent to the situation. For example, a person may respond with extreme anger or distress in response to an apparently small frustration such as having to wait 10 minutes while their social worker finishes a meeting.

> emotional responses that while not heightened are markedly incongruent to the situation. For example, a person laughing when discussing events that appear to be unremarkable or being irritated for no apparent reason (Kitchener et al., 2013). These expressions of emotions are not "one off" responses where there has been a misunderstanding, but will usually be sustained over time.

> sudden and marked change of mood without any apparent environmental cause. For example, a person may suddenly withdraw from communication or express strong emotions such as elation, fear or anger without any apparent reason for this change. Furthermore the expression of the mood may be in extreme form. For example, a person experiencing euphoria associated with mania may demonstrate this by a wide variety of seemingly uncontrolled physical and vocal expressions.

The emotional dysregulation that often accompanies mental health disorders can create many communication challenges. Howe (2008, p. 117) notes that "Emotional dysregulation underpins much of psychopathology. It is difficult to reason with people who find themselves in the grip of powerful feelings and unregulated emotions." In order to sustain the working alliance, the social worker needs to respond skilfully to the emotional dysregulation that often accompanies mental health disorders. Later in this Chapter we discuss skilful communication with people experiencing mental health challenges generally and emotional dysregulation in particular.

Behaviours and communication

Mental health disorders are often associated with behaviours that impact on communication. Some of these behaviours can be directly related to the physiological basis of some mental health conditions. For example, communication behaviours such as changes in tone, pitch and speed of speech can reflect physiological arousal or depression that accompanies some mental health states. Other challenging behaviours can arise as a consequence of the thought disturbances or emotional dysregulation that accompanies mental health disorders. Some behaviours that can arise from mental health disorders include:

> physical or verbal aggression. There are a variety of reasons why mental health conditions can contribute to increased physical or verbal aggression. For example, cognitive distortions may lead a person to systematically interpret the actions of others as hostile and this may lead them to be in an almost constant state of fight or flight.

> self-harm. Self-harm, which is the deliberate infliction of physical pain on the self, is a feature of some mental health conditions. However, the patterns of thinking and emotion that contribute to self-harm can vary among different types of disorders. For example, during a psychotic episode a person may harm themselves because of auditory hallucinations instructing them to do so. People with borderline personality disorder report that self-harm is undertaken to punish themselves or to provide some distraction and emotional relief from their emotional pain (Brown, Comtois and Lineham, 2002).

> impulsive and high-risk behaviours. These behaviours may have ongoing negative consequences for the person. For example, the person experiencing euphoria associated with bi-polar disorder may engage in excessive spending or dangerous driving. Conflict may arise between the worker and client where the worker seeks to address impulsive behaviours.

> social withdrawal. Many mental health disorders result in people isolating themselves and this in turn can intensify the emotional pain associated with the disorder.

> unusual or bizarre behaviours. For example, a person with high anxiety may engage in obsessive compulsive behaviours such as repeated hand-washing in an often vain attempt to contain the anxiety. A person with a delusional belief that they have special powers "to protect them from danger may drive through red traffic lights" (Kitchener et al., 2013, p. 112).

As the above list indicates, mental health challenges can contribute to behaviours that create communication barriers and challenges to the development or maintenance of a working alliance. Indeed, some mental health challenges may result in behaviours such as aggression or social withdrawal that in turn make engagement extremely difficult. Furthermore the person experiencing a mental health disorder may have limited recognition or capacity to contain these behaviours.

Health and welfare professionals sometimes use the term "insight" to refer to the extent to which a person has insight into their mental health disorder and its impact. A person who completely denies their mental health condition with a "dim or fleeting admission of illness" is sometimes referred to as having little or no "insight" (Maxmen et al., 2009, p. 44). When a person lacks insight their challenging behaviours may be particularly difficult to address. This is because from the person's perspective, the behaviour they are exhibiting may be a reasonable response to their circumstance. For example, the person who is experiencing a paranoid delusion is likely to behave in ways that protect themselves from those whom they perceive to be persecuting them, which may include the social worker. Even where a person has insight, they still may find the behaviours difficult to change. For example, a person whose depression is accompanied by feelings of shame and guilt may find it difficult to engage in social interaction because of these feelings.

The episodic nature of some mental health disorders also affects communication. By episodic we refer to differences in signs and symptoms over time, particularly that people experiencing mental health disorders often experience periods of wellness, where symptoms are dramatically reduced or completely absent, between episodes of illness. During periods of wellness, the social worker may seek to develop an understanding with the person about how and by whom they would like decision-making to occur should their condition prevent them from doing so (Kitchener et al., 2013). Before turning to how we as social workers may communicate in ways that address these challenges and builds the working relationship, we will first discuss the role of the social worker in working with people with mental health disorders.

Social work and people with mental health concerns

We turn now to social work practice with people experiencing mental health conditions. Social workers may specialise in practice with people living with mental illness and they may offer a variety of services including: psychotherapy and counselling, case-management, community placement, advocacy and support. However, contact with people experiencing mental health disorders is not limited to mental health social work services.

Mental health challenges may be a contributing factor for people seeking or receiving social work services in any domain of practice. For example, people who experience serious and chronic mental health conditions are more likely to be homeless and have multiple health problems (Gallagher et al., 2006). Mental health challenges may also co-occur with other health conditions, such as alcohol and drug addictions, or life challenges such as living a disability. Social workers in a variety of health, housing or disability services then are likely to communicate with people for whom mental health concerns are part of the life challenges they are facing. Mental health disorders may occur at life transition points, for example, adolescence is a key time when many chronic mental health conditions first emerge. Hence, social workers working in youth justice services, education services and transition from care services may encounter young people experiencing a first episode of mental illness. In addition, life stressors such as being exposed to domestic and family violence can contribute to anxiety and to post-traumatic stress disorder (Okuda et al., 2011, p. 962). Across our fields of practice, we are likely to meet people who experience mental health challenges arising from trauma (see Bowie, 2013; Carello and Butler, 2015; Havig, 2008).

We note that social workers also have legal and ethical obligations when working with people who experience mental health disorders. These obligations include promoting the safety of the person, the prevention of harm to those around them, and taking action to prevent a mental health challenge becoming more serious (Bland et al., 2015; Kitchener et al., 2013). In some contexts, social workers may bear legal obligations to report and refer a person at risk of harm to self or others for treatment including involuntary treatment. But, even in the absence of legal obligations, the social worker has an ethical obligation to promote the safety and well-being of people who are at risk of harm to self or others.

Social workers must also recognise the Human Rights of people with mental health disorders. The UN Convention on the Rights of People Living with Disabilities (2006) recognises the rights of all people to the least intrusive interventions needed to address the challenges they face. Article 12 of the Conventions states that:

> States Parties shall ensure that all measures that relate to the exercise of legal capacity provide for appropriate and effective safeguards to prevent abuse in accordance with international human rights law. Such safeguards shall ensure that measures relating to the exercise of legal capacity respect the rights, will and preferences of the person, are free of conflict of interest and undue influence, are proportional and tailored to the person's circumstances, apply for the shortest time possible and are subject to regular review by a competent, independent and impartial authority or judicial body. The safeguards shall be proportional to the degree to which such measures affect the person's rights and interests.

This means that social workers must ensure that people with mental health challenges are not subject to intrusive interventions, such as involuntary treatment, unless essential to secure their safety and the safety of others, and where such interventions occur it will be "shortest time possible." The Convention stipulates the preferences of the person affected by mental health and other disabilities should be recognised on an equal basis with others. This means that a person experiencing a mental health disorder must not be discriminated against in service choice or method of delivery.

Social workers and other support people also have an important role in promoting the recovery of people living with mental health challenges. According to the Mental Health Commission, NZ (1998, p. 113, cited in Bland et al., 2015, p. 46) to promote recovery is to support people who are, or have been, affected by mental health disorders. It means to support people to live well "in the presence or absence of mental illness and the losses that can associated with it." The Recovery Model is an important and influential approach based on principles of partnership and social inclusion. Peebles et al. (2009, p. 239) describe the recovery model as involving:

> (1) broader treatment goals and aims (beyond symptom-reduction) and different measures of success (i.e., hope, empowerment, life satisfaction), (2) a truly collaborative relationship between provider and consumer of services, and (3) the inclusion of individuals with mental illness, their family members, and advocacy groups as members of treatment team.

The Recovery Model incorporates many principles and values that are consistent with ideas and values underpinning many contemporary practice approaches (see Healy, 2014). The recovery model promotes a holistic approach to practice that is not only focused on the treatment of disorder but also on improving quality of life. This approach is consistent with strengths and solution focused approaches to practice (Healy, 2014). The notion of collaboration central to the Recovery Model is also found in the majority of contemporary social work theoretical perspectives. Furthermore, the importance of partnership to achieving positive mental health outcomes is well established in the mental health literature (Priebe et al., 2011; see also Thompson and McCabe, 2012).

Skilful communication

A variety of studies have found that the working alliance is vital to service user satisfaction and to achieving positive outcomes with people experiencing mental health challenges (see Thompson and McCabe, 2012; see also Bland et al., 2015; Capone, 2016). Here we draw on systematic studies of effective communication with people experiencing mental health disorders (Capone, 2016; McCabe and Priebe, 2004,2008; Priebe et al., 2011; Thompson and McCabe, 2012) and on a range of research informed practice guides (see Aboriginal Mental Health First Aid Training and Research Program; Beyondblue, 2013a; Bland et al., 2015; Kitchener et al., 2013) in outlining principles of skilled communication with people experiencing mental health challenges. We draw also on the themes from our earlier Chapter on communication in contexts of heightened emotions (see Chapter 4). We do this because, as we have noted, mental health disorders often involve heightened emotions or emotional dysregulation (Howe, 2008).

Principle 1: Communicating with confidence, calmness, and non-reactivity

It is important that we respond confidently, calmly, and in a non-reactive manner with people experiencing mental health challenges. We refer to "confidence" as demonstrating a belief in oneself to skilfully manage any challenges that arise. "Calmness" refers to a tranquil and engaged demeanour characterised by the absence of strong emotions. We refer to "non-reactiveness" as an approach that involves looking below the surface level of communication to recognise and respond to the person in a respectful and non-defensive way (Plumb, 2015). When we are non-reactive we are not provoked by the behaviours of others and we are centred in a clear sense of our purpose and values.

By demonstrating confidence, calmness and non-reactively we help to:

➢ **reduce the physiological arousal, that is the fight or flight response that often** accompanies thought disturbance and emotional dysregulation. When a person is experiencing a mental health disorder they can feel out of control of their thoughts, emotions and responses, by modelling calmness you can positively shape the dynamic of the interaction to one of increasing trust and confidence between yourself and the person with whom you are communicating.

➢ **promote mutual understanding.** A person experiencing a mental health disorder can find that their capacity to comprehend or respond to a situation is compromised. By presenting ourselves calmly and speaking clearly we can assist the person to comprehend the situation and to participate in decision-making (Kitchener et al., 2013).

➢ **avoid a cycle of escalation.** As we discussed in Chapters 4 and 5, heightened emotional states are often preceded by an escalation period. If the person has not yet reached the point of escalation, a non-reactive approach in which you demonstrate openness to and interest in the other in ways that can help to reduce the likelihood of further escalation. If escalation has occurred, remaining emotionally present but non-reactive can assist in de-escalation.

Principle 2: Achieving a safe environment

Achieving a safe environment should be a priority in communication in with people experiencing mental health disorders. To point to this is not to suggest that most people living with mental health disorders are dangerous to themselves or others, indeed most are not. Rather it is recognise that, for a variety of reasons, a person experiencing a mental health disorder may be concerned about their safety or that in some circumstances, the mental health disorder may increase the risk to self or others (American Psychiatric Association, 2013).

For the service user, increased concern about one's safety can occur where the mental health disorder contributes to physiological arousal and a consequent "flight" state. Some reasons this can occur include cognitive distortions that increase the person's perception of threat out of reasonable proportion to their risks in the environment. Another reason can be delusions or hallucinations that contribute to an elevated perception of risk. For example, a person may hear voices that tell them they are being pursued and this contributes to a heightened state of arousal.

Some mental health disorders are associated with increased risk of aggression or violence. Physiological arousal associated with mental health conditions can contribute to increased fight response and thus to feelings of irritation and a propensity for aggression. In addition, people experiencing psychoses may be driven by delusions or hallucinations to behave aggressively. Some forms of drug induced psychosis, particularly those associated with methamphetamine use, can be associated with heightened risk of aggression (Milner and Myers, 2007). Strategies for creating a safe environment include:

➤ being aware of physical space around the person. Aim to stay close enough to allow for private conversation but do not crowd the personal space of the person. We need also provide enough space to move away should the person become aggressive.

➤ providing choice in location of meeting. It is important to "find a suitable time and space where you both feel comfortable" (Kitchener et al., 2013, p. 15). While we should choose a location that allows for private conversation, we should avoid environments in which either we or the person with whom we are communicating may feel cornered. For example, in a home visit we may suggest that we talk with the person on the back porch away from public view but yet not in an enclosed space.

➤ asking about their physical well-being and any risks to self, especially if we have any concerns, once some rapport is established.

➤ being aware of potential harms in the environment. Where a person is in a state of emotional distress, it can help to be aware of the possible harms that may inadvertently or otherwise arise. For example, removing objects that might be thrown or sharp implements that might be used to threaten or harm can help to minimise the risk of harm in a potentially escalating situation.

In some instances, the person with a mental health disorder may express suicidal or self-harming intent or intent to harm others. It is important to take these intentions seriously as a mental health disorders can present a strong risk factor suicide completion. Indeed, international research has found that 87 per cent of people who suicide have a mental illness (Arsenault-Lapierre, Kim and Turecki, 2004, cited in Kitchener et al., 2013, p. 94). In some instances, a person may express suicidal or self-harm intent or an intention to harm others, in other instances, their words and actions may indicate this intention. For example, the person giving away large numbers of personal items, indicating they have no sense of purpose in life, significant social withdrawal, or increased drug and alcohol use can be indicators of possible suicide or self-harm risk.

If you believe that a person is a risk of significant harm to themselves or others, it is recommended that you engage a mental health specialist to undertake specialist assessment and intervention. Referring supportive communication with people at risk of suicide, Kitchener et al. (2013, p. 95) propose that we:

➤ tell the suicidal person that you care and that we want to help them.

➤ express empathy for the person and what they are going through.

➤ clearly state that thoughts of suicide are often associated with treatable mental illness as this may instil a sense of hope for the person.

➤ tell the person that thoughts of suicide are common and do not need to be acted on.

In addition, we can also assist people at risk of harm to self or others by inquiring about the nature of the intended harm, such as how long they have felt this way, previous history (harm to self, suicide attempts or harm to others) as this can be a predictor of risk, the extent to which a plan is in place for intention to be realised, and whether the person has access to resources needed to achieve the intention. We should seek to ensure the person is in a safe place until the specialist service arrives or until they have connected to the service. If the risk is high and immediate, it may be necessary to call emergency services or persuade the person to attend an emergency medical facility with you. Do not leave the person alone until assistance has arrived (Kitchener et al., 2013, p. 96).

Principle 3: Promoting collaboration through effective communication

While people with mental health disorders may present and experience communication challenges, the social worker must nonetheless aim to promote collaboration through effective communication. The underlying principles remain similar to the foundations of effective communication outlined earlier in this book though with some different emphases that we outline here.

The first element of collaboration is engaging the person as a person not as an illness or disorder. As Plumb (2015, p. 141) observes:

> See the whole person: when you encounter a person experiencing distress, remember that illness is not their defining feature. They have a past, they have unique experiences, and even if they do not feel them at that moment, they have hopes, preferences and strengths.

Showing an interest in the person's entire life and circumstance, not just their illness is key to developing a working alliance with all people including those experiencing mental health disorders.

A second element of collaboration is that of focusing on the person's concerns, views of their situation and their goals (Bland et al., 2015; Priebe et al., 2011). The worker's concerns about professional purpose, particularly legal and organisational obligations, are important but the service user's concerns need also to take high priority in the formation and maintenance of the alliance. Many commentators urge avoiding disputes about a person's view of the situation particularly in the initial stages of establishing a working alliance (see Kitchener et al., 2013; Zangrilli et al., 2014). Even if we believe a person is demonstrating a distorted or deluded view of their situation, it is unhelpful to dispute this with them. Indeed, disputing their world view may simply communicate to them a lack of regard for them and may damage the working alliance (Zangrilli et al., 2014; McCabe and Priebe, 2004, 2008). Instead we should listen openly to their view, as this will not only build the relationship but also enable us to better understand the situation and next steps required, if any, such as possible involvement of specialist mental health services. We can use empathic listening skills to demonstrate that we are hearing the underlying thoughts and feelings they are conveying, such as "I hear you are feeling really frightened."

A third element of effective communication is demonstrating positive regard and respect. According to Priebe et al. (2011, p. 404), this means that the person "should be valued and respected as a person and his/ her views to be taken seriously and regarded as important." This can be especially important for people with mental health conditions because of the frequent discrimination and stigmatisation they often experience can make them wary of health and welfare professionals.

A fourth element is demonstrating genuineness, warmth and openness (Capone, 2016; Priebe et al., 2011). We demonstrate genuineness, warmth and openness through:

➢ active, non-judgemental listening (Kitchener et al., 2013).

➢ being friendly and interested in the person (Capone, 2016).

➢ appropriate use of self-disclosure. The practitioner's willingness to share some information about themselves is a predictor of client satisfaction with mental health services (Priebe et al., 2011). However, self-disclosure should not undermine the person's confidence in the professionalism or capacity of the service provider nor should it lead to a focus on the service provider's needs or concerns. Priebe et al. (2011), point out that self-disclosures that imply a criticism of the client are also unhelpful to the therapeutic alliance.

➢ expressing positive feelings and showing appreciation of the person's strengths are also indicators of genuineness, warmth and openness.

Principle 4: Prioritising empowerment

Empowerment involves supporting the autonomy of the individual. In practical terms, this requires that people are provided with information and involved in decisions about their care and support (Capone, 2016). Empowerment also requires the social worker to facilitate the person's access the resources they need to reach agreed goals which need not be limited to mental health "treatment" goals (Bland et al., 2015).

We turn first to sharing decision making. People experiencing mental health challenges, like people experiencing other life challenges, often want involvement in decision making in matters concerning them (McCabe and Priebe, 2008). Studies of clinical practice with people experiencing mental health disorders of depression and of schizophrenia have found better mental health outcomes where people had been informed and involved in decisions about their care (Priebe et al., 2011; see also Capone, 2016; Thompson and McCabe, 2012). However, while most people, including people who experience a mental health disorder, usually prefer a partnership model of communication, exceptions and variations to this approach may be required and preferred at some points in the course of the a mental health disorder (Priebe et al., 2011). The practitioner is likely to need to take a stronger decision-making role, where the person's mental health disorder is associated with severe cognitive distortions, emotional dysfunction and/or behavioural problems that place themselves or others at risk of harm. In times of wellness, we discuss with the person their preferences for decision-making in circumstances where their mental health disorder impairs their capacity to participate in decisions. For example, the person may nominate an advocate and we may also outline any protocol we put in place in those circumstances.

Second we turn to engaging the family and social context of the person in supporting the empowerment of the person affected by a mental health disorder. Bland et al. (2015, p. 192) refer to evidence based psychoeducational principles for promoting well-being with individuals experiencing mental health disorders, these include:

➤ family psychoeducation for reducing relapses and rehospitalisations.

➤ supported employment helping people return to the competitive workplace.

➤ social skills training to improve social and community functioning.

➤ integrated treatment for co-occurring substance abuse or dependence.

Bland et al. (2015, p. 193) also observe the importance of supported housing intervention to prevent homelessness among people with mental health disorders.

Each of these interventions addresses the interface between the person and their social environment. Families often play an important role in providing informal support for people living with mental health disorders. For this reason, the workers should aim to work collaboratively with people and their families to develop a shared knowledge of the nature and impact of the person's mental health concern and to build on their lived experience of what works and what does not, in identifying, preventing and addressing challenges associated with the mental health disorder.

Conclusion

In a wide variety of practice settings, social workers are highly likely to meet people experiencing mental health challenges. The development and maintenance of a working alliance remains central to effective social work practice with people experiencing mental health concerns, as it does for practice with people experiencing other life challenges. Yet, as we have outlined mental health challenges can pose unique problems for the working alliance. In this Chapter we have outlined principles for communication that support respectful partnerships between social workers and the people experiencing mental health challenges.

Review questions and exercises

1. What are points for and against social workers recognising the bio-medical construction of "mental health disorders"?

2. What does the term "cognitive distortion" mean and how might a person's cognitive distortion affect communication?

3. Define the terms "delusion" and "hallucination" and discuss what communication a social worker may face in communicating with a person experiencing delusions and hallucinations.

4. Define emotional dysregulation and discuss what communication challenges a person who is experiencing emotional dysregulation might face.

5. Identify the elements of skilful communication outlined in this Chapter and discuss how each element could support the maintenance of the working alliance where a person is experiencing mental health challenges.

Practice exercise

Practice exercise 1

Imagine you are working in a child protection service. You have received a child protection notification regarding Claire Smith, a 28-year-old single mother of two children aged two (Sally) and four years (John). The notification has come from a family member. The notifier states that Claire and her husband, Simon, separated about 12 months ago, though Simon maintains close contact with Claire and the children. The notifier is concerned about the safety and well-being of Claire's children. The notifier says that Claire was hospitalised previously for a psychotic mental health condition and appears to be experiencing psychosis now. When you arrive at the home, Claire is there with her two young children. John, the four-year-old, is at her side and appears to be unclean and to have been crying. Two-year-old Sally is playing in the sandpit close-by to her mother and brother. Claire greets you in a friendly manner and invites you to sit beside her as she watches Sally play. John is clinging to Claire. Claire speaks very quickly and is it hard for you catch everything she is saying. Her train of thought is difficult to follow as she switches topics frequently. Claire tells you that her son and daughter were fathered by a famous television celebrity, who is

▶

◀

refusing to pay child support because he is married and wants to keep their relationship secret. She says that he communicates with her through coded messages on the television because it is too unsafe for them to communicate directly. You notice that Sally has a bottle of water that looks unclean. John asks for a sandwich to which Claire tells him to "Shoosh, I'm talking to someone who is very important." Claire looks behind you suspiciously and asks if you have brought the media with you. When you reassure her that you have not, she replies "That's good, I'm not ready to speak to them yet."

1. What evidence is there that Claire may be experiencing a mental health disorder and what type of disorder(s) may she be experiencing?

2. What would be your priorities in communicating with her?

3. If you were to involve mental health services in this situation how would you do this? (For example, what, if anything would you say to Claire, or to the mental health service providers?).

Practice exercise 2

Imagine you are working in a community health service where you meet Mr Hoc Tran who is 56 years old. Mr Tran has been referred by his general practitioner for supportive counselling to manage the ongoing psycho-social impact of physical injuries Mr Tran sustained in a car accident five years ago. Mr Tran left Vietnam as a teenage refugee with his family in the 1970s. He later met his wife Binh who was also a young refugee at the time they met. Together they built a thriving restaurant business and raised three children, the youngest of whom is still living at home while she completes her university degree. Mr Tran had a car accident five years ago and since that time has had a series of operations on his spine and knee to relieve some of the pain arising from his injuries. Mr Tran continues to experience chronic pain and has been on pain medication for many years. About three months ago the surgeons advised that there was nothing further that they could do to address his ongoing pain from his injuries. They suspect that over time the pain will worsen and that his only medical option now is increased pain medication. Mr Tran says the doctors' views are that his long workdays and heavy workload are contributing to the pain he is suffering. The doctors have recommended to him that he consider retiring from work, or at least reducing his workload. Mr Tran is distressed about this suggestion; his work has been very important to him and has provided a solid income for his family. Mr Tran is devastated that there appear to be no medical options to address his pain other than ongoing pain medication. He is also worried about his financial situation, because while his restaurant is successful he has not yet saved enough for a long retirement for him and his wife. Mr Tran tells you that over the last six weeks, he has experienced disrupted sleep, waking at around 3am and not returning to sleep. He then feels tired and anxious the rest of the day. He yawns repeatedly during his conversation with you, he speaks slowly and maintains little eye contact. Mr Tran says that some days he feels that he is just waiting to die.

▶

◀

1. What mental health disorder(s) might Mr Tran be experiencing and what evidence do you have to support your initial thoughts on his condition?

2. What would be your priorities in communicating with him?

3. How would you communicate with him to develop and build a working alliance and which also addressed your professional purpose, legal and ethical responsibilities and values?

Recommended readings

American Psychiatric Association (2013). *Diagnostic and statistical manual of mental health disorders* (5th edition) Arlington, VA: American Psychiatric Association.

This book is an essential resource on biomedical classifications of mental health disorders. The manual is structured around 20 categories of mental health disorder and outlines the diagnostic criteria for each of these categories. While we share many commentators concerns about the provisional nature of these categories and the limited discussion of the social and structural contexts of the mental health conditions outlined, it nonetheless outlines a dominant framework through which these conditions are understood in many health and welfare settings.

Bland, R., Renouf, N. & Tullgren, A. (2015). *Social Work Practice in Mental Health: An Introduction* (2nd edition). Sydney: Allen and Unwin.

This book is collaboration between two experienced practitioners who are also established academics and a consumer of mental health services. The book provides a practical guide to a systems and recovery informed approach to working with people experiencing mental health disorders. The book includes sections on the systemic contexts of mental health service provision, the legal and ethical obligations of social workers to prevent harm and maximise well-being, information on the lived experience of mental health challenges and how to work with individuals, families and their communities to enable people to live well in the presence or absence of the signs and symptoms of mental health disorder.

Kitchener, B., Jorm, A. & Kelly, C. (2013). *Mental health first Aid manual* (3rd edition). Melbourne: Mental Health First Aid Australia. https://mhfa.com.au/

This is the website for the Mental Health First Aid program. It contains resources and training information, including online training.

Mental Health First Aid is a program designed by a mental health consumer working in partnership with mental health researchers. The program provides an approach to assisting people to support others facing a mental health crisis. The program offers a useful orientation to the content and process of communicating with a person experiencing a mental health disorder. Importantly, the program places a high priority on ensuring the safety of the person experiencing the mental health disorder. The mental health first aid model is not intended for mental health professionals but rather to those who provide general support to people experiencing mental illness. Nonetheless the underlying principles are relevant to the generalist social worker and social work student who is providing support to people experiencing mental health challenges. The themes of promoting safety, prevention, recovery and comfort are relevant to this Chapter on communication with people experiencing serious mental health challenges.

Recommended websites

The International Hearing Voices Network

http://www.intervoiceonline.org/about-intervoice

This is the website of the "Intervoice (International Hearing Voices Projects)." Intervoice supports the international movement of people who hear voices and see visions, and of those who support them. It aims to promote the inclusion of diverse voices in understanding the experiences of those who hear voices and see visions. The movement challenges the dominant biomedical constructions of mental health disorders and aims to include recognition of alternatives to the biomedical approach.

World Federation of Mental Health

http://wfmh.com/index.php

The World Federation of Mental Health was founded in 1948 and, according to its website, its mission includes:

> ➤ the prevention of mental and emotional disorders.

> ➤ the proper treatment and care of those with such disorders.

> ➤ the promotion of mental health.

The Federation describes itself as the only worldwide grassroots advocacy and public education organisation in the mental health field. Its membership includes mental professionals, people who use mental health services, family members and other people interested in promoting mental health and well-being. The website includes many useful resources for those communicating with people experiencing mental health disorders.

10

Differences and Disabilities Affecting Spoken Communication

Social workers often work alongside people who experience challenges with spoken communication. These communication challenges include difficulties in receiving, understanding or expressing oneself in speech. These challenges may be due to physical, sensory or cognitive differences. Many people experiencing challenges with spoken communication are able to communicate effectively when diverse modes of communication are incorporated into our practice (Johansson et al., 2012; Mueller, 2013; Pardoe, 2012). The importance our profession places on the working relationship as the vehicle through which social work practice occurs puts a particular onus on us to develop inclusive forms of communication (Simcock and Castle, 2016).

In this Chapter we focus on three types of barriers to spoken communication. These are challenges in:

1. receiving spoken communication. We refer to hearing or visual challenges or differences that can impact on people's capacity to receive spoken communication.

2. understanding spoken communication. Understanding spoken communications "refers to a person's ability to receive those same expressed messages from the other person." (Pardoe, 2012, p. 119). The term cognitive impairment is often used within the health and social work literature to refer difficulties in understanding are linked to problems in the way incoming information is received and how that information is processed by the person (Buekelman et al., 2007; Levy, 2011; Toglia, 2005).

3. expressing oneself in spoken language: "Expression refers to a person's ability to: make themselves understood, communicate needs and desires, share feelings and emotions, initiate and terminate engagements/encounters." (Pardoe, 2012, p. 119; Joahansson et al., 2010). Disabilities and differences associated with a range of causes including injury, illness and developmental delay can impact on a person's capacities to express themselves through spoken communication.

It is acknowledged that these communication challenges may be independent of each other. For example, a person who experiences hearing loss may experience difficulties in receiving spoken communication but may have no problems in understanding communication or expressing themselves in spoken words. However, a person may experience a combination of challenges. For example, a person with a cognitive impairment that affects their capacity to understand spoken communication may also experience challenges in expressing themselves in spoken words.

Inclusive practice and spoken communication

Many people have differences or impairments that affect their capacity to engage with spoken communication. For example, the World Federation of the Deaf (2016) notes that there are 70 million Deaf people worldwide. Furthermore, the World Health Organization (2017) reports that about 360 million people suffer some form of "disabling" hearing loss. In Chapter 8, we observed that many older adults experience hearing and visual losses. The National Aphasia Association (2017), based in the United States, asserts that over two million people in the United States and at least 250,000 people in the United Kingdom experience aphasia and consequent challenges in expressing themselves in spoken words. Challenges with spoken communication are commonplace and as such should be recognised in social workers' foundations for communication (Simcock and Castle, 2016).

People who experience challenges with spoken communication are often subject to social disadvantage, social exclusion and marginalisation. Communication challenges can significantly impact on quality of life (Beukelman et al., 2007; Johansson et al., 2012). In their review of research on the lived experience of hearing loss (Stephens and Kramer, 2010, p. 79) noted that "isolation, withdrawal, loneliness and depression" were much more common among this group than the general population. Similar findings have been reported with people experiencing challenges in expressing themselves in spoken communication (see Johansson et al., 2012).

We recognise too that the recent developments in Augmentative and Assistive Communication (AAC) technologies have substantially increased opportunities for people with a range of physical, sensory and cognitive differences to engage in spoken communication (Beukelman et al., 2007). Yet despite these developments, we note continuing problems with access, uptake and suitability of AAC (Beukelman et al., 2007). For example, the cost and operational features of some technologies, such as the non-human vocal tone of some vocal output communication aids, may act as barriers to access and uptake of the technology (Simcock and Castle, 2016). Social workers have an important role to play in ensuring equitable access to ACC and to advocating for continuing improvements in these technologies.

The United Nations Convention on the Rights of Persons with Disabilities (United Nations, 2006) asserts the importance of diverse modes of communication for creating social inclusion for people living with significant challenges with spoken communication. Article 21 of the Convention requires that:

> States Parties shall take all appropriate measures to ensure that persons with disabilities can exercise the right to freedom of expression and opinion, including the freedom to seek, receive and impart information and ideas on an equal basis with others and through all forms of communication of their choice, as defined in article 2 of the present Convention, including by:
>
> **a)** Providing information intended for the general public to persons with disabilities in accessible formats and technologies appropriate to different kinds of disabilities in a timely manner and without additional cost.
>
> **b)** Accepting and facilitating the use of sign languages, Braille, augmentative and alternative communication, and all other accessible means, modes and formats of communication of their choice by persons with disabilities in official interactions.

As the UN Convention outlines the right to accessible forms of communication is a human right. As a profession that champions human rights and social justice we need to confront the privilege accorded to spoken communication in our profession and in our societies more generally. To do this, we must develop knowledge and skills for communicating with people who face challenges in spoken communication or who prefer other modes of communication.

The Total Communication approach

Total Communication is an approach to communication that involves "different modalities," including speech, gesture, touch, drawing, pictures and writing, to supplement spoken communication (Johansson et al., 2012, p. 145). Mueller, (2013, p. 3138) observes that:

> Rather than imposing one's own preferred technique and maintaining that technique despite its inadequacies, Total Communication asks us to

be innovative and creative, and to look at all the alternative ways in which messages can be sent and received and employ the most effective approach for the person we are working with.

Total Communication requires us to be flexible and adaptive to the diverse needs of those with whom we communicate.

The Total Communication approach emerged in the 1960s initially among educators with Deaf children. These educators and advocates sought to develop more inclusive forms of education in which non-spoken communication, such as signed and written communication, was valued. The Total Communication approach has been extended to support the diverse communication needs of people experiencing a range of challenges with spoken communication including those with developmental disabilities, acquired brain injuries and conditions affecting communication capacities (see Johansson et al., 2012; Mueller, 2013; Pardoe, 2012). The approach increases our awareness of the value of diverse communication methods for supplementing spoken communication or even for replacing it.

People who experience communication challenges often face discrimination and stigma and so may be reluctant to acknowledge difficulties (Johansson et al., 2012; Stephens and Kramer, 2010). As skilled communicators we need then to be attuned and responsive to signs of communication challenges. As we discuss each type of challenge with spoken communication, we will consider also how we might recognise subtle signs that a person is experiencing challenges in receiving, understanding or expressing themselves. We turn first to challenges in receiving spoken communication.

Challenges in receiving spoken communication

In this section, we refer to impairments in a person's capacity to receive spoken communication. We refer to sensory challenges in hearing and sight. We turn first to hearing challenges. Hearing challenges can range from "minor" hearing loss referring to some loss of hearing range through to profound Deafness. Deafness "implies very little or no hearing" (WHO, 2017, p. 1). Deafness from birth is known as congenital deafness, while Deafness that occurs after birth is called adventitious deafness. Throughout this book, we use the capital D when referring to Deafness and the Deaf community to demonstrate respect for the position of the World Federation for the Deaf that Deafness is a difference rather than a disease or disability. People living with Deafness may identify as part of the Deaf community which has its own language, cultural traditions and norms. We support the position that members of the Deaf community should have access to their preferred language rather than have speaking culture imposed on them.

The term "hearing loss" refers impairments that significantly impact on a person's capacity to receive and process sounds. The WHO (2017, p. 1) defines "Disabling hearing loss" as "loss greater than 40 decibels (dB) in the better hearing ear in adults and a hearing loss greater than 30 dB in the better hearing ear in children." While hearing loss can occur at any age, its impact at different ages is likely to differ. Stephens and Kramer (2010) note that young and middle aged people with hearing loss were particularly affected by loneliness, "most likely due to limited communication with family and friends" (Stephens and Kramer, 2010, p. 91). They also observe that older people with hearing loss may experience poor responsiveness from service providers who may view this loss as part of normal ageing (see also Kampfe, 2015).

In a world where spoken communication is privileged, hearing loss can have profound social consequences. Studies indicate that hearing loss is associated with "changes in intimate contacts and family dynamics, social withdrawal and a reduced social network size" (Stephens and Kramer, 2010, p. 94). Even at relatively low levels of hearing loss, people may experience substantial negative impacts on their capacity to engage in conversation and to participate in social activities (Stephens and Kramer, 2010). People with hearing loss may find it difficult to engage in conversation as hearing impairments lead to difficulties in understanding the content, following the thread of conversation or engaging in usual turn taking.

A range of technologies are available to support people who are Deaf or who experience hearing loss to engage in spoken communication including personal devices, such as hearing aids and communication technologies as well as environmental supports, such as hearing loops. Stephens and Kramer (2010, p. 174) note that " Electromagnetic loop systems have been in use for many years and remain invaluable in public places, where a range of listeners with hearing aids switched to one of the loop pick-up systems can use them." As advocates for social inclusion, social workers should ensure our workplaces and service centres should be accessible to people experiencing hearing loss and deafness. Access can be increased through improved availability of technologies such as hearing loops and enhanced telecommunications facilities.

Many people who experience hearing loss already adapt their communication in ways that enable them to supplement the spoken word with other cues, such as reading the speaker's lips and facial gestures (Evans and Shaw, 2012). From a Total Communication perspective, it is important that the non-deaf conversation partner also adapt their communication to support communication with a person experiencing hearing loss. Better Hearing Australia, Victoria, (2016) proposes the H.E.L.P. acronym to assist in communication with people who experience hearing challenges, this refers to:

➤ Speak with your Head up.

➤ Keep your Eyes on your partner's face.

➤ Learn to monitor the speech of speech and slow down.

➤ Pronounce words clearly.

Supporting communication through the use of pictures, gestures and written communication is often helpful. Being attentive to reducing background noise is also important to supporting communication with people who experience hearing difficulties. Furthermore as hearing loss often involves the upper sound register, it may help to slightly lower your vocal tone, though it is important to retain your normal speaking voice.

In this section we have focused on improving the access of people with hearing loss to spoken communication. We recognise the concerns of many within the Deaf community that the expectation that Deaf people should adapt to spoken communication denies the culture, identity and values of this community. From the perspective of the Deaf community, adaptions of this nature fail to address the privilege accorded to spoken communication. It is this privilege that contributes to discrimination towards people experiencing Deafness. The World Federation for the Deaf proposes that access to Sign Language for all communication, information and education is a basic human right of Deaf people (Murray, 2015). As the World Federation for the Deaf (2016) states:

> Sign language is at the core of Deaf people's lives; sign language makes accessibility for Deaf people possible; without accessibility, Deaf people will be isolated. Thus, full enjoyment of human rights for Deaf people is based on the recognition and respect for Deaf culture and identity. Everywhere in the world, language creates culture and vice versa.

Accordingly, we should ensure that service users have access to Sign Language interpreters. As we discussed in relation to linguistic differences in spoken communication (see Chapter 2), the presence of Sign Language Interpreters is vital to enable the participation of Deaf people in our communication with them.

While we acknowledge the concerns of the Deaf community about the privilege accorded spoken communication, we also recognise that many people who experience hearing loss wish to engage with spoken communication (Stephens and Kramer, 2010). Indeed, the motivation to continue to use spoken communication is likely to be strong among those who have experienced hearing loss over time, who have maintained some level of hearing, and those whose close relationships are with people who use spoken communication. While we recognise the many of the strategies we have discussed, continue to privilege spoken communication they nonetheless have value for promoting the social inclusion of many people we meet in our work who experience hearing loss and Deafness.

We turn now to visual challenges and their impact on people's capacity to receive spoken communication. Visual challenges from low vision to blindness can also interfere with a person's capacity to engage in spoken communication. Non-verbal communication is an important component of communication and a person with visual impairment is likely to experience some limitations on their capacity to recognise non-verbal cues. This can create challenges in interpreting meaning and in engaging in conversational turn taking.

A Total Communication approach involves supplementing visual components with other forms of communication. Vision Australia (2016) recommends the use of additional spoken cues to facilitate conversation with people who experience visual impairment including:

➤ letting the person you are present and also making them aware of any third party to the conversation. We should not assume that the person knows us by our voice.

➤ similarly, letting the person know if you are moving away.

➤ during conversation, remembering to use the person's name to specifically direct turn taking to them. "Susan, what is your view on this?"

➤ remembering to use your usual non-verbal communication as this affects your verbal communication and, in addition, the visually impaired person may have some capacity to see or to sense aspects of this communication.

➤ using accurate and specific information when giving instructions; for example, "Please sit down on this chair which is on your right"

To support communication, it is important to ensure that any written information is formats that are accessible to people with low vision or who are blind. For those with low vision, larger print formats may be helpful, while braille is likely to be needed for those who are blind.

Combined hearing and visual losses

Complex communication issues arise where a person experiences both hearing and visual challenges (Dammeyer, 2010). The degree of these challenges and the time of their onset will impact the degree of communication challenges. One reason these challenges can be profound, is that often a person with a sensory challenge will develop greater acuity in other senses to compensate for hearing or visual challenge. By contrast, those with dual impairments have less opportunity to compensate through the use of visual or hearing senses.

The communication challenges are especially intense for those who experience congenital "deafblindness" which is: "a specific impairment characterised mainly by severe communication problems due to a combined vision and hearing impairment that has existed since birth or at least prior to language acquisition" (Netværk Øst for Praksisledere, 2015, p. 4). Research also indicates that people who experience combined profound hearing and visual challenges are also more likely to experience decreased cognitive function compared to those with only a visual or hearing impairment (Dammeyer, 2010).

Generally a person who experiences congenital deaf-blindness will require a support provider with specialist training "in assistive aids, tactile and bodily forms of communication and how to structure a learning environment that accommodates tactile-bodily perception." (Netværk Øst for Praksisledere, 2015, p. 7). Unless we have developed this specialist communication capacity, as social workers we will need to engage an intermediary, sometimes referred to as an "intervenor," with these specialist skills (Simcock and Castle, 2016, p. 131). It is important that in engaging with the intermediaries we continue to keep our focus on the person who is the primary service user.

Practice exercises: Reflecting on your responsiveness to communication differences

Exercise 1

➤ Describe your natural speaking pitch, speed, and tone.

➤ How might your natural pitch, speech or tone be a challenge for someone experiencing problems in receiving spoken communication?

▶

Exercise 2

The purpose of this exercise is to help you to reflect on how you can communicate in ways that are accessible to people experiencing sensory differences. Divide into pairs or groups of three with one person being the person experiencing a sensory challenge. To simulate the experience of sensory challenge, participants may create a physical barrier to either their hearing or visual senses. For example, to simulate the experience of hearing loss, the person could insert earphones linked to a device conveying low level "chatter" thus making it difficult to hear others. To simulate the experience of sight loss associated with macular degeneration, a person can put on sunglasses with a dot of Vaseline smeared in the centre of the outside of each lens (Kampfe, 2015). The conversation partners are then to engage in a conversation with the person experiencing the communication challenge. Try maintaining a conversation for five minutes. Then reflect on:

➤ how the tone and pace of the conversational partner(s) supported or impeded communication.

➤ points of frustration in the communication for the person experiencing the challenge.

➤ strategies that helped to facilitate communication.

The roles should be rotated so that each participant has the opportunity to experience the sensory challenge and each has the opportunity to play the role of conversation partner.

It is important to acknowledge that simulating the experience of sensory loss is not the same as actually experiencing the loss. Following simulation, we can remove the hearing or visual barriers to communication in a way that a person experiencing these losses cannot. Nonetheless, people undertaking simulations may still experience some distress or discomfort. It is likely to be helpful then to discuss what the experience was like and the emotions that were evoked as part of de-briefing from the exercise.

Challenges in understanding communication: Cognitive impairment

Cognitive impairments refer to ongoing challenges with any of the cognitive functions that enable us "to acquire and use new information" (Toglia, 2005, p. 37). Toglia (2005, p. 37) states that cognitive impairment or dysfunction can be summarised as representing core deficiencies in any of the following domains:

a) The ability to select and use efficient processing strategies to organize and structure incoming information; b) the ability to anticipate, monitor, or verify the accuracy of performance; c) the ability to access previous knowledge when needed; and d) flexible application of knowledge to a variety of situations.

Cognitive impairments refer to challenges associated with attention, memory, organising information, visuospatial function, language, processing information and in problem-solving (Toglia, 2005; see also Beukelman et al., 2007).

The degree to which a cognitive impairment will impact on a person's capacity to communicate relates both to the nature and degree of the impairment as well as to the environment in which the communication occurs. For example, a person who is experiencing dementia related cognitive decline may be able to recall information such as ages or names of family members when in their home environment but may find it difficult to do so when asked in an unfamiliar environment, such as a hospital. Similarly, the degree of impairment will impact on the person's capacity to interpret and process information.

Davis and Collier (2015, p. 125) note that "Cognitive impairment is not associated with any one particular disease or with any one age group." Indeed, cognitive impairments can be associated with a broad range of conditions and life experiences including: some developmental disability, some forms of mental illness, acquired brain injury and disease particularly dementia (see Kampfe, 2015; Levy, 2011; Wolf and Baum, 2011). The person may have experienced cognitive impairment since birth, or a person may experience as sudden loss of cognitive capacity as a result of illness or injury, or a person may experience age related cognitive decline over time as is often the case with dementias.

Cognitive impairments contribute to significant challenges in how a person understands and responds to communication. Davis and Collier (2015, p. 126) point out:

> The very nature of cognitive impairment is that the deficit to mental function-ing make it difficult for the person to relate to others in terms of articulating meanings and interpreting what is being communicated.

These challenges in processing information and interpreting meaning can create several barriers in developing and maintaining a working relation-ship. First, the person with a cognitive impairment may find it difficult to understand our communication. Second, this in turn can contribute to a range of distressing emotional responses such as frustration and fear.

The person's capacity to respond to us may be affected in ways that create challenges for the development and maintenance of the work-ing alliance. It is noted that when people experience some forms of developmental disorder or acquired brain injury, their communication may become "disorganised, confused and disinhibited" (Evans and Shaw, 2012, p. 126). Accepted social conventions around choice of topic and turn taking may be disrupted making it difficult to develop a shared sense of purpose (Evans and Shaw, 2012).

There is a great deal of literature on communication with people experiencing cognitive impairments arising from specific conditions or injuries (Hannon and Clift, 2010; Pardoe, 2012; Davis and Collier, 2015). Across this literature a number of key themes emerge in identifying whether a person is experiencing a cognitive challenge and also in responding to those challenges. Here we have attempted to synthesise that literature.

We turn first to how we can identify whether a person might be experiencing a cognitive impairment. In some instances, we will be informed via case notes, referrals, the person's support person or the person themselves that they experience cognitive impairment. However, in other instances it may not be obvious and the person experiencing these issues may be reluctant to reveal these challenges. Furthermore for a range of reasons, particularly embarrassment or fear of discrimination, the person may conceal cognitive challenges.

Hannon and Clift (2010, p. 104) outline several indicators we can use to identify if a person has a cognitive impairment related to a learning difficulty. The factors they identify are also relevant to indicators of cognitive impairments due to other causes such as brain injury or dementia, these include:

➤ the person chooses the first or last choices offered or the choice that involves the least negotiation. For example, if you ask whether the person would like to meeting Monday, Tuesday or another time, they are most likely to choose Monday. This may be due to memory or language processing difficulties so that they choose the most easy to recall option.

➤ the person has word-finding difficulties in relation to people, objects or events which should be familiar to them. For example, referring to their son-in-law as Leila's husband rather than by his name. The person may also frequently use generic terms such as "you know" or "thingy" to refer to the people, object or event with which they are familiar.

➤ repetitiveness. The person repeats stories without seeming to be aware of having done so can be a sign of cognitive impairment.

➤ acquiescence. Giving answers that they believe the person wants to hear, this may include agreeing to anything the other person asks of them.

> ➤ the person finds it difficult to make choices. To reduce the challenges associated with decision making it is important to provide the person with time to process the information you have provided.

> ➤ Lack of emotional responsiveness. People with some forms of developmental disability, acquired brain injuries or dementias can experience challenges in articulating or identifying emotions.

Facilitating communication

The tone and content of our communication matters for facilitating communication with a person who is experiencing challenges in processing spoken communication. It is important then that:

> ➤ before talking, ensure you have the person's attention. Use the person's name and/or make eye contact to make sure you have their attention.

> ➤ we pace our speech at the appropriate speed to enable the person to process the information and leave room for silence. "Try to keep the nature rhythm and tone of your voice, but just allow more time for the information to be processed" (Pardoe, 2012, p. 120).

> ➤ we are straightforward, our questions should be direct but not closed. Closed questions can lead to incorrect responses as it offers or even forces a choice between options which the person may not fully comprehend.

> ➤ we avoid using abstractions, colloquialisms, metaphors and puns as these can contribute to confusion. What may appear to be everyday terms such as "hop on the bus" or "catch a cab" can create confusion for those whose cognitive challenges lead them to literal interpretations (Diack and Cohen, 2008).

> ➤ similarly, it is important we avoid technical terms and to "check and use the terminology the person uses." (Hannon and Clift, 2010, p. 107). Visual cues can be helpful, pointing to relevant visual cues, photos, or parts of the body relevant to the communication.

> ➤ use consistent terms throughout the conversation. The use of diverse terms for the same concept, can lead to confusion. For example, if you talk about the person's doctor, always use the same name, such as Dr Watson and avoid changing the name such as interchange with other terms such as your "psychiatrist" or "John" (Pardoe, 2012).

➤ we aim for direct communication. Seek to keep sentences short and straightforward. "Negatives in sentences can be easily misunderstood" (Hannon and Clift, 2010, p. 107).

➤ we avoid closed questions that can lead to yes/no responses that are in fact meaningless.

➤ we demonstrate a commitment to inclusion by allowing the person to time to receive, process and respond. Never speak over the person and try not finish the person's sentences (Davis and Collier, 2015, p. 129).

➤ we check concepts. This involves asking the person to tell us have what they have understood. If we believe the person has misunderstood our questions we can also ask the question a second time using different words.

Practice exercise: Expressing ourselves clearly

In communicating with a person experiencing a cognitive impairment, be as straightforward as possible. This means avoiding long and convoluted sentences and avoiding puns or abstractions. It also means being consistent in our language use. Consider the following two examples.

Example 1

It is a public holiday next week and the centre isn't open so we won't be having a playgroup meeting, but I can find other activities for you and your son, David, to do.

Example 2

There is no playgroup on Tuesday. It is a public holiday on that day. Would you like me to find something else for you to do with your son David on Tuesday?

Difficulties with spoken expression

A person's capacity to express themselves in spoken words can be influenced by a range of impairments. Our focus in this section is on communication with people who experience challenges to their capacity to express themselves in words. These challenges are independent of cognitive difficulties. People experiencing impairments in spoken communication may have no trouble in receiving or understanding communication, the challenges they experience may relate only to expressing themselves in speech. Yet we also acknowledge that challenges in spoken expression may co-exist with challenges in receiving or processing spoken communication. For example a person with cerebral palsy who has difficulty with spoken expression may also have hearing problems. Our point is that challenges leading to problems in spoken expression should not be taken to infer difficulties in receiving or processing information without further evidence of co-existing impairments.

We refer to three forms of physical processes that contribute to people experiencing difficulty in expressing themselves in spoken words. The first set of challenges concerns difficulties in co-ordination of the muscles required for speech. The biomedical term "dysarthria" is used to refer "damage to the part of the brain that controls the muscle actions that produce speech...Impairments include loss of voluntary control of muscles, muscle weakness, difficulty controlling lips and swallowing problems" (Evans and Shaw, 2012, p. 128). As a result the person's speech may be slurred, slow and difficult to comprehend. This is a common feature of some health challenges. For example, approximately 90 per cent of people with cerebral palsy experience dysarthria (Schölderle et al., 2016). Other conditions such as motor neurone diseases, brain injuries and brain diseases also can result in dysarthria.

A second challenge is where a brain injury interferes with a person's capacity to express themselves in words. The bio-medical term "aphasia" is used to describe one way in which a brain injury may impact on a person's capacity to communicate (Beukelman et al., 2007). Aphasia involves a range of problems in language comprehension and expression including difficulties in expressing more than one word or phrase at a time or retrieving the correct word and placing "it in the correct order in a sentence" (Evans and Shaw, 2012, p. 127). In their study of people with aphasia, Johansson et al. (2012, pp. 147–148) found that "making small-talk was quite easy, but that it was more difficult or even impossible to engage in deeper discussions." This can create particular problems in communication with health and social welfare professionals where the focus may be on exploration of health or psychosocial concerns.

A third challenge is where a person experiences "damage to the motor planning area that is responsible for the sequence of actions that occur during speech, writing or gesture" (Evans and Shaw, 2012, p. 128). This condition known as "Apraxia of speech" occurs when a person experiences a disruption in transmitting the message from their brain to their mouth (American Speech-Language-Hearing Association, 2017). Apraxia can arise in children and can also occur in adults. Among adults a common cause is stroke and traumatic brain injury, dementia and other neurological disorders (American Speech-Language-Hearing Language Association, 2017).

People who experience challenges in their capacity to express themselves may experience misunderstanding, discrimination and isolation. They often report experiencing social isolation as a result of their limited capacity to express themselves. In a study of people with aphasia's communication support needs, found most informants "appreciated the CP's [conversation partners] use of supportive conversational strategies because that facilitated comprehension and communication." (Johansson et al., 2012, p. 150).

Strategies for communicating well with a person experiencing challenges with spoken communication include:

➤ exploring with the person the best means for supporting communication. Seeking support and advice from the person's support person and other professionals, particularly speech professionals involved with the person. Naturally such advice is only sought with the permission of the person concerned.

➤ consistent with the Total Communication philosophy, supporting spoken communication with visual means, such as drawings, figures and objects and with active use of expressive facial and other non-verbal gestures, such as pointing at relevant objects, signs or symbols to support mutual understanding.

➤ creating a supportive environment. As with other forms of communication challenge, minimising or eliminating background noise is important.

➤ using closed questions can be helpful as the person may find it challenging to answer open questions (Johansson et al., 2012). Whereas where people experience cognitive impairments the use of yes or no questions may lead to confusion, the reverse is the case for people with challenges in spoken expression.

➤ taking time to understand and become accustomed to the person's communication. Disability Employment and Advocacy Services (ND, p. 1) note "that the speech rhythms and voice pitch of someone who has vocal impairment are often very different from those of someone who does not. Once you become familiar with these differences, comprehending the person's speech will be much easier."

➤ allowing more time for communication. People with difficulties in spoken expression often need more time to express themselves. Avoid finishing sentences for the other person or cutting off prematurely.

Putting it all together

When communicating with a person experiencing communication challenges, all the same principles for building the working alliance as outlined in previous Chapters. We need to continue to:

> ➤ listen actively.

> ➤ track the communication through paraphrasing, clarifying and summarising.

> ➤ demonstrate empathy.

> ➤ adopt an open and engaged body posture.

People living with communication challenges associated with disability, illness or injury may be subject to misunderstandings and prejudices by human service professionals. These prejudices can result in workers failing to recognise the communication capacities and rights of people who experience challenges in communicating in spoken or written form. To communicate respectfully we need to be mindful of acknowledging the person's rights and capacities as partners in communication with us.

We need to respond the person holistically, meaning that we should seek to understand the issues that concern them, as well as their strengths. We should be mindful of the language we use to discuss the person and any differences they experience. We should then avoid terms such as "suffering with a disability" or "disabled person" that imply a negative view of the disability or which encompass the person's entire identity by their disability or differences (Simcock and Castle, 2016).

Accepting and respecting differences in communication approaches is important to build the mutual understanding on which the working alliance is founded (Pardoe, 2012). Broussine (2012, p. 105) reminds us of the need to be open to a diverse range of ways in which people with different abilities may engage in a communication encounter:

An individual with autism may give limited or no eye contact, but this should not be misinterpreted as not being interested or aware of their surroundings; a physical impairment can result in idiosyncratic body language that can easily be misunderstood; and someone with a hearing or visual impairment will have problems attending appropriately. Many people with learning disabilities may exhibit some of these non-verbal behaviours and they can compromise understanding, leading to premature termination of a "conversation" or contact, which in turn compromises the caring relationship.

We should accept differences in communication without judgement and without seeking to correct perceived imperfections (Pardoe, 2012).

Consistent with the Total Communication approach we should work with the person to develop and recognise strategies that work in support communication with them. The use of props to support spoken communication, such as pictures, gestures and writing are repeatedly noted as important to supporting communication with people experiencing a range of challenges (Broussine and Scarborough, 2012; Evans and Shaw, 2012). Pardoe (2012, p. 118) notes: "All forms of communication have value and each might be appropriate in particular circumstances and for particular individuals ... might be the most appropriate form of contact and communication."

Other approaches for demonstrating understanding and responsiveness to the person experiencing challenges with spoken communication include:

➤ recognising that emotional and physical state of the person. Communication can be exhausting for people living with challenges such as disability, injury or disease.

➤ ensuring we have the person's attention before commencing active communication.

➤ adjusting our pace, tone and pitch to promote clarity and accessible expression.

➤ allowing time for the communication to occur remembering that a person with communication challenges may need more time to receive, process and/or respond to the person with whom they are communicating.

➤ recognising the continuing importance of non-verbal communication. Do not interfere with the person's space without their permission. Pardoe (2012, p. 118) notes that the use of pre-verbal/pre-intentional communication or early gestures – such as touch, eye-contact, smiles and other significant facial gestures, pointing or indicating" can be helpful.

➤ ensuring information is available in a variety of accessible formats, which may include large print, colour-coded information, picture symbols and photographs (SCOPE, 2015).

Friends or family members and other support people may play a significant role in life of the person living with challenges in spoken communication. The term communication partner is used to refer to someone who has understands the communication needs of the person living with the communication challenges (see Johansson et al., 2012). The communication partner may offer a bridge to the social world (see Johansson et al., 2012). While we should recognise the service user as primary focus, involving the communication partner(s) can also be important. The communication partner may be able to provide insights into the best strategies for adapting communication to the needs of the people experiencing challenges to spoken communication.

Creating a physical environment which is welcoming, quiet and calming has been found to support communication with people experiencing challenges to receiving, understanding or expressing themselves (see Vision Australia, 2016; Johansson et al.,2012). People with some forms of developmental disability, particularly autism spectrum disorder, may be distressed by visually stimulating environments where there are lots of bright colours or lights. If a person is experiencing challenges in engaging, understanding or responding to communication, it is advisable to ask the person about the environment that would be helpful to them and take the initiative by assisting the person to move to a more private, quiet and calm environment.

Conclusion

The right to accessible communication is a fundamental human right. As social workers we need to be responsive to the challenges people experience in receiving and understanding spoken communication and expressing themselves through speech. As a profession that has long depended on spoken communication as a core vehicle for creating and maintaining the working relationship there is much we have to learn about adapting our communication approaches. The Total Communication approach offers a framework for adaptable communication that is responsive to the needs of differently abled people. In this Chapter we have considered practical strategies for communication with people with diverse needs and capacities.

Review Questions

1. What is the Total Communication approach?

2. How can you create an environment which facilitates spoken communication with people experiencing challenges with hearing and with vision?

3. What are three strategies you might use to assess whether a person with whom you are communicating experiences difficulty in understanding spoken expression?

4. What are three strategies you can use to promote effective communication with a person who finds it difficult to express themselves in spoken words?

Practice exercises

Exercise 1

Imagine that you work at a neighbourhood house providing general information, support and referral to people living in the community. The house offers a variety of social support activities, such as playgroups, art spaces, and literacy and numeracy support. Your service recently conducted a community survey that indicated there are many people living in the area who have sensory challenges but, as you are aware, very few of these people visit the community services centre. What strategies could you establish to ensure that the neighbourhood house is a welcoming environment for people living with sensory challenges?

Practice exercise 2

Imagine that you work as a social worker providing support services to people at risk of homelessness. You are just about to meet Peter, a man in his mid-40s who is well known to your service but this is the first time you are meeting him. Peter moved to the area about a year ago following the death of his mother from a heart attack. Peter's mother had been his carer, a role she shared with Peter's father until Peter's father died three years ago. Peter has had a mild cognitive impairment due to a birth injury. The impairment affects him in a variety of ways. He has trouble with processing information, has limited literacy and has difficulty maintaining social relationships. Following his mother's death, Peter moved away from the regional town where he and his parents had lived to search for work in the area where you are based. Peter says that he had previously worked in manual jobs such as basic farm work but has not had paid work in the last five years. Case-notes indicate that Peter has difficulty in maintaining housing and has over the past 12 months moved house on four occasions. It is also noted that his living conditions are unhygienic, with a worker who recently visited his room stating that there was rotting food and rubbish throughout the apartment. The worker has noted that Peter's main concern is with finding work. Peter is seeing you today after an argument with a person at the boarding house where he has been living for the past month. Peter says he needs somewhere else to live and, even more importantly he says, he needs to find a job.

➢ What do you see as the main communication challenges you might encounter?

➢ How would you manage these challenges?

➢ How would you build an effective working alliance with Peter?

Recommended Books

Broussine, E. & Scarborough, K. (Eds.) (2012). *Supporting people with learning disabilities in health & social care* London: Sage. doi: 10.4135/9781446288191

This edited collection provides a comprehensive introduction to policy and practice with people experiencing learning disabilities. The book includes Chapters on forming working alliances with people experiencing learning disability and their families. These principles are applied to a wide variety of contexts including mental health, health and palliative care and in criminal justice.

Katz, N. (Ed.) (2011). *Cognition, occupation and participation across the lifespan: Neuroscience, neurorehabilitation and models of intervention in occupational therapy*. Bethesda, MD: American Occupational Therapy Association.

Although written for occupational therapists, this edited collection provides an excellent overview of current research on cognitive challenges and responses for improving the quality of life of people living with these challenges. The book provides a useful evidence base in bio-psycho-social aspects of cognitive disabilities and differences.

Simcock, P. & Castle, R. (2016). *Social work and disability: Social work theory and practice*. Cambridge: Polity.

This book offers a critical analysis of the disability and practical guide to collaborative practice with people living with disabilities.

Recommended websites

The American Foundation for the Blind

http://www.afb.org/

The American Foundation for the Blind is an advocacy network for people living with vision impairment and blindness. The Foundation's priorities include policy reform to promote services and equal access to resources and services for people living with vision impairment. A key objective of the Foundation is to remove the technological and systemic barriers to prevent people living with vision loss from fully participating in society. The website includes tip sheets for people living with vision loss and for the people around them as well as information on emerging technological aids for assisting those with vision loss to live independent and socially engaged lives.

The International Association for the Scientific Study of Intellectual and Developmental Disabilities

https://www.iassidd.org/

The International Association for the Scientific Study of Intellectual and Developmental Disabilities is the first and only world-wide group dedicated to the scientific study of intellectual disability. The website includes a range of reports and resources for promoting the human rights and dignity of people living intellectual disability.

World Federation of the Deaf

https://wfdeaf.org

World Federation of the Deaf is an international body advocating for the human rights of Deaf people and for the recognition of sign language in all aspects of life. The website includes information and resources for respectful communication with people who are Deaf.

11

Becoming a Skilled Communicator: Key Themes and Future Directions

Skilled communication enables us to form working relationships with people at points of distress and difficulty and with people who have diverse communication capacities and needs. In this Chapter we summarise key themes of skilled communication. We will also discuss future directions for building the communication base of social work.

We recognise communication in social work involves both art and science. The development of a working alliance is, in part, a creative act that involves the thoughtful and adaptive use of self. The foundations of the working alliance are formed even before we meet the service user as we critically analyse our practice context, the capacities we bring to the situation and as we anticipate the service user's likely abilities and needs. The formation of the working alliance requires the social worker to demonstrate: non-possessive warmth; genuineness; accurate empathy; and helpfulness (Sheldon and Macdonald, 2009; see also Healy and Darlington, 2009). We can draw on the formal communication knowledge and skill base of our profession to demonstrate these qualities. Yet we need also to relate authentically to the service user in ways that build on our unique communication capacities as well as those of the service user.

While there is an artistic element to the formation of the working alliance, science is important too. By science we refer to the large and diverse body of empirical research in the social and behavioural sciences including in social work that can inform the communication base of social work.

The emerging body of social and behavioural sciences research on emotions is an area of particular interest to us. We acknowledge that social work has a long tradition of recognising emotions, particularly emotions that support the working alliance such as empathy (see Folgheraiter, 2004; Jensen et al., 2010). Over the past three decades a body of research on emotions has emerged that is challenging our profession to extend its understanding of the contribution of emotions to many aspects of social work (see Howe, 2008; Munro, 2011). This research is challenging the dualism between rationality and emotions by highlighting the value of emotions to all aspects of practice. Keinemans (2014, p. 2179) argues that rather than seek to disregard or suppress our emotions, "social work professionals should examine the emotions they experience in daily practice, as their [our] moral judgements, decisions and actions are influenced by them." This research draws our attention also to heightened emotional states, including "negative" states, as part of the spectrum of human emotional experience (Fox, 2008). We can see then, that the capacity to understand and respond to heightened emotional states in ourselves and in others needs to be an essential component of the communication base of social work. Developing our capacity to communicate skilfully in response to people experiencing heightened emotions is important to strengthening the working alliance and to build our confidence and resilience in the face of challenging communication encounters.

A second theme is that we recognise diversity in people's communication capacities and needs as a usual condition of social work practice. Regardless of the contexts in which we practice, we will communicate with people from different cultural and linguistic groups to our own, with people at different points in the life course, with people who experience mental health challenges and people for whom spoken communication is either challenging or a non-preferred means of communication. The skilled communicator needs a broad foundation of communication knowledge and skills to build and maintain the working alliance with people in diverse circumstances and with varied needs and preferences.

Recognition of diverse communication capacities involves unsettling some of our profession's taken for granted assumptions about communication. One such assumption is that spoken communication is an adequate mode of communication in the majority of social work interactions. In this book, we have highlighted that many people face challenges with spoken communication and that the skilled communicator needs to be responsive to the need to supplement or replace spoken communication in many communication encounters. While challenges in relation to spoken communication may be most apparent in some circumstances, such as where a person experiences a sensory loss or cognitive impairment, people may experience many other barriers to accessing or processing spoken communication or in expressing themselves through talk. For example, where people experience heightened emotional states or mental health disorders their capacity to receive or process spoken communication may be limited. As a separate illustration, we have pointed out that children and young people often demonstrate a preference for creative communication in which spoken communication is supplemented by play or artistic expression. Similarly, as we have demonstrated in Chapter 8, older adults may benefit from communication strategies that are responsive to the changing sensory capacities frequently associated with the ageing process.

The Total Communication strategies, discussed in Chapter 10, are relevant to consider in all communication situations. Total Communication involves supplementing spoken communication with other modalities which may include written information, use of gestures and creative techniques, such as the use of pictures (Johansson et al., 2012, p. 145). For example, a child protection social worker might supplement a discussion of safety goals by providing a service user with a visual chart that they can take with them to monitor their own progress against agreed goals. In practice many social workers may intuitively adapt their practice to complement spoken communication with other modalities. The Total Communication philosophy calls on us to do so more deliberately and systematically (see Chapter 10).

Our third theme is core principles of communication with people facing life challenges. We have returned in several Chapters to four key principles of communication to build and maintain the working alliance in social work practice. These principles are predicated on our recognition that in social work practice we are often communicating with people who are experiencing life challenges and this is frequently accompanied by elevated emotional states. The four principles we suggest are:

(a) communicating confidence, calmness and non-reactivity. By communicating confidence and calmness we can reassure the service user of our capacity to be helpful and emotionally available to them. We refer to non-reactivity to reflect on our and others' emotional states and to incorporate this awareness into our response in ways that support the working alliance (see also Kitchener et al., 2013; Plumb, 2015). As we have highlighted, confidence, calmness and non-reactivity are vital for several reasons including that: the worker is communicating a sense of self-confidence and confidence in the other person; the modelling of calm behaviour encourages the other person to do the same; by regulating our own emotional state we also promote our capacity to use problem-solving skills and act in a thoughtful manner as we are informed by our emotions but not controlled by them.

(b) promoting physical and emotional safety. Social workers often communicate with people facing acute emotional distress associated with life challenges. The challenges can often trigger a fight or flight response in the person. We can reduce the impact of these responses on communication by creating an environment of physical and emotional safety. We refer to creating an environment that is calming, welcoming and supportive of the person's communication needs. This includes reducing the amount of stimulation in the environment through limiting ambient noise or other intrusions. We create a welcoming and supportive environment by removing symbols or signs that might be emotional triggers for a person, for example, political or religious symbols should be avoided except where the person is aware and has sought out a service aligned with a specific political or religious approach. Creating an emotionally safe environment also involves the worker being alert and responsive to the other's emotional reactions to them or their environment (see Havig, 2008). Consistent with the Total Communication approach we need also to ensure that there is sufficient light and appropriate seating arrangements for the person to view visual cues to support communication, that written material is in accessible formats, and that protocols are in place for arranging interpreter support or culturally advisory support if needed.

(c) collaborative communication. Consistent with our profession's emphasis on partnership in practice, we seek to involve the service user in negotiating our shared purpose and the processes by which it will be achieved.

(d) prioritising empowerment. We aim here to maximise service user's control over their situation. This means supporting the service user's development of knowledge and skills to respond to their situation and to enhance their involvement in the decision-making at each step of the social work process.

Finally, we recognise that social work is an emotionally demanding occupation. We need to develop emotional resilience both to promote our own longevity in the field and also to ensure that we remain emotionally available to the service user. As discussed in Chapter 2, supportive supervision is important to promoting emotional resilience and practice knowledge and skill. Supportive supervision involves emotional support and also enables the social worker to critically reflect on their practice to develop their knowledge and skill (Karvinen-Niinikoski, 2004; Saxby, 2016). Supportive supervision has been found to reduce burnout and turnover (Saxby, 2016).

Future directions

We turn now to consider future directions in developing the communication knowledge and skill base of social work. We turn first to broadening the evidence base of communication in social work. In this book we have sought to demonstrate how some of the emerging insights from the growing body of social and behavioural research on emotions can inform skilled communication in social work. Other social work researchers have drawn too on this rich body of research on emotions to build knowledge for practice (see Howe, 2008; Keinemans, 2014; Munro, 2011). We believe that more work is needed to examine how this diverse body of research may contribute to the evidence base of our practice. We also consider that our profession also has much to offer in building interdisciplinary understanding of emotions and emotional regulation given our profession's exposure to people experiencing a wide variety of life challenges and the emotional states generated by these experiences.

Communication research is another area of potential exchange between social work and other social and behavioural science disciplines. Communication research is the study of the processes and strategies through which people communicate with each other and includes a range of methodologies such as conversation analysis, discourse analysis and semiotic analysis. Despite social work's emphasis on communication in practice, as a discipline we draw very little on communication research and also make very limited contribution to it (Hall, Slembrouck and Sarangi, 2006). This has led to gaps in our knowledge about how social workers effectively respond to commonplace but challenging communication encounters. Similar absences have been noted in other health and human services disciplines. For example, psychiatry researchers McCabe and Priebe (2008, pp. 404–405) note: "Despite the fact that communication about psychotic symptoms is a frequent challenge and regarded as fascinating by many clinicians, there is little systematic, theoretically informed training on how clinicians should respond." It seems that scope exists for social workers to contribute to interdisciplinary collaborations in developing a much needed evidence base about communication in contexts of challenge and diversity.

The role of ICT

The role of ICT in social work communication is another area requiring development. We acknowledge the growing use of Information and Communication technologies (ICT) in social work and the substantial controversy about whether the communication skills used in face to face interaction directly translate to technology mediated interactions (see Chan and Holosko, 2016; Haxell, 2012; Richards and Viganó, 2013; Shaw, 2012)

ICT is a broad term referring to a range of technologies that support communication and includes technologies such as video conferencing, cell phones including texting facilities, chat rooms, purpose built websites and email. In the context of social work and human services, ICT mediated service delivery refers to services delivered primarily through ICT, such as e-counselling or text based counselling, and services enhanced by ICT such as purpose built websites to support social work interventions (Chan and Holosko, 2016; Harrison and Melville, 2009). ICT also offers many advantages in service delivery particularly in terms of increasing convenience and access to many groups of service users (Harrison and Melville, 2009; Richards and Viganó, 2013). Furthermore, while the evidence base is slim, a small number of studies suggest comparable outcomes in face to face and online human services (Chan and Holosko, 2016; Richards and Viganó, 2013).

ICT is transforming human service delivery in ways never before thought possible. For example, Haxell (2012) describes a youth counselling service in New Zealand that has offered counselling by text messaging since 2004. Similarly in their systematic review of ICT social work intervention, Chan and Holosko (2016) refer to enhanced community education programs designed to enable service users to access self-paced education packages, engage in online discussion with other service users and with service providers, and access a range of web-based resources. In addition, as we have discussed in Chapters 8 and 10 of this book, advances in augmentative and assistive technologies have provided new communication opportunities for people with sensory losses and differences.

Despite the opportunities provided by ICT, there are also reservations about its extension into social work and other areas of human services practice. One issue is the "digital divide," referring to the much reduced access to ICT experienced by some populations such as disadvantaged and geographically remote populations, compared to more advantaged groups (Shaw, 2012). The digital divide means that some of those most likely to benefit from the convenience of ICT mediated social work services are less likely to be able to access them. Concerns exist too around privacy considerations and the potential of ICT to extend State surveillance of vulnerable populations (Harrison and Melville, 2009). ICT communications often leave a "digital footprint" that is a record of the communication between the social worker and the service user that is not usually the case in face to face interactions. Concerns are raised also about the utility of ICT for complex communication situations. For example, Hadziabdic and Hjelm (2013, p. 21) say language interpretation is best offered in face to face mode, because this mode offers superior opportunities for observation of non-verbal and paralingual cues compared to other modes. In their systematic review of the use of ICT in social work interviews, Chan and Holosko (2016) noted concerns about the devaluing and removal of professional creativity as services offered online become more standardised and shaped by the technology through which they are delivered.

Still there can be little doubt that "as the pervasiveness of technology in people's lives grows" so too will demand for ICT mediated services (Richards and Viganó, 2013, p. 1005). However the implications for the communication base of social work are unclear. Does ICT require an entirely different framework for communication or only adaption of the existing approaches? Haxell (2012, p. 280) warns against regarding technology as merely a tool, as she notes "Communications alter with different media, and these alterations for better or worse, affect professional practice."

The extent to which our use of communication skills differs in an ICT mediated environment compared to face to face interaction may depend on the form the ICT used. For example, text based services such as text messaging and online chat lose the non-verbal elements that are integral to face to face communication. But even with forms of ICT that incorporate both visual and auditory elements of communication, some differences in skill use are likely. For example, Richards and Viganó (2013, p. 1002) propose that "Online counseling is characterized by unique features and behaviors such as apparent anonymity, disinhibition, distance, time delay, convenience, and loss of social signaling" (Richards and Viganó, 2013, p. 1002). Some of these communication differences may have benefits. For example, people who wish to remain anonymous may prefer some forms of ICT mediated support over face to face communication. Overall, while we can assume that some of the fundamentals of the social work remain unchanged, such as the continuing importance of the working alliance, we need to be responsive to possible alterations to communication skill use in ICT mediated communication (Richards and Viganó, 2013). Further research is needed to develop an evidence base for ICT mediated social work and human service delivery (see Chan and Holosko, 2016; Haxell, 2012; Richards and Viganó, 2013).

Conclusion

Becoming a skilled communicator in social work is a life-time journey. Social workers communicate with people in a variety of circumstances and with people who have a broad range of communication capacities and needs. As a profession we have much to gain and much to contribute to interdisciplinary knowledge and skills about communication in complex and diverse situations. Skilled communication lies at the base of everything we do in social work; it provides the foundation through which we work in partnership with others to achieve meaningful change with them. We hope this book has provided a useful foundation for skilled communication in the diverse and challenging contexts of social work practice.

References

Aboriginal mental health first aid training and research program (2010). *Problem drug use: Guidelines for providing mental health first aid to an Aboriginal or Torres Strait Islander Person.* Melbourne: Mental Health First Aid Australia and Beyondblue.

Allen, G. & Langford, D. (2008). *Effective interviewing in social work and social care: A practical guide.* Basingstoke: Palgrave Macmillan.

Altman, N. (2014). The color of whiteness and the paradox of diversity. In J. Rosenberger (Ed.), *Relational social work practice with diverse populations* (pp. 55–66). New York, NY: Springer.

American Foundation for the Blind (2008). Key Definitions of Statistical Terms. http://www.afb.org/info/blindness-statistics/key-definitions-of-statistical-terms/25.

American Psychiatric Association (2013). *Diagnostic and statistical manual of mental health disorders* (5th edition). Arlington, VA: American Psychiatric Association.

American Speech-Language-Hearing Language Association (2017). *Apraxia of Speech in Adults.* http://www.asha.org/public/speech/disorders/ApraxiaAdults/.

Anderson, C. A. (2000). Violence and aggression. In A. Kadzin (Ed.) *Encyclopedia of Psychology, 8,* (pp. 162–169). New York, NY: Oxford University Press.

Arnd-Caddigan, M., & Pozzuto, R. (2008). Use of self in relational clinical social work. *Clinical Social Work Journal, 36*(3), 235–243.

Arsenault-Lapierre, G., Kim, C. & Turecki, G. (2004). Psychiatric diagnoses in 3275 suicides: A meta-analysis. *BioMed Central Psychiatry, 4*(1), 37. doi: 10.1186/1471-244X-4-37.

AUSIT (2007). *AUSIT Guidelines for Health Professionals Working with Interpreters.* http://ausit.org/AUSIT/Documents/Guidelines_For_Health_Professionals.pdf.

AUSIT (2016). *Interpreters: Getting it Right.* http://ausit.org/AUSIT/Documents/gir_interpreting.pdf, retrieved 3/6/17.

Australian Association of Social Workers (2010). *Code of Ethics.* https://www.aasw.asn.au/document/item/1201.

Bacon, V. (2013). Yarning and listening: Yarning and learning through stories. In B. Bennett, S. Green, S. Gilbert & D. Bessarab (Eds.), *Our voices: Aboriginal and Torres Strait Islander social work* (pp. 136–165). South Yarra: Palgrave Macmillan.

Banks, S. (2012). *Ethics and values in social work* (4th ed., Practical social work series). Houndmills, Basingstoke ; Palgrave Macmillan.

Barker, B., Alfred, G., Kerr, T. (2014). An uncaring state? The overrepresentation of First Nations children in the Canadian child welfare system. *Canadian Medical Association, 186*(14), pp. E533–E555.

Bartels, L. (2015). *Indigenous specific court initiatives to support Indigenous defendants, victims and witnesses. Briefing paper 17.* Sydney: Indigenous Justice Clearinghouse. http://www.indigenousjustice.gov.au/wp-content/uploads/mp/files/publications/files/brief017.pdf.

Bauman, M., Bliss-Moreau, E., Machado, C. & Amaral, D. (2011). The neurobiology of primate social behavior. In J. Decety & J. Cacioppo (Eds.), *The Oxford handbook of social neuroscience* (pp. 683–701). New York, NY: Oxford University Press.

Bennett, B., Green, S. Gilbert, S. & Bessarab, D. (2013). *Our voices: Aboriginal and Torres Strait Islander social work.* South Yarra: Palgrave Macmillan.

Bessarab, D. & Crawford, F. (2013). Trauma, grief and loss: The vulnerability of Aboriginal families in the child protection system. In B. Bennett, S. Green, S. Gilbert & D. Bessarab (Eds.), *Our voices: Aboriginal and Torres Strait Islander social work* (pp. 93–113). South Yarra: Palgrave Macmillan.

Bessarab, D. & Ng'andu, B. (2010). Yarning about yarning as a legitimate method in Indigenous research. *International Journal of Critical Indigenous Studies, 3*(1), 37–50.

Better Hearing Australia, Victoria (2016). *Communication Strategies.* http://www.betterhearing.org.au/about-hearing-loss/communication-strategies/.

Beukelman, D. R., Fager, S., Ball, L. & Dietz, A. (2007). AAC for adults with acquired neurological conditions: A review. *Augmentative and Alternative Communication, 23*(3), 230–242.

Beyondblue (2013a). Beyondblue guide to the management of depression in primary care. Available at: https://das.bluestaronline.com.au/api/prism/document?token=BL/0484.

Beyondblue (2013b). Understanding anxiety. Available at: http://resources.beyondblue.org.au/prism/file?token=BL/0384.

Biestek, F. P. (1961). *The casework relationship.* London: Allen & Unwin.

Bird, S. (2010). Failure to use an interpreter. *Australian Family Physician, 39*(4), 241.

Biron, M. & van Veldhoven, M. (2012). Emotional labour in service work: Psychological flexibility and emotion regulation. *Human Relations, 65*(10), 1259–1282.

Bland, R., Renouf, N. & Tullgren, A. (2015). *Social work practice in mental health: An introduction* (2nd edition). Sydney: Allen & Unwin.

Blackman, L. (2001). *Hearing voices: Contesting the voice of reason.* London: Free Association Books.

Bloom, S. L. (2013). *Creating sanctuary: Toward the evolution of sane societies.* New York, NY: Routledge.

Bosly, F. (2007). *Frontline service workers'* conceptualisation of client anger and how it shapes their practice. Unpublished Masters thesis. St Lucia: The University of Queensland.

Bosly, F. (2012). *'I wouldn't want my kids around him': How men who use violence in their intimate relationships perceive themselves as fathers.* Unpublished PhD thesis. St Lucia: The University of Queensland.

Bowie, V. (1996). *Coping with violence: A guide for the human services*. London: Whiting & Birch.

Bowie, V. (2013). Trauma-informed care. *Youth Studies Australia [online], 32*(4), 81–83.

Boyle, S., Hull, G., Mather, J., Smith, L. & Farley, O. W. (2006). *Direct practice in social work*. Boston, MA: Pearson Education Inc.

Briggs, L. (2009). Collaborative assessment from a cross-cultural perspective. In J. Maidment & R. Egan (Eds.), *Practice skills in social work and welfare: More than just common sense* (pp. 170–180). Crows Nest: Allen & Unwin.

Brisset, C., Leanza, Y. & Laforest, K. (2011). Working with interpreters in health care: A systematic review and meta-ethnography of qualitative studies. *Patient Education and Counseling, 91*(2), 131–140.

Broussine, E. (2012). Building positive relationships with people with learning disabilities. In E. Broussine & K. Scarborough (Eds.), *Supporting people with learning disabilities in health & social care* (pp. 99–115). London: Sage. doi: 10.4135/9781446288191.n7.

Broussine, E. & Scarborough, K. (Eds.) (2012). *Supporting people with learning disabilities in health & social care*. London: Sage. doi: 10.4135/9781446288191

Brown, T. N. (2003). Critical race theory speaks to the sociology of mental health: Mental health problems produced by racial stratification. *Journal of Health and Social Behavior*, 44, 292–301.

Brown, M. Z., Comtois, K. A. & Linehan, M. M. (2002). Reasons for suicide attempts and nonsuicidal self-injury in women with borderline personality disorder. *Journal of Abnormal Psychology, 111*(1), 198–202.

Brulle, R. J. & Pellow, D. N. (2006). Environmental justice: Human health and environmental inequalities. *Annual Review of Public Health, 27*, 103–124.

Butler, E., Lee, T. & Gross, J. (2007). Emotion regulation and culture: Are the social consequences of emotion suppression culture-specific? *Emotion, 7*(1), 30–48.

Bywater, J., Hughes, J., Ryden, N. & O'Loughlin, S. (2012). Direct work with children and young people. In M. O'Loughlin & S. O'Loughlin (Eds.), *Social work with children and families* (3rd edition, pp. 81–106). London: Sage.

Capone, V. (2016). Patient communication self-efficacy, self-reported illness symptoms, physician communication style and mental health and illness in hospital outpatients. *Journal of Health Psychology, 21*(7), 1271–1282.

Carello, J. & Butler, L. D. (2015). Practicing what we teach: Trauma-informed educational practice. *Journal of Teaching in Social Work, 35*(3), 262–278.

Casey, W. (2003). Therapeutic journeys: Counselling Aboriginal clients and their families. In *Series three alcohol and drug counselling*. Perth: Sushi Productions.

Chalmers, D. (2016). *Communication with Children from Birth to Four Years*. London: Routledge.

Chan, C. & Holosko, M. J. (2016). A review of information and communication technology enhanced social work interventions. *Research on Social Work Practice, 26*(1), 88–100.

Chand, A. (2005). Do you speak English? Language barriers in child protection social work with minority ethnic families. *British Journal of Social Work, 35*(6), 807–821.

Chen, M.-W. & Han, Y. S. (2001). Cross-cultural group counseling with Asians: A stage-specific interactive approach. *The Journal for Specialists in Group Work, 26*(2), 111–128.

Coffin, J. (2007). Rising to the challenge in Aboriginal health by creating cultural security. *Aboriginal and Islander Health Worker Journal, 31*(3), 22.

Compton, M. T., Broussard, B., Hankerson-Dyson, D., Krishan, S., Stewart, T., Oliva, J. R. & Watson, A. C. (2010). System-and policy-level challenges to full implementation of the Crisis Intervention Team (CIT) model. *Journal of Police Crisis Negotiations, 10*(1–2), 72–85.

Connolly, M., Crichton-Hill, Y. & Ward, T. (2006). *Culture and child protection: Reflexive responses.* London: Jessica Kingsley Publishers.

Conradie, L. & Golding, T. (2013). *A short guide to working with children and young people.* Bristol: Polity Press.

Corbin, J. R. (2007). Reactive attachment disorder: A biopsychosocial disturbance of attachment. *Child and Adolescent Social Work Journal, 24*(6), 539–552.

Corenblum, B. & Armstrong, H. D. (2012). Racial-ethnic identity development in children in a racial-ethnic minority group. *Canadian Journal of Behavioral Science, 44*(2), 124–137.

Cornish, U. & Ross, F. (2004). *Social skills training for adolescents with moderate learning difficulties.* London: Jessica Kingsley Publishers.

Corporal, S. (2007). Getting to know the community. In Y. Darlington, L. Garland & K. Hall (Eds.), *Listening with respect: Strengthening communication with Aboriginal and Torres Strait Islander Australians* (pp. 11–15). St Lucia, Brisbane: School of Social Work and Human Services, University of Queensland.

Cottingham, M. D. (2015). Learning to 'deal' and 'deescalate': How men in nursing manage self and patient emotions. *Sociological Inquiry, 85*(1), 75–99.

Criss, P. (2010). Effects of client violence on social work students: A national study. *Journal of Social Work Education, 46*(3), 371–390.

Crone, E. (2015). *The adolescent brain: Changes in learning, decision-making and social relations.* London: Routledge.

Czaika, M. & de Haas, H. (2014). The globalization of migration: Has the world become more migratory? *International Migration Review, 48*(2), 283–323.

Daining, C. & DePanfilis, D. (2007). Resilience of youth in transition from out-of-home care to adulthood. *Children and Youth Services Review, 29*(9), 1158–1178.

Dammeyer, J. (2010). Interaction of dual sensory loss, cognitive function, and communication in people who are congenitally deaf-blind. *Journal of Visual Impairment & Blindness, 104*(11), 719.

Daniel, B., Wassell, S. & Gilligan, R. (2010). *Child Development for Child Care and Protection Workers* (2nd edition). London: Jessica Kingsley Publishers.

Davis, S. & Collier, A. (2015). Communicating with people with cognitive impairment. In R. Iedema, D. Piper & M. Manidis (Eds.), *Quality and safety in health care* (pp. 124–135). Melbourne: Cambridge University Press.

Deacon and Open University (2016). *How to die: Simon's choice.* London: Minnow Films.

Delaney, K. R. & Johnson, M. E. (2006). Keeping the unit safe: Mapping psychiatric nursing skills. *Journal of the American Psychiatric Nurses Association, 12*(4), 198–207.

Dewall, C. N., Anderson, C. A. & Bushman, B. J. (2012). Aggression. In I. Weiner (Ed.), *Handbook of psychology* (2nd edition, Volume 5, pp. 449–466). New York, NY: Wiley.

Diack, G. & Cohen, H. (2008). Effective communication. In L. Clark & P. Griffiths (Eds.), *Learning disability and other intellectual impairments: Meeting needs throughout health services* (pp. 41–54). London: Wiley.

Doka, K. (1989). *Disenfranchised grief.* Lexington, MA: Lexington Books.

Dolan, R. (2002). Emotion, cognition and behaviour. *Science, 298,* 1191–1194.

Dombo, E. A., Gray, C. & Early, B. P. (2013). The trauma of moral injury: Beyond the battlefield. *Journal of Religion & Spirituality in Social Work: Social Thought, 32*(3), 197–210.

Dominelli, L. (2002). Anti-oppressive practice in context. In R. Adams, L. Dominelli & M. Payne (Eds.), *Social work: Themes, issues and critical Debates* (2nd ed., pp. 3–19). Basingstoke: Palgrave Macmillan.

Dominelli, L. (2012). Globalisation and Indigenisation: Reconciling the Irreconcilable. In. K. Lyons, T. Hokenstad, M. Pawar, N. Huegler and N. Hall (Eds.), *The SAGE handbook of international social work*, pp. 41-55. London: Sage.

Drescher, J. (2015). Out of DSM: Depathologizing homosexuality. *Behavioral Sciences, 5*(4), 565–575.

Driedger, S. M., Cooper, E., Jardine, C., Furgal, C. & Bartlett, J. (2013). Communicating risk to Aboriginal Peoples: First Nations and Metis responses to H1N1 risk messages. *PLOS One, 8*(8), e71106.

Duperouzel, H. (2008). It's OK for people to feel angry' The exemplary management of imminent aggression. *Journal of Intellectual Disabilities, 12*(4), 295–307.

Dvir, Y., Ford, J. D., Hill, M. & Frazier, J. A. (2014). Childhood maltreatment, emotional dysregulation, and psychiatric comorbidities. *Harvard Review of Psychiatry, 22*(3), 149.

Eades, D. (2008). Language and disadvantage before the law. In J. Gibbons & M. T. Turrell (Eds.), *Dimensions of forensic linguistics* (pp. 185–195). Amsterdam: John Benjamins Publishing Company.

Eades, D. (2013). *Aboriginal ways of using English.* Canberra: Aboriginal Studies Press.

Egan, G. (2010). *The skilled helper: A problem-management and opportunity-development approach to helping* (9th edition). Belmont, CA: Brooks/Cole Cengage Learning.

Epps, K., Moore, C. L. & Hollin, C. R. (1999). Prevention and management of violence in a secure youth centre. *Nursing and Residential Care, 1*(5), 261–267.

Evans, M. & Shaw, S. (2012). Access and communication. In S. Shaw, A. Haxell & T. Weblemore (Eds.), *Communication across the lifespan* (pp. 124–140). South Melbourne: Oxford University Press.

Fadden, L. & LaFrance, J. (2010). Advancing Aboriginal English. *Canadian Journal of Native Education, 32,* 143–153.

Fallot, R. & Harris, M. (2009). Creating cultures of trauma-informed care (CCTIC): A self-assessment and planning protocol. *Community Connections, 2,* 1–17.

Fauteux, K. (2010). De-escalating angry and violent clients. *American Journal of Psychotherapy, 64*(2), 195–213.

Ferdenzi, C., Roberts, S. C., Schirmer, A., Delplanque, S., Cekic, S., Porcherot, C., Cayeux, I., Sander, D. & Grandjean, D. (2013). Variability of affective responses to odors: Culture, gender, and olfactory knowledge. *Chemical Senses, 38*(2), 175–186.

Ferguson, H. (2011). *Child protection practice.* Basingstoke: Palgrave Macmillan.

Ferrazzi, P. & Krupa, T. (2016). 'Symptoms of something all around us': Mental health, Inuit culture, and criminal justice in Arctic communities in Nunavut, Canada. *Social Science & Medicine, 165,* 159–167.

Fischer, A. H., Manstead, A. S., Evers, C., Timmers, M. & Valk, G. (2004). Motives and norms underlying emotion regulation. In P. Philippott & R. S. Feldman (Eds.), *The regulation of emotion* (pp. 187–210). Mahweh, NJ: Lawrence Erlbaum Associates.

Folgheraiter, F. (2004). *Relational social work: Toward networking and societal practices.* London: Jessica Kingsley Publishers.

Fook, J. (2013). Critical reflection in context: Contemporary perspectives and issues. In J. Fook & F. Gardner (Eds.), *Critical reflection in context: Applications in health and social care* (pp. 1–11). Abingdon: Routledge.

Fook, J. & Gardner, F. (2007). *Practising critical reflection: A resource handbook.* Maidenhead: Open University Press.

Fook, J. & Gardner, F. (Eds.) (2013). *Critical reflection in context: Applications in health and social care.* Abingdon: Routledge.

Fook, J., Ryan, M. & Hawkins, L. (2000). *Professional expertise: Practice, theory and education for working in uncertainty.* London: Whiting & Birch.

Forrester, D. & Harwin, J. (2011). *Parents who misuse drugs and alcohol: Effective interventions in social work and child protection.* Chichester: Wiley.

Fox, E. (2008). *Emotion science: Cognitive and neuroscientific approaches to understanding human emotions.* Basingstoke: Palgrave Macmillan.

France, K. (2007). *Crisis intervention: A handbook of immediate person to person help.* London: Charles C. Thomas Publishers.

Froemming, K. J. & Penington, B. A. (2011). Emotional triggers: Listening barriers to effective interactions in senior populations. *International Journal of Listening, 25*(3), 113–131.

Gallagher III, B. J., Jones, B. J., McFalls, J. A. & Pisa, A. M. (2006). Social class and type of schizophrenia. *European Psychiatry, 21*(4), 233–237.

Gendron, T. L., Welleford, E. A., Inker, J. & White, J. T. (2016). The language of ageism: Why we need to use words carefully. *The Gerontologist, 56*(6), 997–1006.

Gil, S., & Weinberg, M. (2015). Secondary trauma among social workers treating trauma clients: The role of coping strategies and internal resources. *International Social Work, 58*(4), 551–561.

Green, S. & Baldry, E. (2008) Building Indigenous Australian social work. *Australian Social Work, 61*(4), 289–402.

Green, L. (2017). The Trouble with Touch? New Insights and Observations on Touch for Social Work and Social Care. British Journal of Social Work, 47(3), 773–792.

Gross, J. J. (2008). Emotion regulation. In M. Lewis, J. Haviland-Jones & L. Feldman Barrett (Eds.), *Handbook of emotions* (3rd edition). New York, NY: Guilford Press.

Gross, J. J. (2015). Emotion regulation: Current status and future prospects. *Psychological Inquiry, 26*(1), 1–26. and Social Psychology, 85(2), 348.

Gross, J. J., & Thompson, R.A. (2007). Emotion regulation: Conceptual foundations. In J. J. Gross (Ed.), Handbook of emotion regulation (pp. 3-26). New York: Guilford.

Hadziabdic, E. & Hjelm, K. (2013). Working with interpreters: Practical advice for use of an interpreter in healthcare. *International Journal of Evidence Based Healthcare, 11*(1), 69–76.

Hall, C., Slembrouck, S. & Sarangi, S. (2006). *Language practice in social work: Categorisation and accountability in child welfare.* London: Routledge.

Hannon, L. & Clift, J. (2010). *General hospital care for people with learning disabilities.* Hoboken, NJ: Wiley.

Hargie, O. (2011). *Skilled interpersonal communication: Research, theory and practice* (5th edition). Hove, East Sussex: Routledge.

Harms, L. (2015*). Working with people: Communication skills for reflective practice* (2nd edition). South Melbourne: Oxford.

Harris, J. & White, V. (2014). *A dictionary of social work and social care* (online edition). Oxford: Oxford University Press.

Harrison, G. & Melville, R. (2009). *Rethinking social work in a global world.* Basingstoke: Palgrave Macmillan.

Harwood, J. (2007). *Understanding communication and ageing: Developing knowledge and awareness.* Los Angeles, CA: Sage.

Havig, K. (2008). The health care experiences of adult survivors of child sexual abuse: A systematic review of evidence on sensitive practice. *Trauma, Violence, & Abuse, 9*(1), 19–33.

Haxell, A. (2012). The electronic message. In S. Shaw, A. Haxell & T. Weblemore (Ed.), *Communication across the lifespan* (pp. 269–282). South Melbourne: Oxford University Press.

Hayslip, B., Blumenthal, H. & Garner, A. (2015). Social support and grandparent caregiver health: One-year longitudinal findings for grandparents raising their grandchildren. *The Journals of Gerontology Series B: Psychological Sciences and Social Sciences, 70*(5), 804–812.

Healy, K. (2012). *Social work methods and skills: The essential foundations of practice.* Basingstoke: Palgrave Macmillan.

Healy, K. (2014). *Social work theories in context: Creating frameworks for practice.* Basingstoke: Palgrave Macmillan.

Healy, K. & Darlington, Y. (2009). Service user participation in diverse child protection contexts: Principles for practice. *Child & Family Social Work, 14*(4), 420–430.

Heiting, G. (2016). How your vision changes as you age. http://www.allaboutvision.com/over60/vision-changes.htm.

Hochschild, A. R. (2012). *The managed heart: Commercialization of human feeling.* Berkeley, CA: University of California Press.

Howe, D. (2008). *The emotionally intelligent social worker.* Basingstoke: Palgrave Macmillan.

HREOC (1997). *Bringing them home report: Report of the national inquiry into the separation of Aboriginal and Torres Strait Islander children from their families.* Sydney: Human Rights and Equal Opportunity Commission.

Hurston, Z. N. (2008). *Mules and men.* NewYork: Harper Perennial Modern Classics.

Intervoice (2017). *About voices.* http://www.intervoiceonline.org/about-voices.

Jandt, F. (2016). *An introduction to intercultural communication: Identities in a global community* (8th edition). Los Angeles, CA: Sage.

Jasper, J. M. (2011). Emotions and social movements: Twenty years of theory and research. *Annual Review of Sociology, 37,* 285–303.

Jensen, T. K., Haavind, H., Gulbrandsen, W., Mossige, S., Reichelt, S. & Tjersland, O. A. (2010). What constitutes a good working alliance in therapy with children that may have been sexually abused? *Qualitative Social Work, 9*(4), 461–478.

Johansson, M. B., Carlsson, M. & Sonnander, K. (2012). Communication difficulties and the use of communication strategies: From the perspective of individuals with aphasia. *International Journal of Language & Communication Disorders, 47*(2), 144–155.

Johnson, Y. M. & Munch, S. (2009). Fundamental contradictions in cultural competence. *Social Work, 54*(3), 220–231.

Kahneman, D. (2011). *Thinking, fast and slow.* New York, NY: Farrar, Straus and Giroux.

Kampfe, C. M. (2015). *Counseling older people.* Alexandria, VA: American Counseling Association.

Karliner, L. S., Jacobs, E. A., Chen, A. H. & Mutha, S. (2007). Do professional interpreters improve clinical care for patients with limited English proficiency? A systematic review of the literature. *Health Services Research, 42*(2), 727–754.

Karvinen-Niinikoski, S. (2004). Social work supervision: Contributing to innovative knowledge production and open expertise. In N. Gould & M. Baldwin (Eds.), *Social work, critical reflection and the learning organization* (pp. 23–40). London: Routledge.

Keinemans, S. (2014). Be sensible: Emotions in social work ethics and education. *British Journal of Social Work, 45*(7), 2176–2191.

Kernsmith, P. (2005). Exerting power or striking back: A gendered comparison of motivations for domestic violence perpetration. *Violence and Victims, 20*(2), 173–185.

Killian, K., Hernandez-Wolfe, P., Engstrom, D., & Gangsei, D. (2017). Development of the vicarious resilience scale (VRS): A measure of positive effects of working with trauma survivors. *Psychological trauma: theory, research, practice, and policy, 9*(1), 23–31.

Killen, K. (1996). How far have we come in dealing with the emotional challenge of abuse and neglect? *Child Abuse and Neglect, 20*(9), 791–795.

Kitchener, B., Jorm, A. & Kelly, C. (2013). *Mental health first aid manual* (3rd edition). Melbourne: Mental Health First Aid Australia.

Knight, C. (2015). Trauma-informed social work practice: Practice considerations and challenges. *Clinical Social Work Journal, 43*(1), 25–37.

Kring, A. & Sloan, D. (Eds.) (2010). *Emotion regulation and psychopathology*. New York, NY: The Guilford Press.

Köberlein, J., Beifus, K., Schaffert, C. & Finger, R. P. (2013). The economic burden of visual impairment and blindness: A systematic review. *British Medical Journal Open, 3*(11), e003471.

Koprowska, J. (2014). *Communication and interpersonal skills in social work* (4th edition). London: Sage.

Lago, C. (2006). *Race, culture and counselling: the ongoing challenge (2nd edition)*. Maidenhead, England: Open University Press.

Laming, L. (2003). *Inquiry into the death of Victoria Climbié*. London: Stationery Office.

Le Riche, P. (1998). The dimensions of observation: Objective reality or subjective interpretation. In P. Le Riche & K. Tanner (Eds.), *Observation and its application in social work: Rather like breathing* (pp. 17–38). London: Jessica Kingsley Publishers.

Lefebvre, M. F. (1981). Cognitive distortion and cognitive errors in depressed psychiatric and low back pain patients. *Journal of Consulting and Clinical Psychology, 49* 517–525.

Lefevre, M. (2010). *Communicating with children and young people: Making a difference*. Bristol: The Policy Press.

Leudar, I. & Thomas, P. (2000). *Voices of reason, voices of insanity: Studies of verbal hallucination*. London: Routledge.

Levitan, C. A., Ren, J., Woods, A. T., Boesveldt, S., Chan, J. S., McKenzie, K. J., Dodson, M., Levin, J., Leong, C. & van den Bosch, J. J. (2014). Cross-cultural color-odor associations. *PloS One, 9*(7), e101651.

Levy, L. (2011). Cognitive information processing. In N. Katz (Ed.) (2011). *Cognition, occupation and participation across the lifespan: Neuroscience, neurorehabilitation and models of intervention in occupational therapy* (pp. 93–116). Bethesda, MD: American Occupational Therapy Association.

Liaw, S. T., Lau, P., Pyett, P., Furler, J., Burchill, M., Rowley, K. & Kelaher, M. (2011). Successful chronic disease care for Aboriginal Australians requires cultural competence. *Australian and New Zealand Journal of Public Health, 35*(3), 238–248.

Liberman, K. (1981). Understanding Aborigines in Australian courts of law. *Human Organization 40*, 247–255.

Lishman, J. (2009). Communication in social work (2nd ed). Basingstoke: Palgrave.

Liu, J. (2004). Concept analysis: Aggression. *Issues in Mental Health Nursing, 25*(7), 693–714.

Liu, S., Volčič, Z. & Gallois, C. (2014). *Introducing intercultural communication: Global cultures and contexts*. London: Sage.

Lowenstein, L. (1999) *Creative interventions for troubled children and youth*. Toronto: Hignell Book Printing.

Lowenstein, L. (2002). *More creative interventions for troubled children and youth.* Toronto: Hignell Book Printing.

Lowenstein, L. (2006). *Creative interventions for bereaved children.* Toronto: Hignell Book Printing.

Lynch, R. & Garrett, P. M. (2010). 'More than words': Touch practices in child and family social work. *Child & Family Social Work, 15*(4), 389–398.

Maiter, S., Palmer, S. & Manji, S. (2006). Strengthening social worker-client relationships in child protection services: Addressing power imbalances and 'ruptured' relationships. *Qualitative Social Work, 5*(2), 161–186.

Manktelow, R. (2011). Working with irrationality and dangerousness in mental health. In B. Taylor (Ed.), *Working with aggression and resistance in social work* (pp. 94–101). London: Sage.

Maxmen, J., Ward, N. & Kilgus, M. (2009). *Essential psychopathology and its treatment* (3rd edition). New York, NY: W.W. Norton.

McCabe, R. & Priebe, S. (2004). The therapeutic relationship in the treatment of severe mental illness: A *review* of methods and findings. *International Journal of Social Psychiatry, 50*(2), 115–128.

McCabe, R. & Priebe, S. (2008). Communication and psychosis: It's good to talk, but how? *British Journal of Psychiatry, 192*(6), 404–405.

McDonnell, A. & Sturmey, P. (2011). *Managing aggressive behaviour in care settings: Understanding and applying low arousal approaches.* Somerset: Wiley.

McRae, K., Ochsner, K. N., Mauss, I. B., Gabrieli, J. J. & Gross, J. J. (2008). Gender differences in emotion regulation: An fMRI study of cognitive reappraisal. *Group Processes & Intergroup Relations, 11*(2), 143–162.

Mende-Siedlecki, P., Kober, H. & Ochsner, K. (2011). Emotion regulation: Neural bases and beyond. In J. Decety & J. Cacioppo (Eds.), *The Oxford handbook of social neuroscience* (pp. 277–291). New York, NY: Oxford University Press.

Miletic, T., Piu, M., Minas, H., Stankovska, M., Stolk, Y. & Klimidis, S. (2006). *Guidelines for working effectively with interpreters in mental health settings.* Melbourne: Transcultural Psychiatry Unit. http://www.imiaweb.org/resources/mentalhealth.asp.

Miller, R. (2009). Engagement with families involved in the statutory system. In J. Maidment & R. Egan (Eds.), *Practice skills in social work and welfare: More than just common sense* (2nd edition, pp. 114–130). Crows Nest: Allen & Unwin.

Milner, J. & Myers, S. (2007). *Working with violence: Policies and practices in risk assessment and management.* Basingstoke: Palgrave Macmillan.

Monds-Watson, A. (2011). Defining key concepts: Aggression, ambivalence and resistance. In B. Taylor (Ed.), *Working with aggression and resistance in social work* (pp. 1–13). Exeter: Learning Matters.

Morrison, T. (2007). Emotional intelligence, emotion and social work: Context, characteristics, complications and contribution. *British Journal of Social Work, 37*(2), 245–263.

Moss, M. & Moss, S. (2003). Doubly disenfranchised: grief in old age. *Grief Matters: The Australian Journal of Grief and Bereavement, 6*(1), 4–6.

Mueller, V. (2013). Total communication (TC) approach. In F. Volkmar (Ed.), *Encyclopedia of autism spectrum disorders* (pp. 3138–3143). New York, NY: Springer.

Munro, E. (1996). Avoidable and unavoidable mistakes in child protection work, *British Journal of Social Work, 26*(6), 793–808.

Munro, E. (2008). *Effective child protection.* London: Sage.

Munro, E. (2011). *The Munro review of child protection: Final report.* London: United Kingdom Government. https://www.gov.uk/government/uploads/system/uploads/attachment_data/file/175391/Munro-Review.pdf.

Murphy, M. L. (2016). Minding your pleases and thank-yous in Britain and the US: Verbal manners don't always travel well, *English Today, 128, 32*(4), 49–53.

Murray, J. J. (2015). Linguistic human rights discourse in deaf community activism. *Sign Language Studies, 15*(4), 379–410.

NASW (2008). *Code of ethics.* http://www.naswdc.org/pubs/code/code.asp.

National Aphasia Association (2017). Aphasia factsheet. https://www.aphasia.org/aphasia-resources/aphasia-factsheet/.

National Federation of the Blind (2016). *Are you struggling with vision loss?* https://nfb.org/seniors-brochure.

Netværk Øst for Praksisledere (2015). *Congenital deaf-blindness: In light of the UN's Convention on the rights of persons with disabilities, Article 3.* http://dbf-konventionen.dk/wp-content/uploads/2015/05/D%C3%B8vblindf%C3%B8dt_folder_ENG_endelig1.pdf.

Neven, R. S. (2010). *Core principles of assessment and therapeutic communication with children, parents and families.* Hove, East Sussex: Routledge.

Nevo, I. & Slonim-Nevo, V. (2011). The myth of evidence-based practice: Towards evidence-informed practice. *British Journal of Social Work, 41*(6), 1176–1197.

Nicholls, D. (2012). Touch. In S. Shaw, A. Haxell & T. Weblemore (Eds.), *Communication across the lifespan* (pp. 187–196). South Melbourne: Oxford University Press.

Nussbaum, J. F. & Fisher, C. L. (2009). A communication model for the competent delivery of geriatric medicine. *Journal of Language and Social Psychology, 28*(2), 190–208.

Okuda, M., Olfson, M., Hasin, D., Grant, B. F., Lin, K. & Blanco, C. (2011). Mental health of victims of intimate partner violence: Results from a national epidemiologic Survey. *Psychiatric Services, 62*(8), 959–962.

OSHA (2015). *Guidelines for preventing workplace violence for healthcare and social service workers.* Washington, DC: US Department of Labor.

Pachana, N. A. (2016). *Ageing: A very short introduction.* South Melbourne: Oxford University Press.

Palmer, A. D., Newsom, J. T. & Rook, K. S. (2016). How does difficulty communicating affect the social relationships of older adults? An exploration using data from a national survey. *Journal of Communication Disorders, 62*, 131–146.

Pardoe, R. (2012). Promoting effective communication. In E. Broussine & K. Scarborough (Eds.), *Supporting people with learning disabilities in health & social care* (pp. 116–130). London: Sage.

Payne, M. (2011). Humanistic social work: core principles in practice. Basingstoke: Palgrave Macmillan.

Peace, S. Dittmann-Kohli, F., Gerben, J., Westerhof, G. & Bond. (2007). The aging world. In J. J. Bond, S. M. Peace, F. Dittmann-Kohli & G. Westerhof (Eds.), *Ageing in society* (pp. 1–14). London: Sage.

Peebles, S., Mabe, A., Fenley, G. Buckley, P., Bruce, T., Narasimhan, M., Frinks, L. & Williams, E. (2009). Immersing practitioners in the recovery model: An educational program evaluation. *Community Mental Health Journal, 45*(4): 239–245.

Peter, D., Robinson, P., Jordan, M., Lawrence, S., Casey, K. & Salas-Lopez, D. (2015). Reducing readmissions using teach-back: Enhancing patient and family education. *Journal of Nursing Administration, 45*(1), 35–42.

Petr, C. G. (2003). *Social work with children and their families: Pragmatic foundations.* New York: Oxford University Press.

Petrie, P. (2011). *Communication skills for working with children and young people: Introducing social pedagogy.* London: Jessica Kingsley Publishers.

Plumb, J. (2015). Therapeutic communication with people experiencing mental illness. In R. Iedema, D. Piper, M. Manidis (Eds.), *Quality and safety in health care.* Melbourne: Cambridge University Press.

Price, O. & Baker, J. (2012). Key components of de-escalation techniques: A thematic synthesis. *International Journal of Mental Health Nursing, 21*(4), 310–319.

Priebe, S., Richardson, M., Cooney, M., Adedeji, O. & McCabe, R. (2011). Does the therapeutic relationship predict outcomes of psychiatric treatment in patients with psychosis? A systematic review. *Psychotherapy and Psychosomatics, 80*(2), 70–77.

Priebe, S. & Mccabe, R. (2008). Therapeutic relationships in psychiatry: The basis of therapy or therapy in itself? *International Review of Psychiatry, 20*(6), 521–526.

Rao, D. V., Warburton, J. & Bartlett, H. (2006). Health and social needs of older Australians from culturally and linguistically diverse backgrounds: Issues and implications. *Australasian Journal on Ageing, 25*(4), 174–179.

Reimer, E. C. (2013). Relationship-based practice with families where child neglect is an issue: putting relationship development under the microscope. *Australian Social Work, 66*(3), 455–470.

Richards, D. & Viganó, N. (2013). Online counseling: A narrative and critical review of the literature. *Journal of Clinical Psychology, 69*(9), 994–1011.

Richter, D. (2006). Nonphysical conflict management and de-escalation. In D. Richter & R. Whittington (Eds.), *Violence in mental health settings: Causes, Consequences and Management* (pp. 125–144). New York: Springer.

Roberton, T., Daffern, M. & Bucks, R. S. (2012). Emotion regulation and aggression. *Aggression and Violent Behavior, 17*(1), 72–82.

Robson, A., Cossar, J. & Quayle, E. (2014). Critical commentary: The impact of work-related violence towards social workers in children and family services. *British Journal of Social Work, 44*(4), 924–936.

Ronan, G. F., Dreer, L., Maurelli, K., Ronan, D. & Gerhart, J. (2013). *Practitioner's guide to empirically supported measures of anger, aggression, and violence.* New York, NY: Springer Science & Business Media.

Rose, P. (2013). *Cultural competency for the health professional.* Burlington, MA: Jones & Bartlett Learning.

Rosenberger, J. (2014. Introduction. In J. Rosenberger (Ed.), *Relational social work practice with diverse populations* (pp. 3–12). New York, NY: Springer.

Savaya, R., Gardner, F. & Stange, D. (2011). Stressful encounters with social work clients: A descriptive account based on critical incidents. *Social Work, 56*(1), 63–71.

Saxby, C. (2016). *Clinical supervision, burnout and intent to leave: An Australian mixed methods study of community-based allied health professionals.* Unpublished PhD Thesis. St Lucia: University of Queensland.

Scope (2015). *How to design a communication aid.* http://www.scopeaust.org.au/wp-content/uploads/2017/03/Necas-aid-design-handout.pdf.

Schölderle, T., Staiger, A., Lampe, R., Strecker, K. & Ziegler, W. (2016). Dysarthria in adults with cerebral palsy: Clinical presentation and impacts on communication. *Journal of Speech, Language, and Hearing Research, 59*(2), 216–229.

Schraer, R. (2014). 85% of social workers were assaulted, harassed or verbally abused in the past year. *Community Care.* http://www.communitycare.co.uk/2014/09/16/violence-social-workers-just-part-job-70-incidents-investigated/.

Shaw, S. (2012). Care at a distance. In S. Shaw, A. Haxell & T. Weblemore (Eds.), *Communication across the lifespan* (pp. 322–332.). South Melbourne: Routledge.

Shay, J. (2014). Moral injury. Psychoanalytic Psychology, 31(2), 182-191.

Sheldon, B. & Macdonald, G. (2009). *A textbook of social work.* London: Taylor and Francis.

Sheppard, M. & Charles, M. (2015). Head and heart: An examination of the relationship between the intellectual and interpersonal in social work. *British Journal of Social Work, 45*(6), 1837–1854.

Shulman, L (1999). The skills of helping individuals, families, groups and communities, 4th edition. Itasca, IL: Peacock.

Simcock, P. & Castle, R. (2016). *Social work and disability: Social work theory and practice.* Cambridge: Polity.

Skuse, V. (2007). It's not what you do but how you do it. In Y. Darlington, L. Garland & K. Hall (Eds.), *Listening with respect: Strengthening communication with Aboriginal and Torres Strait Islander Australians* (pp. 21–27). St Lucia, Brisbane: School of Social Work and Human Services, University of Queensland.

Slater, C., Lambie, I. & McDowell, H. (2015). Youth justice co-ordinators' perspectives on New Zealand's youth justice family group conference process. *Journal of Social Work, 15*(6), 621–643.

Small, J., Chan, S. M., Drance, E., Globeman, E., Hulko, W., O'Connor, D., Perry, J., Stern, L. & Ho, L. (2015). Verbal and nonverbal indicators of quality of communication between care staff and residents in ethnoculturally and linguistically diverse long-term care settings. *Journal of Cross-Cultural Gerontology, 30*(3), 285–304.

Smith, R. (2012) Tips for social workers: Working with interpreters, *Community Care,* June 26, 2012. http://www.communitycare.co.uk/blogs/childrens-services-blog/2012/06/working-with-interpreters/.

Spratt, T., & Callan, J. (2004). Parents' views on social work interventions in child welfare cases. *British Journal of Social Work, 34*(2), 199–224.

Sprigg, C. A., Armitage, C. J. & Hollis, K. (2007). Verbal abuse in the National Health Service: Impressions of the prevalence, perceived reasons for and relationships with staff psychological well-being. *Emergency Medicine Journal, 24*(4), 281–282.

Stephens, D. & Kramer,. S. E. (2010). *Living with hearing difficulties*. Hoboken, NJ: John Wiley & Sons. http://ebookcentral.proquest.com/lib/uql/detail.action?docID=454350.

Stewart, D., Bowers, L., Simpson, A., Ryan, C. & Tziggili, M. (2009). Manual restraint of adult psychiatric inpatients: A literature review. *Journal of Psychiatric and Mental Health Nursing, 16*(8), 749–757.

Storlie, T. (2015). *Person-centered communication with older adults: The professional provider's guide*. Burlington, MA: Academic Press.

Stubbs, B., & Dickens, G. (2008). Prevention and management of aggression in mental health: An interdisciplinary discussion. *International Journal of Therapy & Rehabilitation, 15*(8), 351–357.

Stubbs, B., & Dickens, G. (2009). Physical assault by patients against physiotherapists working in mental health settings. *Physiotherapy, 95*(3), 170–175.

Sturmey, P. & McDonnell, A. (2011). *Managing aggressive behaviour in care settings*. Hoboken, NJ: Wiley.

Sue, D. W. & Sue, D. (1977). Barriers to effective cross-cultural counseling. *Journal of Counseling Psychology, 24*(5), 420–429.

Tanner, K. (1998). Introduction. In P. Le Riche & K. Tanner (Eds.), *Observation and its application to social work: Rather like breathing* (pp. 9–16). London: Jessica Kingsley Publishers.

Taylor, B. (2011). Avoiding assault and defusing aggression. In B. Taylor (Ed.). (2011). *Working with aggression and resistance in social work* (pp. 35–50). London: Sage.

Thompson, L. & McCabe, R. (2012). The effect of clinician-patient alliance and communication on treatment adherence in mental health care: A systematic review. *BMC Psychiatry, 12*(1), 87.

Thompson, R. A. & Goodman, M. (2010). Development of emotion regulation: More than meets the eye. In A. Kring & D. Sloan (Eds.), *Emotion Regulation and Psychopathology* (pp. 38–58). New York, NY: The Guilford Press.

Tilbury, C. (2009). The over–representation of indigenous children in the Australian child welfare system. *International Journal of Social Welfare, 18*(1), 57–64.

Toglia, J. P. (2005). A dynamic interactional approach to cognitive rehabilitation. In N. Katz (Ed.), *Cognition and occupation across the life span: Models for intervention in occupational therapy* (pp. 29–72). Bethesda, MD: American Occupational Therapy Association.

Trevithick, P. (2005). *Social work skills: A practice handbook* (2nd edition). Buckingham: Open University Press.

Trotter, C. (2002). Worker skill and client outcome in child protection. *Child Abuse Review, 11*(1), 38–50.

Trotter, C. (2004). *Helping abused children and their families* (2nd edition). St Leonards: Allen & Unwin.

Trotter, C. (2013). *Collaborative family work: A practical guide to working with families in the human services*. Crows Nest: Allen & Unwin.

Trotter, C. (2015). *Working with involuntary clients: A guide to practice* (3rd edition). Crows Nest: Allen & Unwin.

Trowell, J. & Miles, G. (1991). *The place of an introduction to child to young child observation in social work training*. London: CCETSW.

Tuckey, M. R. & Scott, J. E. (2014). Group critical incident stress debriefing with emergency services personnel: A randomized controlled trial. *Anxiety, Stress & Coping, 27*(1), 38–54.

United Nations (1989). *United Nations Convention on the rights of the child.* https://www.unicef.org/crc/.

United Nations (2006). *United Nations Convention on the rights of persons with disabilities.* https://www.un.org/development/desa/disabilities/convention-on-the-rights-of-persons-with-disabilities.html.

US Department of Health and Human Services (2007). *A profile of older Americans: 2007.* https://www.acl.gov/sites/default/files/Aging%20and%20 Disability%20in%20America/2007profile.pdf.

Vertovec, S. (2007). Super-diversity and its implications. *Ethnic and Racial Studies, 30*(6), 1024–1054.

Vision Australia (2016). Inclusive communication strategies. https://www. visionaustralia.org/business-and-professionals/print-accessibility-services/ inclusive-communication-strategies.

Von Braun, T., Larsson, S., & Sjblom, Y. (2013). Narratives of clients experiences of drug use and treatment of substance use-related dependency. *Substance use & misuse, 48*(13), 1404–1415.

Wang, D. (2012). The use of self and reflective practice in relational teaching and adult learning: A social work perspective. *Reflective Practice, 13*(1), 55–63.

Warburton, J. & Chambers, B. (2007). Older Indigenous Australians: Their integral role in culture and community. *Australasian Journal on Ageing, 26*(1), 3–7.

Ward, J. (2012). Ward, J. (2012). *The student's guide to social neuroscience*. Hove, East Sussex: Psychology Press.

Watkins, J. (2008). *Hearing voices: A common human experience*. South Yarra: Michelle Anderson Publishing.

Werner, K. & Gross, J. (2010). Emotion regulation and psychopathology: A conceptual framework. In A. Kring & D. Sloan (Eds.), *Emotion regulation and psychopathology* (pp. 13–37). New York, NY: The Guilford Press.

Williams, K. N., Herman, R., Gajewski, B. & Wilson, K. (2009). Elderspeak communication: Impact on dementia care. *American journal of Alzheimer's Disease and Other Dementias, 24*(1), 11–20.

Winkielman, P., Berridge, K. & Sher, S. (2011). Emotion, consciousness and social behaviour. *The Oxford handbook of social neuroscience* (pp.195–211). New York, NY: Oxford University Press.

Wolf, T. & Baum, C. (2011). Impact of mild cognitive impairments on participation: Importance of early identification of cognitive loss. In N. Katz (Ed.), *Cognition, occupation and participation across the lifespan: Neuroscience, neurorehabilitation and models of intervention in occupational therapy* (pp. 41–50). Bethesda, MD: American Occupational Therapy Association.

Wolvin, A & Coakley, C. G. (1996). *Listening* (5th edition). Madison, WI: Brown & Benchmark Publishers.

World Federation for the Deaf (2016). Human Rights. https://wfdeaf.org/human-rights. Retrieved 25/10/16

World Health Organization (2014). Mental disorders (fact sheet). http://www.who.int/mediacentre/factsheets/fs396/en/.

World Health Organization (2016). Mental health and older adults. http://www.who.int/mediacentre/factsheets/fs381/en/.

World Health Organization (2017). Deafness and hearing loss factsheet. http://www.who.int/mediacentre/factsheets/fs300/en/.

Yip, K. S. (2004). A Chinese cultural critique of the global qualifying standards for social work education. *Social Work Education, 23*(5), 597–612.

Yorkston, K. M., Bourgeois, M. S. & Baylor, C. R. (2010). Communication and aging. *Physical Medicine and Rehabilitation Clinics of North America, 21*(2), 309–319.

Zangrilli, A., Ducci, G., Bandinelli, P. L., Dooley, J., McCabe, R. & Priebe, S. (2014). How do psychiatrists address delusions in first meetings in acute care? A qualitative study. *BMC Psychiatry, 14*(1), 178.

Zubrzycki, J. & Crawford, F. (2013). Collaboration and relationship building in Aboriginal and Torres Strait Islander social work. Bennett, B., Green, S. Gilbert, S. & Bessarab, D. Eds), *Our voices: Aboriginal and Torres Strait Islander social work* (pp. 191–205). South Yarra: Palgrave Macmillan.

Index